THE EIGHTIES

Joseph A. Palermo
California State University, Sacramento

Boston Columbus Indianapolis New York San Francisco Upper Saddle River Amsterdam
Cape Town Dubai London Madrid Milan Munich Paris Montreal Toronto Delhi
Mexico City São Paulo Sydney Hong Kong Seoul Singapore Taipei Tokyo

Editor-in-Chief: Dickson Musslewhite
Publisher: Charlyce Jones Owen
Senior Assistant: Maureen Diana
Vice President, Director of Marketing: Brandy Dawson
Marketing Manager: Maureen Prado Roberts
Production Manager: Meghan DeMaio
Creative Director: Jayne Conte
Cover Designer: Suzanne Behnke
Cover Image: Pop icon Madonna. b91/ZUMA Press/Newscom
Composition and Full Service Project Management: Nitin Agarwal/Aptara®, Inc.

Photo Credits: Courtesy Ronald Reagan Library, p. 12; Bernard Gotfryd/Premium Archive/Getty Images, p. 30; NATO via CNP/Newscom, p. 32; TRIPPETT/SIPA/Newscom, p. 48; Dennis Brack/Dennis brack/Newscom, p. 55; The Library of Congress, p. 62; 20th Century Fox Film Corp., 1983, All rights reserved./The Everett Collection, p. 70; Pictorial Press/Pictorial Press Ltd / Alamy, p. 77; Lee Jaffe, p. 83; Handout/Getty Images, p. 86; BOB LARSON/UPI /Landov, p. 96; Photos 12/Alamy, p. 99; Bettmann/Corbis, p. 102; Justin Leighton / Alamy, p. 116; Cynthia Johnson/Time & Life Pictures/Getty Images, p. 121; cover, b91/ZUMA Press/Newscom

Library of Congress Cataloging-in-Publication Data

Palermo, Joseph A.
   The eighties/Joseph A. Palermo.
     p. cm.
   Includes bibliographical references and index.
   ISBN-13: 978-0-205-74249-3
   ISBN-10: 0-205-74249-1
   1. United States—Politics and government—1981–1989.   2. United States—Foreign relations—1981–1989.   3. United States—Social conditions—1980–   4. Nineteen eighties.   I. Title.
   E876.P36 2012
   973.927—dc23

                                                                                                2011047157

ISBN-10: 0-205-74249-1
ISBN 13: 978-0-205-74249-3

Dedicated to Jannette Dayton Palermo, Gianna Isabella Palermo, and Lorayne Mary Palermo

CONTENTS

PREFACE

On January 28, 1986, the U.S. space shuttle, *Challenger*, burst into a giant fireball 73 seconds after liftoff over the Atlantic near the central Florida coast. On the night of the disaster, which killed seven crewmembers (including the first teacher in space, Christa McAuliffe), President Ronald Reagan spoke to American schoolchildren who were watching it on TV as part of their science curriculum: "I know it is hard to understand," he said, "but sometimes-painful things like this happen. It's all part of the process of exploration and discovery. It's all part of taking a chance and expanding man's horizons. The future doesn't belong to the fainthearted; it belongs to the brave. The *Challenger* crew was pulling us into the future, and we'll continue to follow them." The president's brief remarks to the nation that evening displayed not only his talent as a communicator, but also his inherent optimism.

Given that Reagan was sworn in as the nation's 40th president in January 1981 and served until January 1989, his presidency coincided with the decade itself. Periodizing "decades" is always problematic, but the historian must compartmentalize time in order to digest the immense political, social, cultural, and technological changes that take place. It is impossible to write about the United States in the 1980s without looking at Reagan's influence. However, at the same time we shouldn't limit our analysis only to a study of his presidency. In this book, I attempt to present a short yet comprehensive overview of the politics and foreign policy of the era, while also describing some of the major changes that took place involving social movements, technology, and popular culture.

With Reagan's victory in 1980, the decade opened with the country signaling a move toward conservatism. At the same time, millions of baby boomers were reaching an age where building a career, starting a family, and possibly buying a home took priority over fighting for social causes. The deep economic recession of the early 1980s also focused their attention on material pursuits. Politically, the decade is marked by the election of the oldest and first divorced president; the biggest Electoral College landslide in history; and the first sitting vice president to win the presidency through election in 152 years. There were violent conflicts in Central America, Afghanistan, Angola, and elsewhere, and the United States used its military directly in Lebanon, Grenada, Libya, and Panama. A president narrowly escaped assassination, the AIDS epidemic swept an unprepared world, and the word "Chernobyl" became synonymous with disaster. The president's party never controlled the House of Representatives, and divided government meant that the legislative achievements of Presidents Reagan and George Herbert Walker Bush were possible only with support from the "opposition."

The Equal Rights Amendment (ERA) failed to win ratification and the women's movement met with a powerful backlash from well-organized social conservatives; but there was also the first ever woman candidate nominated on the presidential ticket of a major political party. There was an unraveling of the consensus on environmental policies, but also a proliferation of activist groups that lobbied on behalf of environmental protection. There were many years of rising nuclear tensions between the United States and the Soviet Union, but also the first nuclear arms control treaty that eliminated an entire category of weapons.

With the invention of the Political Action Committee (PAC), the "sound-bite," and the 24-hour news cycle, American politics underwent some lasting changes. The term "to be Borked" entered the American political lexicon meaning to be rejected for a high government post based largely on political grounds; "Dukakis-in-a-tank" became short-hand for any embarrassing photo-op that takes place in the heat of a campaign; and the name "Willie Horton" connotes the dark arts of negative campaign tactics. The 1980s began with the people of East Berlin walled off behind the world's preeminent symbol of police-state repression, and Nelson Mandela stuck in a South African prison; but by the first years of a new decade both the East German dictatorship and the apartheid regime had been tossed into the ashbin of history. The 1980s revealed the potential costs of financial deregulation to American taxpayers, and the criminal convictions of some of Wall Street's most celebrated personalities showed that even "free" markets needed a cop on the beat.

Questions about America in the 1980s that we might wish to consider are: What were the legacies of the Reagan administration and the profound changes in both domestic and foreign policy? What technological, cultural, and economic transformations begun in the 1980s have had the most lasting effects? Why have so many of the public policy prescriptions of the 1980s continued to be tried again in later decades? How have the outcomes of the political and cultural battles of that era affected our contemporary public discourse? And what can we learn today about the role of government, free markets, and America's place in world affairs by looking back at the 1980s?

In the chapters that follow I have attempted to construct a narrative that unfolds chronologically yet takes thematic detours along the way to go deeper into topics that should be of interest to college students. In the Introduction, I place Jimmy Carter and Ronald Reagan in the political and social context leading up to the 1980 campaign and offer a biographical sketch of Reagan. Chapter 1 provides an overview of how the new administration and Congress altered the nation's course, as well as an account of the Reagan administration's style of governance. Chapter 2 analyzes U.S. foreign policy including the nuclear arms build up, the events leading up to the October 1983 Marine barracks bombing in Lebanon, and the invasion of Grenada. In Chapter 3, I examine the election of 1984 and the wider social movements of the period involving African Americans and women as well as the nation's response to a new and deadly disease. Chapter 4 shifts gears to evaluate the revolution that was taking place in the realm of technology and popular culture as well as the "culture wars." In Chapter 5, I return to foreign affairs with an emphasis on some of the democratic transformations that were taking place, as well as the rise in the Soviet Union of a leader who would ultimately abandon the Cold War altogether. Chapter 6 covers the most serious crisis of Reagan's presidency and chronicles his administration's deft maneuvers out of it as well as some of the other scandals that engulfed high-profile figures outside the administration. Finally, Chapter 7 dissects the 1988 presidential election; traces the events sweeping Eastern Europe, which gave birth to a "new world order"; and analyzes the implications of the U.S. invasion of Panama that ousted an anti-communist government. It is my hope that this work deepens our understanding, in some small way, of a truly extraordinary period in American history and will pique readers' curiosity to learn more about the 1980s.

ACKNOWLEDGMENTS

I would like to thank the following scholars who took the time to offer me helpful advice and constructive criticism of chapter drafts as I was working on the book:

George Edgar, *Modesto Junior College;*
Shane Hamilton, *University of Georgia;*
Lucien Mott, *SUNY, New Paltz;*
John Turner, *University of South Alabama.*

For me, writing about the 1980s was an intriguing endeavor because it was during that decade when I earned my first college degrees, began my career in teaching, and had three children. I want to thank the series editor, Terry Anderson, for his comments and sage advice, and Richard Polenberg of Cornell University for his close reading of the manuscript. I'd like to convey my appreciation for the hard work of Charlyce Jones-Owen, Maureen Diana, Sanchita Massey, Nitin Agarwal, and the whole team at Pearson who were enjoyable to work with and kept this project moving along.

The Department of History chair at California State University (CSU), Sacramento, Aaron Cohen, gave me valuable research support as well as the opportunity to teach a graduate seminar on the 1980s that was very helpful to me in focusing my thoughts on the period. I want to thank him and all my students at CSU over the course of writing this book (undergraduate and graduate alike) who helped me see the 1980s from their perspective. I would also like to thank the cash-strapped CSU for a sabbatical semester that allowed me to get the book started. And, a special thanks to Dr. Stan Oden, my colleague in the Government Department, for some great conversations about the 1980s; to my close friend, Brian Burman, for reading drafts of some of the early chapters; and to my brother, Christopher Palermo, for our discussions about the popular culture of the era.

Finally, I would like to express my deepest love and appreciation to my wife, Jannette Dayton Palermo, for putting up with me during the writing process; and to my nursery school-age daughter, Gianna Isabella Palermo, for letting me use her little bedroom as a study.

THE MOMENT YOU KNOW

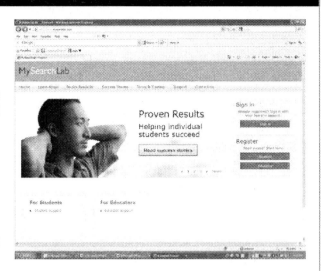

www.mysearchlab.com

MySearchLab with eText delivers proven results in helping individual students succeed. Its automatically graded assessments and interactive eText provide engaging experiences that personalize, stimulate, and measure learning for each student. And, it comes from a trusted partner with educational expertise and a deep commitment to helping students, instructors, and departments achieve their goals.

PERSONALIZE LEARNING

Writing, Research and Citing Sources

- Step by step tutorials present complete overviews of the research and writing process.
- Instructors and students receive access to the EBSCO ContentSelect database, census data from Social Explorer, Associated Press news feeds, and the Pearson bookshelf. Pearson SourceCheck helps students and instructors monitor originality and avoid plagiarism.

Etext and more

- **Pearson eText**—An e-book version of *The Eighties* is included in MySearchLab. As with the printed text, students can highlight and add their own notes as they read their interactive text online.
- **Chapter quizzes and flashcards**—Chapter and key term reviews are available for each chapter online and offer immediate feedback.
- **Primary and Secondary Source Documents**—A collection of documents, organized by chapter, are available on MySearchLab. The documents include head notes and critical thinking questions.
- **Gradebook**—Automated grading of quizzes helps both instructors and students monitor their results throughout the course.

MySearchLab Connections

At the end of each chapter in the text, a special section, *MySearchLab Connection: Sources Online*, provides a list of the documents included on the MySearchLab website that relate to the content of the chapter. See pages xi–xii for a full list of the sources listed in the text.

MYSEARCHLAB CONNECTIONS: SOURCES ONLINE

INTRODUCTION

The Demise
of the Me Decade

CHAPTER OUTLINE

America Held Hostage
Ronald Reagan
Governor Reagan

Presidential Candidate
The 1980 Campaign

AMERICA HELD HOSTAGE

In the summer of 1979, at a time when his approval rating was plummeting, President James Earl Carter spoke to the nation in a primetime television address where he described the insecurity that was gripping American society. "It is a crisis of confidence," he said. "It is a crisis that strikes at the very heart and soul and spirit of our national will. We can see this crisis in the growing doubt about the meaning of our own lives and in the loss of a unity of purpose for our nation." The president seemed dour and tendentious while the language he used exuded an air of hopelessness. The press dubbed it the "malaise" speech (though he never used the word), and it was an unmitigated political disaster. *The New Republic* editorialized that the speech had "put the finishing touches on a failed presidency." In 1976, Carter, the nuclear engineer and Georgia's peanut farmer governor, had come to Washington as a fresh face promising to lead the country out of the depressing era of Vietnam and Watergate. Three years later, he had become heavily identified with a dreary status quo.

Carter's bleakness had a lot to do with events in Iran during the previous year over which he had little control. Throughout 1978, the shah of Iran, Reza Pahlavi, a stalwart U.S. ally for 25 years, fought to preserve his government from a tapestry of revolutionary organizations and guerrilla groups. By January 1979, it was clear that his reign was coming to an end and the shah and the rest of the royal family had no choice but to leave the country. Thereafter, the shah found himself isolated when nation after nation, fearing the domestic political response, refused him sanctuary. He first fled to Egypt only to be forced out after his presence there caused problems for his friend President Anwar Sadat. The shah and his entourage then lived briefly in Morocco, followed by the Bahamas, and then Mexico. Wherever they landed, millions of dollars had to be spent on security because the new "Islamic Republic of Iran" had offered a substantial bounty for his assassination.

1

The overthrow of the shah should not have come as a surprise. He had ruled Iran since August 1953 when the CIA helped install him in a coup d'etat against the government of Prime Minister Mohammed Mossedegh. The shah had been a poor representative of America's stated foreign policy goal of upholding democracy and Carter's more specific intent to defend human rights. And although he claimed to care deeply about his country and his people, the shah had squandered much of the nation's oil wealth, enriched a tiny elite, and aided by a CIA-trained secret police, SAVAK, repressed his political opponents. A month after the shah's departure, when Ayatollah Ruhollah Khomeini arrived in Tehran from Paris, millions of Iranians greeted him on the streets. Khomeini was not only the supreme Shia cleric in Iran, but also a life-long adversary of the shah's regime who had lived in exile for years and disseminated incendiary lectures via underground audiotapes. A Shia theocracy rapidly stepped in to fill the power vacuum.

Carter sought bipartisan advice about how best to deal with the revolution that had engulfed Iran. His national security advisor, Zibgniew Brzezinski, as well as former Secretary of State Henry Kissinger, and David Rockefeller (a close friend of the shah) of Chase Manhattan Bank lobbied the president to allow the ousted king, who had been battling pancreatic cancer, to come to the United States for medical treatment. The shah deserved no less, they argued, because he had been a loyal anti-Communist ally in the Persian Gulf. There emerged a consensus, trumpeted in newspaper editorials, that to bar the shah asylum would show weakness toward the Soviet Union and sow seeds of doubt about America's other commitments abroad. Carter decided to admit the shah for "humanitarian" reasons, and he came to New York to undergo a battery of cancer tests and treatments. Infuriated, the revolutionary leaders in Tehran demanded the shah's extradition.

On November 4, 1979, militant Iranian students who had been monitoring the U.S. Embassy in Tehran stormed the compound and took 66 American hostages. Inside the embassy they discovered shredded documents, pirated vehicle license plates, and lists of Iranian citizens who were contacts or targeted for surveillance. The students brought in rug weavers from the countryside, mostly older women, who deployed their hand-eye coordination to reassemble some of the documents. The evidence convinced many Iranians that Carter's State Department and the CIA were manipulating the power struggles within the fledgling regime just as the CIA had done in 1953.

The seizing of the hostages outraged Americans and television news shows began counting down the days of their captivity. ABC's *Nightline*, which chronicled Iran-related events, evolved into a fixture of evening television news programming and an audience of millions became caught up in the unfolding drama. Journalists interviewed friends and family members of the hostages as well as a contentious assortment of ever-changing spokespeople from the Iranian government. The shah's prognosis was terminal, and after receiving medical care in New York he bid farewell to the United States in December 1979, bound for Panama.

The shah had departed but the hostage crisis dragged on. Facing withering criticism for his inaction Carter launched a risky military action in April 1980 to try to rescue the 52 remaining hostages. (Among the original 66 hostages, the Iranians had released the women, blacks, and those in ill health.) The objective of the intervention, called "Operation Eagle Claw," was to commandeer the U.S. Embassy, gather up the Americans, and whisk them to safety on helicopters. But as the military units amassed in a desert rendezvous point outside Tehran, a blinding sandstorm caused one of the helicopters to slam into a C-130 transport plane. The resulting explosion killed eight servicemen and Carter aborted the mission. Secretary of State Cyrus Vance, who opposed the plan from the start, resigned in protest. Political commentators blasted Carter for being an incompetent commander in chief, a warmonger (or both), and for bungling an operation that in hindsight looked foolhardy. The Khomeini regime divided the hostages into smaller groups and scattered them to safe houses dispersed throughout Tehran, ensuring the failure of any future attempt to free them.

The shah believed he could live out his remaining days on the Isla Contadora in Panama, but after the Iranian ambassador to Panama presented a 450-page extradition request to the Panamanian government he returned to Egypt. He died there on July 27, 1980, at the age of 60. President Sadat gave him a state funeral. The shah was dead and buried but the Iranians still held the American hostages. Carter beefed up the U.S. military presence in the region and stipulated that the United States would stand against any nation that threatened its "vital interests" in the Persian Gulf, which became known as the "Carter Doctrine."

The Carter administration might have weathered the foreign policy storm had it not come at a time when the nation's economy was entering a terrible slump. The Iranian Revolution contributed to the downturn by disrupting oil production. In little over a year the price of oil rose from $13 a barrel to $30 a barrel, and gas prices nearly tripled at the pump. The shortages not only produced long lines at service stations throughout the United States, but also exacerbated inflation by hiking the prices of other commodities. Between December 1978 and November 1980, inflation ate away at Americans' buying power dropping real wages by 8 percent. Other bad economic news for Carter included a weak dollar, rising unemployment, and high interest rates that dried up consumer credit.

In the 1970s, a new phenomenon had taken hold that economists called "stagflation," high unemployment *and* high inflation. To squeeze the inflation out of the U.S. economy Federal Reserve Chair Paul Volcker, whom Carter appointed in August 1979, implemented a series of sharp increases in the federal funds rate (the rate the central banks charge other financial institutions). By the spring of 1980, this interest rate stood at 17.6 percent, and the interest on thirty-year mortgages climbed to 13.7 percent. Carter was seeking reelection in a year when economic growth was flat and inflation was approaching 13 percent. The collapse of the consumer economy dovetailed perfectly to wreak maximum political damage on the Democratic administration as well as the Democrats who controlled Congress. The president's record of achievement was slender and he seemed incapable of giving the American people even the symbolic sense that better days lay ahead.

RONALD REAGAN

More than any other individual, Ronald Reagan put his stamp on the tone and tenor of America in the 1980s. Book titles often refer to the period as "the Reagan Era," "Reagan's America," "the Age of Reagan," or "Morning in America" (a Reagan campaign slogan). Since he served as president from 1981 to 1989 his persona loomed over the entire decade. "Reagan does not argue for American values," the scholar Garry Wills wrote in 1987, "he embodies them." But along with the growing historiography that places Reagan at the center of the eighties there are also many books on the subject with words like "Illusion," "Daydream," or "Sleepwalking" in their titles, suggesting there was also an element of suspending disbelief. Even Reagan's highly sympathetic biographer, Lou Canon, subtitled his exhaustive work on Reagan's presidency, *The Role of a Lifetime.* Any discussion of the eighties, therefore, must begin by looking at the extraordinary life of this personality who was, by any measure, a pivotal figure.

Ronald Wilson Reagan was born on February 6, 1911, in Tampico, Illinois, a town of about 800 people in the northwestern part of the state. His Irish-American father, John Edward "Jack" Reagan, was a fairly successful salesman but bouts with alcoholism hindered his achievements. Reagan's mother, Nelle, was an active member of the Disciples of Christ church, which in the Midwest at the time was a relatively lenient denomination. Throughout his life Reagan was not known to be particularly pious, but his mother was devout and she instilled in her younger of two sons a deep sense of self-confidence. In 1920, the Reagan family relocated to Dixon, Illinois, a town about ten times the size of Tampico that Reagan would always call his hometown. It was in Dixon where Nelle encouraged her son to take acting parts in church plays and other community theater productions. His home life could be tough, especially when his father became unemployed during the Great Depression. As a child, Reagan recalled seeing his father pass out from drink. (His father gave him the nickname "Dutch" because of the Dutch-boy haircut he sported as a youngster.) It was President Franklin D. Roosevelt's (FDR) federal relief programs that allowed Jack Reagan to support his family during the worst years of the Depression. As a young man Reagan voted for FDR and he identified himself as a liberal Democrat.

Reagan attended Eureka College in Illinois, an intimate liberal arts school linked to the Disciples of Christ that is located about twenty miles northwest of Peoria. He was a popular figure on campus who starred in school plays, played football, and was elected student body president his senior year. After graduating from Eureka in June 1932, he pursued a career in the new broadcast media of radio and landed a job announcing college football games for WOC, a tiny station in Davenport, Iowa. After proving to his employers and listeners that he had an innate talent for radio work WOC offered him a full-time position. When WOC merged with WHO, a larger station that broadcast out of Des Moines, Reagan's voice reached over a hundred thousand people and made him a celebrity in the Midwest; he earned a salary of $75 a week, which in the 1930s was a salary equal to that of a physician or a lawyer.

In 1937, while covering the spring training of the Chicago Cubs in southern California the ambitious young Reagan hired an agent to arrange a screen test for him at Warner Brothers studios. The studio was so impressed with his abilities that it signed him to a motion picture deal that paid him $200 a week. During his first year under contract Reagan was a workhorse thespian appearing in 13 movies. He broke out of B-movie status with *Knute Rockne—All American* playing the role of George Gipp, the legendary Notre Dame football player. In the film, Reagan utters the famous line: "Win one for the Gipper" that he used throughout his political career. Thereafter, he was often called "the Gipper." In 1940, he married the A-list actress, Jane Wyman, and the couple had one child, Maureen, and adopted another, Michael. Reagan received his highest critical acclaim as a screen actor for his performance as Drake McHugh in the 1942 movie *Kings Row*. The most memorable scene is where Reagan's character discovers that a nefarious doctor had punished him by needlessly amputating his legs. "Where's the rest of me?" he asks when he awakens in horror, which became the title of Reagan's 1981 autobiography.

The outbreak of World War II derailed Reagan's Hollywood career and he would never again have the chance to star in a film of the quality of *Kings Row*. He had joined the Army reserve in Des Moines, Iowa, long before the Japanese attack on Pearl Harbor and he was called to active duty in April 1942. He spent the war stateside making training films for the army. Despite Warner Brothers signing him to a seven-year, million-dollar contract, the war was a huge setback for his acting career. In the early postwar years, the studio badly miscast Reagan in a series of forgettable B movies, such as playing the sidekick to a wily chimpanzee in *Bedtime for Bonzo* (1951). While Reagan's movie career floundered, his wife Jane Wyman's flourished, especially after she won an Academy Award for Best Actress in 1948 for her performance as a deaf woman in *Johnny Belinda*. Their marriage ended in divorce the following year in an era where even in Hollywood such break ups were frowned upon. Reagan spent a few unhappy years until he met Nancy Davis, whose birth name was Anne Francis Robbins, and who was also an actor doing bit parts for MGM Studios. The couple married in March 1952 and from then on Nancy Reagan became an indispensable teammate throughout Reagan's public career. They had two children—Patricia and Ronald Jr.

During the 1950s, Reagan gained a coveted acting spot as the public relations spokesman for the General Electric (GE) Corporation. He traveled to every GE plant in the country, meeting with executives and workers, and making contacts with local officials of the Republican Party and the Chamber of Commerce. His free market ideology was cemented while giving virtually the same speech over and over again to like-minded audiences. In 1954, GE hired him to host a new television show, *General Electric Theater*, which became the top-rated Sunday night broadcast. Reagan became a household name and was paid $125,000 a year. General Electric remodeled his house with state-of-the-art appliances to advertise the "fully electric home." There were limits, however, to how far the company would allow Reagan to go in articulating his *laissez faire* philosophy, such as when GE censored a speech he gave impugning FDR's Tennessee Valley Authority (TVA) as "socialistic." It turned out that GE did not want to lose the TVA as a major buyer of its electrical equipment.

GOVERNOR REAGAN

Reagan's most important executive role prior to entering politics was his six terms as president of the Screen Actors Guild (SAG). He was SAG president during the McCarthy era, which was a time when anti-Communist crusaders in Congress and in the statehouse in Sacramento "blacklisted" Hollywood directors, producers, and actors who they saw as tainted by their associations with communism. Amidst the bipartisan effort to weed out alleged Communists and Soviet spies from government, educational institutions, and private industry, Reagan headed SAG at one of its most difficult moments. The accusations of Communist influence of the House Committee on Un-American Activities (HUAC) bitterly divided the entertainment industry with actors, producers, and directors pointing fingers at each other or defying Congress by refusing to cooperate. Directors Alfred Hitchcock, John Huston, and Otto Preminger as well as many famous actors, including Humphrey Bogart, Lauren Bacall, Katherine Hepburn, and Judy Garland, pushed back against HUAC by forming the "Committee for the First Amendment."

Given the potential power of film and television to manufacture left-wing propaganda, anti-Communist politicians and government officials, including FBI Director J. Edgar Hoover, believed that Hollywood needed to purge itself of subversive elements. As SAG president Reagan at first stood up against the congressional red-baiting of his members at a time when HUAC held prominent writers, actors, and directors in contempt for not cooperating. But as the anti-Communist atmosphere heated up Reagan testified before HUAC saying that communist sympathy was indeed a problem in Hollywood, and he passed on tips to the FBI about the political connections of some SAG members.

Following his years as SAG president Reagan grew more conservative, changed his party affiliation, and threw himself into California's Republican politics. In 1960, he campaigned for his fellow Californian, Vice President Richard Nixon, in his close presidential loss to Massachusetts Senator John F. Kennedy. Two years later, he again went out on the stump for Nixon in his unsuccessful bid to unseat California Governor Edmund G. "Pat" Brown. But it was on October 27, 1964, when Reagan spoke on behalf of the Republican presidential candidate, Senator Barry Goldwater of Arizona, when he tapped into a truly national political following. The Goldwater campaign ran the speech, "A Time for Choosing," on television, and it was a resounding success that raised over a million dollars in campaign donations. The hundreds of speeches he had given on behalf of GE had honed Reagan's oratorical skills, and he had a screen actor's ability to convey his message effectively and with feeling.

After the 1964 election, where the incumbent President Lyndon B. Johnson trounced Barry Goldwater by nearly 16 million votes, a group of wealthy southern Californian businessmen who were active in Republican politics goaded Reagan to run for governor in 1966. The developers Holmes Tuttle and Henry Salvatori organized a "Friends of Ronald Reagan" committee to raise money and popularize his candidacy. The committee hired a media consultant, Stuart Spencer, who ran a firm called BASICO, and pulled together a team of public relations specialists that compiled hundreds of policy note cards for Reagan to study. They understood that unseating the incumbent governor would not be easy, especially with a candidate who had never run for public office, and they conceded that Brown had a better understanding than Reagan of the intricacies of state government. When a reporter asked Reagan what kind of governor he would be, he quipped: "I don't know, I've never played a governor." Reagan's opponents claimed he was too extreme and inexperienced to be a serious candidate, but those conclusions would prove to be grossly oversimplified.

In the fall of 1964, students at the University of California (UC), Berkeley, many of whom were active in the civil rights movement, organized large demonstrations against the UC administration demanding greater freedom of political speech on campus. The free speech movement rocked Berkeley for the better part of the academic year. The student unrest alienated many suburban swing voters, and in August 1965, when one of the most destructive riots in U.S. history broke out in the Watts section of South-Central Los Angeles, Governor Brown bore considerable political heat for not doing enough to prevent the violence. In 1966, the Reagan campaign skillfully exploited the student agitation as well as the African-American uprising in Watts for maximum political benefit. Reagan positioned himself as the "law-and-order" candidate who would draw the line against those who seemed to be tearing California apart. Reagan defeated Governor Brown by nearly a million votes, which was a stunning achievement given that two years earlier the Republican candidate for president (Goldwater) had lost the state by 1.3 million votes. Reagan embodied the shifting mood of California's electorate, and he built a well-financed campaign organization from his base in southern California that took the Democratic establishment by surprise. It was a decisive win but the legislature remained in Democratic hands.

Early in Reagan's governorship his office was disorganized, and he delegated authority so widely that it gave the impression he was overly dependent on his executive staff. His first chief of staff, Philip Battaglia, was not up to the task and by the end of Reagan's first summer in office he was edged out. Governor Reagan replaced him with a more competent figure, William P. Clark Jr., who had staying power as one of his top advisers. Clark's staff drew up "mini-memos" for the governor that streamlined policy choices with brief summaries of state matters. Reagan could check a box at the bottom of each memo to approve, reject, or send back for further review. This system worked well for Reagan and he used it throughout his career.

As Governor, Reagan was often a pragmatist who was willing to compromise and broker deals that cut against his conservative ideological orthodoxy. By doing so, he sustained his popularity in what was still a liberal-leaning state. For example, he would sometimes later say he had shrunk the size of California's government, but during his two terms as governor from 1967 to 1975 spending doubled from under $5 billion per year to $10 billion. He also signed one of the largest tax increases in the state's history in 1967, which reflected his realism on California's perennial budget shortfalls; and a health law that protected a woman's right to choose. (He later said he never intended to relax restrictions on abortion by signing the bill.) Law and order was another matter. Governor Reagan did not hesitate to order in the National Guard to put down demonstrations he believed had grown too unruly as he did in Berkeley in September 1969 when helicopters sprayed teargas on hundreds of student protesters; "if it takes a bloodbath, let's get it over with," Reagan said. Yet while Reagan often berated the state's college students and their disruptive activities—(he once said "a hippie is someone who looks like Tarzan, walks like Jane, and smells like Cheetah")—state spending on public higher education rose steadily during his tenure. He assailed the students but stayed on the good side of their parents by fully funding the state's popular colleges and universities.

　　Governor Reagan's style of governance and active role in Republican politics fueled speculation that he was building a successful record as a chief executive to use it as a springboard for a future presidential bid. In 1968, after serving little more than a year, he put out feelers to Republican primary voters. But former Vice President Nixon had a lock on the nomination that year. After Nixon's victory Reagan was well-positioned to make a presidential run in 1976 following Nixon's second term. But the Watergate scandals and Nixon's early resignation in August 1974 erected a new set of problems for Republican presidential candidates. When President Gerald Ford chose New York Governor Nelson Rockefeller, who was identified with the northeastern liberal wing of the party, to be his vice president and running mate, the conservatives in the party rallied around Reagan. Reagan challenged Ford in some of the 1976 primaries, and although unsuccessful, he won several important states, including California and kept his name in the limelight. The effort moved him one step closer to being the front-runner for the 1980 nomination. When Georgia Governor Jimmy Carter defeated Ford, it indirectly helped Reagan by furnishing an example of an "outsider" governor winning the White House.

PRESIDENTIAL CANDIDATE

As Carter's presidency unfolded he failed to satisfy his critics from both sides of the political spectrum. The liberal Massachusetts Senator Edward Kennedy ran in the primaries testing the incumbent president's popularity among Democratic base voters. "Our leaders have resigned themselves to defeat," he declared. Competition with Kennedy added a new dimension to Carter's predicament: He could neither appease his critics on the Right who were coalescing around Reagan nor could he stave off his detractors from the Left, like Ted Kennedy, who believed he had betrayed core Democratic principles. Carter survived the intraparty rivalry but it gave the impression of disunity. Making the 1980 race all the more volatile was a new way of financing campaigns: "Political Action Committees" (PACs). PACs were invented to sidestep the post-Watergate campaign finance reform laws and get around spending limits. Republican and Democratic operatives became experts at utilizing PAC money as well as other new techniques, most notably the conservative activist Richard Viguerie's pioneering direct mail operation that used computers to connect with voters.

　　In addition to the PACs and the direct mail innovations, a new socially conservative constituency was taking shape. Outraged by the liberalization of abortion laws and other cultural influences of the 1960s, Christian evangelicals became active in Grand Old Party (GOP) politics. They formed their own PACs and became a significant base for Reagan's 1980 presidential bid. The Reverends Oral Roberts, Pat Robertson, Jimmy Swaggart, Jerry

Falwell (who had his own "Moral Majority" PAC), and the husband-and-wife team of Jim and Tammy Faye Bakker drew large audiences for their radio and television shows. In 1980, an estimated 60 to 100 million viewers tuned in each week to one or more of the "televangelists" as well as to dozens of lesser-known personalities who broadcast in local media markets. Their mastery of the new media and their ties to the wider Conservative movement turned these TV preachers into leaders of a formidable *bloc* inside the Republican Party. Reagan, who moved comfortably in Hollywood circles that Christian conservatives loved to flog, still cultivated the solid support of prominent religious personalities and through them gained access to their sizeable followings.

Amidst the ferment of the 1980 political season another event took place that would alter the media landscape. In June 1980, the investor and entrepreneur Ted Turner launched the nation's first 24-hour television news channel, the Cable News Network (CNN), headquartered in Atlanta, Georgia. Americans who subscribed to cable could tune-in and get news and information from around the world with live updates and a "news crawl" with the latest headlines. CNN spawned a legion of imitators and competitors over the years that changed the face of television news. Turner eventually sold the enterprise but not before his network had institutionalized the 24-hour news cycle as a mainstay of American journalism. These new political forces—the PACs, the Christian broadcasters, and cable news—remodeled the communications environment of American politics just when Reagan, the former actor, bounded onto the stage.

Reagan's rise came at a time when demographic and cultural changes were moving the ideological center of American politics rightward. His message indirectly catered to the needs of a large segment of the baby boom generation who were part of a remarkable population bubble of 76 million babies born between 1946 and 1964. In the 1960s and 1970s, baby boomers had expressed themselves in colorful protests revolving around civil rights, feminism, and the war in Vietnam. By the 1980s, however, economic tough times had hit just as millions of them were ready to build careers, buy homes, and start families. The conservatives had the wind at their backs, in part, because their agenda was perfectly timed when this new social reality was kicking in. The wretched state of the economy of the Carter years bred fear and a lack of confidence while the cold hand of the market enforced a new austerity. Gone were the days when young people could take their economic security for granted. Getting your "piece of the pie" was now a key concern, even something to celebrate. The genius of Reagan's brand of conservatism was that it combined self-interest with living for the "here and now" through unapologetic consumption, thereby appropriating some of the hedonistic and libertine cultural impulses that had characterized the previous two decades.

Not only did the new conservatism fit well with the careerist necessities of an aging baby boom population, but young people too began to adapt their allegiances. College Republican clubs proliferated, published their own newspapers, and organized lecture series with the help of conservative think tanks, such as the Heritage Foundation and the American Enterprise Institute. Back in the sixties, 85 percent of college students told pollsters that they hoped their education would empower them to "develop a philosophy of life." By the mid-eighties, only 44 percent exuded such idealism while the majority said they wanted to "earn a lot of money." Not since the Eisenhower era had so many young people adopted the sensibilities of Republican conservatism. Even the popular culture mirrored this rise of young conservatives with the highly-rated NBC television sit-com, *Family Ties* (1982–1989), whose lead character, played by Michael J. Fox, was a young Republican rebelling against his left-leaning parents.

THE 1980 CAMPAIGN

Reagan entered the 1980 Republican primaries as the clear front-runner. His only credible challenger was the former CIA Director George Herbert Walker Bush (who ended up joining him on the ticket). In July, upon receiving his party's nomination at the Republican National Convention in Detroit, Reagan stepped forward as the optimistic alternative to Carter's dreariness and restated his belief that America's best days lay ahead: "The American people, the most generous on earth, who created the highest standard of living, are not going to accept the notion that we can only make a better world for others by moving backwards ourselves." On August 3, he began his presidential bid by appearing at a rally in Philadelphia, Mississippi. Sixteen years earlier the town had been the site of the abduction and murder of three young civil rights volunteers who were registering black voters as part of "Freedom Summer." Spokespeople for the Reagan-Bush campaign denied that choosing Mississippi for their first campaign event had any hidden meaning, but some political commentators saw it as evidence that Reagan was replaying Nixon's "Southern Strategy" of 1968. Nixon had lined up the backing of white southerners who had left the Democratic Party in droves after Presidents Kennedy and Johnson threw their support behind civil rights. In the 1970s, Nixon had harshly criticized the federal government for imposing what he called racial "quotas" on employers that cost white workers their jobs. The often-false perceptions around "affirmative action" also pushed white voters in Reagan's direction. In 1980, the South's electoral votes could be decisive for a Reagan victory.

In Mississippi, Reagan told an overwhelmingly white audience: "I believe in states' rights. I believe we have distorted the balance of our government today by giving powers that were never intended to be given in the Constitution to that federal establishment." The Reagan-Bush campaign hoped to win not only regional voters away from the South's native son, Jimmy Carter, but also white people outside the South, such as blue-collar workers who polls showed believed too much attention had been given to black grievances over the previous decade. Throughout the campaign, Reagan also blasted Carter for his "softness" toward the Soviet Union, his handling of the Iranian hostage crisis, and his agreement with General Omar Torrijos to place the Panama Canal under Panamanian sovereignty at the end of 1999. Carter was "handing over what is rightfully United States territory," he said. (Some high-profile conservatives disagreed with Reagan's stand on the canal issue because they respected Torrijos as an anti-Communist ally in Latin America.) But the canal debate fanned the flames of national pride and it served the campaign well.

On October 28, in Cleveland, Ohio, Reagan's sole debate with Carter took place at a time when the election was still up for grabs. Given that Carter had all of the advantages of incumbency the goal of the Reagan-Bush campaign was to use the nationally televised event to reintroduce its candidate to the American people. The news media latched on to one exchange that occurred after Carter finished a short disquisition on national health care policy. Reagan retorted, cocking his head to the side and smiling facetiously: "There you go again." His belittling attitude toward the president elevated Reagan's stature by implying that he had the self-confidence to know he could do a better job. It surfaced later that someone on the White House staff had leaked to the Reagan-Bush campaign the three-ring binder of notes and summaries Carter had used to prepare for the debate. The disclosure of "Debategate" caused a minor brush up when the FBI as well as a congressional committee opened investigations. However, nothing came of it and the political press treated the story as little more than a schoolyard prank.

Reagan won with 51 percent of the popular vote to Carter's 44 percent, and handily whipped the incumbent president in the Electoral College, 489 to 49. To the chagrin of West Coast Democrats, Carter had given his concession speech hours before the polls closed in California (which Reagan easily won). The 50.7 percent voter turnout in the 1980 election was the lowest in 32 years, and nearly 40 percent of voters told pollsters they would have cast their ballots for any candidate simply for not being Carter. The third party candidacy of John Anderson, the 10-term liberal Republican representative from Illinois who ran as an independent, tended to help Reagan. Anderson won 7 percent of the popular vote (but no electoral votes). The Reagan-Bush team won by 8,423,115 votes and carried 44 states.

Reagan also had coattails. The Republicans won 12 Senate seats gaining control of a chamber of Congress for the first time in 26 years. The Senate flipped from a 59 to 41 Democratic majority to a 52 to 48 Republican advantage. Not since 1958, did a party pick up so many Senate seats in a single election. Conservative PACs had targeted seven liberal Democratic senators for defeat: George McGovern of South Dakota; Frank Church of Idaho; John Culver of Iowa; Birch Bayh of Indiana; Warren Magnuson of Washington; Gaylord Nelson of Wisconsin; and Alan Cranston of California. Among them only Cranston survived. In the House of Representatives, the GOP won 34 net seats and also made big gains in governorships and in state legislatures. The Democrats held on to their majority in the House, but it had been cut to half. The Reagan campaign's "Southern Strategy" paid off as well: among white voters Reagan won 59 percent.

The Iranian hostage crisis dragged on through Carter's lame-duck period while his National Security Council worked tirelessly to secure the release of the remaining 52 hostages. Secretary of State Warren Christopher, a Washington insider and veteran of several Democratic administrations who replaced Cyrus Vance, had been in charge of negotiating the terms. The day before Reagan's inauguration, Secretary Christopher had succeeded in reaching a deal with the Islamic Republic of Iran to end the stand-off. Carter spent sleepless nights pushing for the compact (called the "Algerian Accords") and hoped to leave office with securing the hostages' freedom as his final official act as president. The United States agreed not to intervene in Iran and to lift the freeze on Iranian assets, among other concessions.

Carter had a deep emotional commitment to resolve the crisis on his watch but the Iranians controlled the timing. They despised him for giving sanctuary to the shah and violating their sovereignty with "Operation Eagle Claw." As payback, they waited until the moment Carter was no longer president to authorize the departure of the plane carrying the hostages bound for Germany. The television networks juxtaposed Reagan's inaugural events with heartwarming scenes of the hostages reuniting with their loved ones after 444 days in captivity. In the eyes of the nation it was Reagan, not Carter, who freed the Americans.

An audience of about 41 million television viewers watched as Chief Justice Warren Burger swore in Reagan as the 40th U.S. president. The inaugural celebrations gave off an air of ebullience and optimism as well as ostentatious displays of wealth. Never before had a former movie star won the presidency and the Reagans' Hollywood connections were on full display. The lavish galas gave the distinct impression that show business had come to Washington. A-list celebrities were in attendance, and the stylish parties brought an elegance to the White House not seen since the Kennedy years. On the inauguration night, First Lady Nancy Reagan wore a James Galanos hand-beaded gown valued at $22,500, which she later donated to the Smithsonian Institution. "I felt like Cinderella," she said.

REVIEW QUESTIONS

1. What major domestic and foreign policy crises proved to be the most damaging to President James Earl Carter's one-term presidency?
2. What concrete steps did the Carter Administration take diplomatically and militarily in confronting the problem of the U.S. Embassy takeover in Tehran, Iran?
3. What does Ronald Reagan's long career as a Hollywood actor and a California politician before he won the presidency in 1980 tell us about his worldview and how it was shaped?
4. As Governor of California (1967-1975) what were some of Reagan's actions that illustrate a pragmatic approach to governance? What were some of his more "ideological" stands on the issues of the day?
5. What demographic or social organizations, as well as political techniques, were mobilized during the 1980 presidential campaign that were relatively new and innovative? How did the Cable News Network (CNN), political action committees (PACs), and computerized direct mail operations change American politics in 1980? How would you characterize the new ethos that the Reagans brought to Washington in January 1981?

mysearchlab CONNECTIONS SOURCES ONLINE

READ AND REVIEW

Review this chapter by using the study aids and these related documents available on MySearchLab.

Study Plan

Chapter Test

Essay Test

Documents

Jimmy Carter, The "Malaise" Speech (1979)
Carter talks of a malaise of the American spirit.

Ronald Reagan, Republican Party Nomination Acceptance (1980)
Candidate Reagan discusses the values of the conservative Republican Party and his goals if elected president.

Ronald Reagan, First Inaugural Address (1981)
President Ronald Reagan speaks on reducing taxes, government spending, and the size of the federal government.

Richard Viguerie, Why the New Right is Winning (1981)
Ultra conservative writer talks about the 1980 election.

RESEARCH AND EXPLORE

Use the databases available within MySearchLab to find additional primary and secondary sources the topics within this chapter.

Video

Jimmy Carter and the Crisis

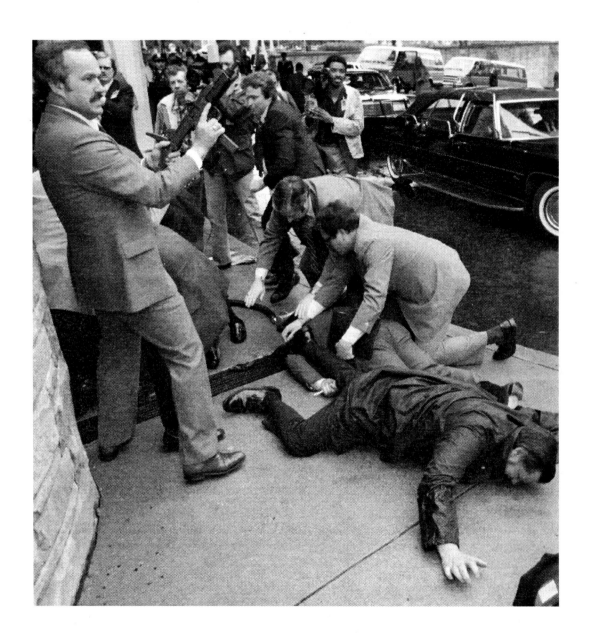

1

The Reagan Revolution

CHAPTER OUTLINE

Assassination Attempt
Reagan and the Press
Reagan in Power

Deregulation
The New Economic Orthodoxy
The Environment

ASSASSINATION ATTEMPT

Sixty-nine days into his presidency, on March 30, 1981, Ronald Reagan was leaving the Washington Hilton Hotel after addressing an AFL-CIO conference when a deranged gunman lunged out of the crowd on the sidewalk and emptied his .22 caliber pistol. One bullet ricocheted off the presidential limousine and hit Reagan just under his left armpit. His press secretary, James Brady, was shot in the forehead. A Secret Service agent, Tim McCarthy, and a Washington DC police officer, Tom Delahanty, were also wounded. Secret Service agents threw Reagan into the car after brandishing their Uzi submachine guns and rushed him to George Washington University Hospital. Brady was paralyzed and would spend the rest of his life in a wheelchair. Along with his wife Sarah, he became a fierce advocate for stricter gun control.

The 25-year-old assailant, John Hinckley Jr., had fired wildly in the president's direction using exploding bullets. Hinckley claimed to have been obsessed with the movie *Taxi Driver* and believed that if he assassinated a leading political figure, like the storyline of the film, he would become a hero in the eyes of the actor Jodie Foster who

This photograph captures the moment on March 30, 1981, just after a deranged gunman, John Hinckley Jr., emptied his .22 caliber pistol in the direction of President Reagan outside the Washington Hilton Hotel. Fragments of one of the bullets struck Reagan and he spent 12 days recovering in George Washington University Hospital. His press secretary, James Brady, suffered a paralyzing head wound.

played the role of an underage prostitute. The Academy Awards show had been scheduled to air on television that evening and Hinckley asked one of the arresting officers if the broadcast would be cancelled because of the shooting, which it was.

At the White House, news of the shooting stirred a sense of pandemonium. Secretary of State Alexander M. Haig Jr. held an ill-fated press conference where he proclaimed: "I am in control here." The press quickly pointed out that Haig was wrong. The vice president, the Speaker of the House, and the Senate Pro Tem were in line to succeed the president before the secretary of state. It was an embarrassing gaffe that gave credence to the idea already circulating among some of Reagan's close advisers, that the former general might not be the right person for the job.

Reagan had been very lucky he caught a ricochet. The 70-year-old president suffered a punctured lung and a severe loss of blood. He sustained three hours of surgery and spent the next 12 days in the hospital. He handled his ordeal with humor and aplomb displaying grace under pressure. "I forgot to duck," he told his wife Nancy; "Please tell me you're all Republicans," he chided the doctors. His lightheartedness amidst danger endeared him with an American public that was deeply concerned about losing another leader to senseless gun violence. Telegrams, cards, and letters flooded the White House wishing the president well, and the period of Reagan's recovery set up a sympathetic relationship with the American people and the press that served him well in the political battles that followed. Reagan's optimistic nature, even while healing from a gunshot wound that could have taken his life, got the nation behind him early on in his presidency. Two weeks after he was discharged from the hospital, he spoke to a joint session of Congress where he was given a hero's welcome and several lengthy standing ovations. Polls showed that after the assassination attempt Reagan's popularity skyrocketed past his 77 percent approval rating before he was shot. Speaker of the House Tip O'Neill conceded: "We can't argue with a man as popular as he is."

REAGAN AND THE PRESS

The White House Communications Office became expert at framing media coverage to further its legislative and foreign policy goals. Throughout 1981, when President Reagan was trying to pass his agenda through a divided Congress, he used polished television presentations to great effect. It was this combination of Reagan's acting abilities and the skills of his public relations (PR) specialists that brought the "bully pulpit" into the modern media age. Opinion polls suggested the president was more popular personally than many of his policies, such as a CBS/*New York Times* poll showing that the public favored a balanced budget over broadened military spending and opposed tax cuts for the wealthy and corporations. Cuts in public transportation, environmental programs, and assistance to college students were equally unpopular as well as the building of new nuclear power plants. The response from the White House was to bend these political realities by deploying compelling narratives.

In his speeches, Reagan often evoked patriotic themes similar to those he had been delivering since his days as a spokesman for General Electric (GE). He had a talent for tailoring his remarks and timing them perfectly for television sound bites. He started the practice of giving a short radio address every Saturday morning and hoped they would be as effective as Franklin D. Roosevelt's (FDR's) fireside chats. The White House assembled a crack team of media professionals to manage every aspect of the president's image. Michael Deaver and Chief of Staff James Baker III ran a PR shop that left little to chance. At the dawn of the 24-hour news cycle, they stressed "message discipline" and a "line of the day" approach to press management. High-profile administration figures would fan out and hammer away at a single theme to have White House prerogatives dominate the topic of discussion among the press and television news outlets. They utilized visual imagery as no other previous administration and limited Reagan's unscripted access to the press. During his first year in office Reagan held only six press conferences.

Donald Regan, who served as both treasury secretary and White House chief of staff, said of Reagan's persona: "Every moment of every public appearance was scheduled, every word scripted, every place where Reagan was expected to stand was chalked with toe marks . . . He has been learning his lines, composing his facial expressions, hitting his toe marks for half a century." These efforts paid political dividends. Michael Deaver said that Reagan "enjoyed the most generous treatment by the press of any president in the postwar era." Some frustrated independent journalists started calling Reagan the "Teflon" president because no matter how unpopular some of his policies were, they never seemed to "stick" to him. Even factual gaffes he was seldom called out on, like when he said "80 percent of our air pollution stems from hydrocarbons released by vegetation," or his claim in 1983 that the United States had "as much forest as there was when Washington was at Valley Forge." So smitten was the Beltway press with the new charismatic president that journalist Mark Hertsgaard dedicated an entire book to critiquing its lagging performance titled *On Bended Knee.* "Upon Reagan's ascension to power in 1981," Hertsgaard noted, "The press quickly settled into a posture of accommodating passivity from which it never completely arose."

Yet as the recession dragged on into 1982, with unemployment peaking at 10.8 percent, even slick public relations and a compliant press corps were not enough to keep Reagan's magic from wearing thin; that summer the president's approval rating slipped to 42 percent.

REAGAN IN POWER

Throughout the 1970s, stagflation had so pummeled the American middle class that it gave the incoming administration a virtual blank slate to try out radically new economic ideas as long as they departed from the status quo. Few administrations in history had been given such a chance to rewrite the script of the nation's economy. The first budget that President Reagan sent to Congress called for $41.4 billion in cuts and a $7.2 billion boost in defense spending. His party controlled the U.S. Senate for the first time in decades, but he did not have a rubberstamp in the Democratic-controlled House of Representatives. The White House had to work with House Speaker Thomas "Tip" O'Neill, the liberal stalwart from Massachusetts. But Speaker O'Neill had to contend with 47 or so "moderates" in his own caucus, mostly from the South (sometimes called "Boll Weevils"), who the Republicans could count on to cross party lines to pass Reagan's agenda, especially regarding taxes, the economy, and defense.

When Reagan was a presidential candidate his chief domestic policy adviser, Martin Anderson, authored "Policy Memorandum No. 1," which formulated a blueprint for what later became known as "Reaganomics." The centerpiece of Anderson's policy prescription was a large tax cut for the wealthiest Americans and corporations with the goal of freeing up capital for new investment. Reagan needed little convincing. As a successful Hollywood movie actor he found himself in the top tax bracket, which could be as high as 94 percent. This tax burden, he claimed, coerced him to pass on new acting roles because he had little incentive to earn more money given that at some point during the year he felt he was no longer working for himself, but for the Internal Revenue Service. Reagan's view of taxes mirrored his own intuitive and experiential understanding of economics. But the stories he told about his own tax burden were often misleading since the highest rate he paid was during World War II (90 percent) and that was only on income above $100,000. And the tax cuts that Reagan advocated mostly concerned the top 2 percent of incomes, not the vast majority of working Americans.

Reagan had not only come to power in the middle of an economic crisis that gave him great leeway to maneuver, but he also possessed a detailed master plan that conservative social planners had been tinkering with since the 1920s. The president's economic advisers seized upon the "supply-side" theories of Arthur Laffer, Jude Wanniski, George Gilder, and others. In his best-selling book, *Wealth and Poverty* (1981), Gilder had offered a spirited defense of *laissez-faire* capitalism. "A successful economy depends on the proliferation of the rich," he wrote, "to help the poor and middle classes, one must cut the taxes of the rich." In the Congress, the New York Representative Jack Kemp, a former National Football League quarterback and rising star in the GOP, dedicated his career to furthering the cause of "supply-side" economics. Supply-siders believed in the self-regulating nature of markets and regarded government intrusion into the economy with outright contempt. They argued that by cutting the taxes of the top earners and corporations an economic boom would follow that would fill the coffers of the federal treasury. In a reversal of the Robin Hood ethic, the richer you were the bigger the tax break. Instead of larger budget deficits and a bigger national debt, they confidently predicted that tax cuts for high earners would bring about greater revenues.

Early on, Reagan recognized the political usefulness of the supply-side theory, which was consistent with what conservatives had been advocating for years: tax cuts to reward wealth creation and to deny government the resources to meddle with the private sector. The White House tapped into a well-connected cadre of supply-siders from conservative think tanks that operated outside the universities. At the start of his 1980 campaign, after undergoing cram sessions with enthusiasts of the new theory, Reagan told an interviewer: "An across the board reduction in tax rates, every time it has been tried, it has resulted in such an increase in prosperity . . . that even government winds up with more revenue." It was this assertion that, during the Republican primaries, George H. W. Bush labeled "voodoo economics."

The Reagan administration harnessed the boundless energy of a young corporate lobbyist named Wayne Valis to marshal congressional backing for the new tax plan. In February 1981, Valis gathered together nearly a hundred of his colleagues who were among the most effective lobbyists on Capitol Hill, and he prodded them to join the administration in its tax-cutting crusade. "Like the Confederacy, you have only won defensive victories," he said. "That leads to defeat. If you will march with us this time, you will win offensive victories!" Valis's call to arms set the tone for the administration's combativeness in pushing through its economic agenda. These efforts paid off six months later with the passage of the Economic Recovery Tax Act (ERTA) of 1981.

Democratic members of the Ninety-seventh Congress understood the political peril of inaction in a down economy and they worked with the new administration. On

August 13, 1981, Reagan held an outdoor signing ceremony for the ERTA at his 688-acre ranch outside Santa Barbara. Forty-eight House Democrats crossed over to unite with the Republicans to overhaul the nation's tax code. The new legislation reduced marginal income tax rates for all Americans by 25 percent. The wealthiest people, who paid 70 percent in 1981, would see their tax rate lowered to 50 percent. Rates for lower-income people fell more modestly, from 14 percent to 11 percent. The ERTA was the biggest tax cut in American history and it was intended to be permanent. It cut corporate taxes by $747 billion over five years, and it also lowered the capital gains tax from 28 percent to 20 percent. The threshold for estate taxes shot up from $165,625 to $600,000.

Journalist Thomas Edsall, writing in *The Washington Post* on the day Reagan signed the ERTA, reported that the new tax law "heavily rewarded traditional Republican constituencies" and sharply curtailed "federal taxes on such forms of income as business profits, capital gains, interest on income and oil revenues, as well as on inheritances." Edsall pointed out that the new tax law "left the government more dependent than ever on taxes on ordinary wage and salary income." The ERTA, as proposed, freed up money for the wealthiest Americans, Wall Street investors, and big business to invest to get the economy moving again. The wealthy reaped the greatest windfall from the changes in the tax code. And during the "sausage-making" mark up of the legislation representatives and senators from both parties larded the bill with billion-dollar tax breaks for corporations, oil conglomerates, and other special interests. Many supporters of the new tax law also demanded from Congress deep cuts in domestic programs, and since the administration also requested substantial increases in defense spending, the debate generally prioritized military expenditures over health and human services.

But before the ink was dry on Reagan's signature of the ERTA, his top budget adviser, Office of Management and Budget (OMB) Director David Stockman, sounded the alarm about a pending fiscal train wreck. Stockman, who was a hard-charging 34-year-old former Michigan congressman, calculated that looming on the horizon were the biggest peacetime deficits in U.S. history. Many of the conservatives who populated Reagan's economic brain trust had an innate aversion to deficits. They feared that after years of high interest rates devoted to controlling inflation their own tax policies might set the stage for a new inflationary cycle. Running up their own deficits had the added political liability of undercutting one of Reagan's central critiques of Jimmy Carter's economic policies. Stockman knew the administration's "rosy scenario" that a balanced budget would be achieved by 1984 was totally unrealistic.

However, running up big deficits could also have the potential to be used politically to serve as an excuse to "starve the beast" and impel the Democrats in Congress to pare down expenditures that served their core constituencies. Reagan wanted to "cut off their allowance" (he liked to say). The Omnibus Reconciliation Act of late 1981 included $136 billion in budget cuts for the 1982 to 1984 period. More than 200 federal programs were on the chopping block. Hit the hardest were appropriations for education, the environment, health, housing, aid to the cities, food stamps, research on synthetic fuels, and the arts.

OMB Director Stockman and other deficit hawks championed dispensing with what they called "pork barrel" projects. But many Grand Old Party (GOP) members of Congress were not about to go along with cutting transportation, farm subsidies, and other federal disbursements that benefited them politically in their home states or districts. Over the course of Reagan's first term, the structural deficits that emerged were largely the result of cutting taxes while increasing military spending. Proposals for zeroing out whole categories of federal subsidies that Stockman sent to Congress were "dead on arrival." Polls persistently showed that there was little popular support for eviscerating domestic programs. These constraints set up a political atmosphere where the Republican administration and the Democratic Congress cobbled together budgets that attempted to fund both "guns" and "butter."

The administration and Congress worked together on a defense buildup that was among the largest in American history in peacetime. Secretary of Defense Casper Weinberger, who had been Nixon's OMB director where his cost-cutting zeal had earned him the nickname "Cap the Knife," now that he was in charge of the Pentagon seemed to lose his characteristic parsimony. Each year during Reagan's first term, Weinberger asked Congress for record-setting amounts of money; the military outlays rose by 34 percent, going from $171 billion to $229 billion. By the end of the decade, the defense buildup had totaled nearly $2 trillion.

These supplementary expenses did not necessarily mean the United States was getting the greatest "bang for the buck." The hasty growth of weapons systems could be duplicative and wasteful and opened up opportunities for profiteering. It wasn't long before congressional investigators were looking into cost overruns, no-bid contracts, and the activities of well-connected individuals and corporations. In the latter half of the decade, procurement scandals besieged the Capitol, which included the infamous $600 toilet seats and $7,000 coffee makers. Forty-five of the largest defense contractors eventually came under criminal investigation for illegal kickbacks and overcharges.

On the campaign trail Reagan had repeated an apocryphal story about an individual who personified the undeserving poor. (He often used yarns and personal anecdotes to illustrate larger points.) There was a woman in Chicago he called a "welfare queen" who "had eighty names, thirty addresses, twelve Social Security cards" and "collected veterans' benefits on four nonexistent husbands." He said that her tax-free income was "over $150,000." The subtext of the story was that government relief aimed at the poor should be slashed due to rampant waste and abuse. The tale became a motif indicting the failures of Lyndon Johnson's Great Society social programs. But when reporters scrutinized the case, they could find only one woman in Chicago who had been convicted in 1977 of using two aliases to pick up welfare checks totaling about $8,000.

Reagan differentiated between what he called the "truly needy" and the "truly greedy," and sometimes talked about "a welfare queen in designer jeans." He continued to use the "welfare queen" trope as president, and in 1981 when he told it to a gathering of members of the Congressional Black Caucus they stormed out of the Oval Office. It marked a significant departure in trying to understand the causes and consequences of poverty in America. When the administration later proposed counting ketchup as a "vegetable side dish" to save money in the federal school lunch program it backtracked after facing public scorn. Throughout the previous two decades, the plight of the poor had been a major concern in American politics. In 1961, middle-class Americans were shocked when CBS aired Edward R. Murrow's documentary *Harvest of Shame* on the day after Thanksgiving exposing the living conditions of migrant farm workers in rural Florida. The following year Michael Harrington published *The Other America*—about poverty in America—which caught the attention of President Kennedy. Lyndon Johnson's "war on poverty" followed, and alleviating poverty was the centerpiece of both Robert F. Kennedy and Martin Luther King Jr.'s public work in their final years. Reagan's attitude had a potent effect on the national dialogue on poverty. It changed the focus from shaming the nation for failing the poor to breeding indifference, or worse, blaming the victims of poverty themselves. The revamped conservative ideology that Reagan brought to Washington went a long way toward realigning the dominant culture's interpretation of poverty as well as the government's role (if any) in lessening its effects.

The Reagan administration not only reconfigured the nation's perception of the working poor, but also raised fundamental questions about the legitimacy of labor unions and their collective bargaining rights. Throughout the post–World War II era Americans had accepted labor unions and their attendant rights as a normative part of modern industrial relations. Since the 1930s the National Labor Relations Board (NLRB) had acted as a reasonably neutral arbiter in most capital-labor disputes. Reagan's NLRB, however, favored management over labor more so than previous administrations. Companies now had greater latitude to impose speed-ups, hire scab workers, and violate labor contracts. No battle illustrates this new order in labor relations better than the manner in which Reagan handled a strike by the Professional Air Traffic Controllers Organization (PATCO) that occurred early in his presidency.

In 1980, PATCO had been one of three national labor unions that had endorsed Reagan for president (the other two were the Teamsters and the Airline Pilots Association). In August 1981, PATCO's rank and file voted for a strike action to address long-festering grievances relating to their pay scale, hours of activity, and stressful working conditions. During the previous decade, strikes by public workers were usually settled quickly with good-faith negotiations and federal arbitration. In a period of high unemployment, the PATCO strike by relatively well-paid, highly skilled professionals failed to glean much public sympathy. Although the airlines were highly unionized at the time, no other union in the industry took meaningful action in solidarity. Reagan gave PATCO 48 hours to end the strike and when the workers refused, he fired all 11,600 PATCO workers. He then brought in supervisors and air traffic controllers from the U.S. military to break the strike. The Department of Justice arrested some of the union leaders and criminally prosecuted them. In a few short weeks PATCO was history. It was the most aggressive stand against organized labor by the federal government since the passage of the antilabor Taft-Hartley Act of 1947.

The PATCO episode became a new template in the 1980s for labor relations that drove home the point that the federal government would no longer tolerate strikes by its employees. The president's decisive stand against PATCO afforded a context for a string of private sector strikes that ended badly for the unions. Not long after the PATCO action, the Greyhound Bus Company and Eastern Airlines fired striking workers and replaced them with nonunion substitutes. The labor leader and cofounder of the United Farm Workers, Dolores Huerta, noted: "We found that right after the PATCO people were fired the United Auto Workers Union accepted an agreement to freeze their wages. That put a lot of pressure on the other unions to do the same thing. So, what you had was a tremendous weakening of the power of labor."

The Reagan administration also had a very different viewpoint toward federal regulatory agencies than its predecessor. This new ideological orientation drove the appointment of lobbyists, corporate lawyers, and executives from the regulated industries themselves to pivotal positions. For example, John Van de Water, who previously ran a West Coast consulting firm that specialized in union busting, became the head of the NLRB. During his confirmation hearing an excerpt of one of Van de Water's speeches was read into the congressional record: "Good faith bargaining simply means that you listen to the union's argument with yours. That's all that good faith bargaining is. You don't have to give a cent."

Other similar appointments followed, such as C. W. McMillian, vice president of the National Cattleman's Association, who became the head of the Department of Agriculture's inspection division; and Richard Lyng, a lobbyist for the American Meat Institute, who was named an undersecretary of agriculture. The assistant secretary of energy for conservation and renewable energy, Joseph Tribble, came from the Georgia Pulp and Paper Company, a corporation that had been prosecuted for dumping toxic waste into rivers. James Watt was appointed secretary of the Interior who had been a lawyer for the Mountain States Legal Foundation, a law firm that represented mining and timber corporations. Anne Gorsuch (Burford) was put in control of the Environmental Protection Agency (EPA) who, like Watt, came from Colorado and built her career fighting against environmental regulations as a state legislator. Secretary of Labor Raymond Donovan was a construction company executive who instructed the agencies under his jurisdiction, including the Mine Safety and Health Administration (MSHA), to promote "voluntary" compliance with health and safety laws.

The Occupational Safety and Health Administration (OSHA), in charge of protecting Americans who worked in dangerous industries and enforcing workplace safety, Reagan called "one of the most pernicious of the watchdog agencies" that was poised "to minimize the ownership of private property in this country." OSHA's budget was slashed by 10 percent, and Thorne Auchter was installed as assistant secretary of the agency whose family-run construction business in Jacksonville, Florida, had been leveled with 48 safety violations. A Wall Street insider, John Shad, chaired the Securities and Exchange Commission (SEC), and he labored to remake the agency into a partner in the prerogatives of brokerage houses and investment banks. During his seven-year tenure at the SEC, Shad froze the number of investigators at its 1981 level even though the number of stock traders nearly doubled in that period. The SEC's budget was also cut by roughly 30 percent, and the enforcement division's staff fell from 200 inspectors to 50. Reagan's secretary of the Treasury, Donald Regan, entered government directly from his post as CEO of Merrill Lynch, and, like Shad, pushed to deregulate financial services. And so it went with many of Reagan's top appointees.

DEREGULATION

In February 1981, Reagan signed Executive Order 12291 mandating that all federal regulations undergo a "cost-benefit" analysis. Proposals for new guidelines were to be submitted to David Stockman's OMB to determine their effects on business. Any rule that business didn't like would be subjected to an industry-friendly review. The OMB possessed new powers to reject "burdensome" regulations and Jim Tozzi, a corporate lobbyist, became the deputy administrator of the Office of Information and Regulatory Affairs (OIRA), a division of OMB. Tozzi had specialized in finding ways around federal rules for his clients and now, as a high-ranking official, he could "review" many of the same directives he had battled against. The administration also notified Chambers of Commerce around the country to appeal directly to the White House and go over the heads of federal agencies if they were not satisfied with the government's handling of their regulatory obligations.

Reagan appointed J. Peter Grace, chief of W. R. Grace & Company, to lead a commission called the "President's Private Sector Survey on Cost Control" to formulate a comprehensive analysis of all existing federal regulations. The Grace Commission's executive committee consisted of CEOs from some of the nation's largest corporations and it worked behind closed doors; when Congress requested a full list of its members the panel refused to cooperate. The Grace Commission weathered some embarrassment when in the mid-eighties W. R. Grace & Company had to settle a civil lawsuit that accused it of poisoning the groundwater in Woburn, Massachusetts. Health officials attributed the leukemia deaths of five children and one adult to Grace's pollution. (A book on the Woburn case became a best seller and was made into a Hollywood movie titled *A Civil Action*.)

The Grace Commission's final report concluded that removing federal regulations on business would fetch $424 billion in savings in three years, and would recoup an astounding $1.9 trillion per year by the year 2000. The nonprofit watchdog group, *Public Citizen*, believed these assertions were wildly exaggerated: "The implicit philosophy of the commission's report is that if American corporations were free of various federally mandated environmental, health and safety regulations, they could operate in a more cost-effective and publicly responsible manner. But Grace's own company's environmental and workplace record illustrates the pitfalls of weakening or abandoning such laws." Studies from both the Government Accounting Office (GAO) and the Congressional Budget Office echoed *Public Citizen's* conclusions. Later, the White House conceded that the Grace Commission report was "riddled with inaccuracies and vastly overstated potential savings."

One tragic example of the consequences of the administration's deregulatory zeal entailed the pharmaceutical industry. Beginning in the 1960s, medical studies linked aspirin that was used to relieve the symptoms of childhood diseases, such as chicken pox, with a higher risk of developing Reye's syndrome, a disease that can cause severe damage to the brain and liver as well as lead to death. Pediatricians had been warning parents not to give their children aspirin when they had chicken pox or other viral infections. In 1981, the Department of Health and Human Services (HSS) decided to alert consumers about the danger, and the Food and Drug Administration (FDA) followed suit, citing a "consensus of the scientific experts" that new warning labels were in order for children's aspirin. The Centers for Disease Control and Prevention (CDC) and the American Academy of Pediatrics also favored new labels. But business associations aligned with the pharmaceutical industry reacted negatively and funded a group of their own called the "Committee on the Care of Children" that aggressively lobbied against the new rule. Assessing the potential costs to drug companies, Jim Tozzi of the OIRA squashed any attempt to compel them to print new labels for aspirin. In November 1982, Reagan's HSS secretary, Richard Schweiker, withdrew the labeling mandate saying the idea had been "premature."

The battle over the warning labels continued until 1986 when the administration succumbed to public pressure and introduced the new guidelines. In 1980, there had been 555 reported cases of Reye's syndrome; the year after the labeling requirement went into effect there were only 36 reported cases. A study by the National Academy of Sciences and the School of Public Health at the University of California, Berkeley, found that of the hundreds of children who died of Reye's syndrome between 1981 and 1986, 1,470 might have been saved if aspirin had been properly labeled. "These 1,470 deaths were especially tragic," the report concluded, "because they were, typically, healthy children who never recovered from the viral infection of chicken pox."

THE NEW ECONOMIC ORTHODOXY

The budget deficit projections compelled Reagan to raise taxes to stave off fiscal disaster. In August 1982, he signed the Tax Equity and Fiscal Responsibility Act (TEFRA), which raised $98 billion in new revenues over three years by modifying some of the original breaks that had been part of the ERTA. Some of the new levies were not only aimed at the business community, but they also included excise taxes on tobacco, airports, communications, and other sources of revenues peppered throughout the complicated tax code. Reagan insisted that the TEFRA was not a tax hike but a loophole closing measure, which in the long run was true because the ERTA, even with the passage of TEFRA, lowered overall tax revenues. The new law reimbursed about one-quarter of the taxes the administration and Congress had abolished the previous year. Also in 1982, Reagan signed the Highway Revenue Act, which contained a new levy on gasoline designed to raise $3.3 billion.

Reagan's signing of the TEFRA and other tax bills disappointed acolytes of supply-side economics, but the need for revenue enhancement measures tugged at Reagan's pragmatic side as well as his political intuition that told him how far he could go. In the midterm elections that November the GOP lost 27 seats in the House of Representatives. Had they lost seven more they would have been back to their pre-1981 level. When the Ninety-eighth Congress was sworn in two months later, the president's approval rating stood at 47 percent, signifying the lingering effects of the recession still exacted a political toll.

From the time President Franklin D. Roosevelt first enacted the federal minimum wage law in 1938 there had been regular raises to keep up with inflation and give the lowest-paid workers a share of society's productivity gains. Reagan never liked the idea of the government dictating wages and said during the campaign that the minimum wage caused higher unemployment, especially among African–American teenagers. He was determined to make sure there would be no increases on his watch. Just before leaving office Carter signed legislation raising the minimum from $2.30 to $3.35 an hour, which took effect in 1982; but thereafter, as promised, there were no further augmentations of the minimum wage during Reagan's two terms. The result was that in the 1980s inflation ate away at the minimum wage's real value until it had fallen 25.2 percent by 1990. Allowing the minimum wage to drop in value by one-fourth over the course of the decade put additional downward pressure on wages and generally gave businesses greater access to cheaper labor. Moreover, the share of private sector workers who belonged to unions fell from close to 20 percent in 1980 to 12.1 percent in 1990. (By the 2000s, it had dropped to about 7 percent.) The decline in real wages, along with lower interest rates and global oil prices, assisted in bringing down the rate of inflation. When the inflation that crippled the economy finally began to recede, going from 12.5 percent in 1980 to only 3.8 percent by early 1983, Reaganomics was widely heralded as a success.

In early 1981, secretary of human services, Richard Schweiker, caused a stir when he called for reducing Social Security benefits as well as new requirements to punish early retirees. Reagan had criticized Social Security throughout his public career, sometimes denouncing it as an arm of "coercive" government. There was not a high level of public trust in a Republican administration's ability to manage fundamental changes to Social Security. Reagan responded to this political reality by appointing a 15-member commission headed by one of the administration's favorite free market economists, Alan Greenspan, to examine the condition of Social Security and make recommendations.

Greenspan had been a close associate of the free-market guru and *Atlas Shrugged* author, Ayn Rand, and, along with Milton Friedman, was among the academic economists most famous for holding an almost religious devotion to the precepts of *laissez-faire* capitalism. By 1983, there was a bipartisan consensus in Washington that tinkering with the payroll tax was warranted to shore up the Social Security system. The Greenspan Commission allowed President Reagan to get his bearings on Social Security before running headlong into a confrontation with the Democratic House over the future of one of the nation's most beloved programs. The sheer complexity of the long-term fiscal health of Social Security as well as the trust fund's popularity required due diligence from politicians from both parties. The commission idea had an air of necessity to it since in early 1983, two months after the Republicans had lost seats in the midterm elections, Reagan's approval rating had sunk to 35 percent. Some of his political aides attributed this slide in the polls to his mixed signals on his plans for Social Security.

The Greenspan Commission recommended imposing higher payroll taxes, which after enacted by Congress accounted for about half of the hike in taxes from 1984 to 1989. The enhanced payroll taxes increased the burden on most working people. Additionally, cash-strapped states and local governments raised taxes to offset the effects of the recession and the reductions in federal assistance. When evaluated in the context of the lower tax rates for the highest income earners, the changes in the tax code of the early 1980s amounted to one of the largest redistributions of wealth upward in U.S. history.

Throughout Reagan's two terms the defense buildup totaled nearly $2 trillion, and all eight of the administration's budgets ran deficits. The smallest was in fiscal year 1982, which was $127.9 billion; and the largest was in fiscal year 1986, which was $221.2 billion. In 1983, the deficit reached a peacetime record up to that time of 6.3 percent of GDP. The national debt went from roughly $900 billion in 1980 to $2.9 trillion in 1989. Had the administration's 1981 tax cuts stood without subsequent remedies in the form of revenue "enhancements" the deficits would have grown even larger. A bipartisan coalition in Washington had set the nation on a budgetary course that was drenched in red ink.

Throughout the post–World War II period the United States had run modest trade surpluses with the rest of the world. But on September 16, 1985, the Department of Commerce announced that the United States had become a debtor nation. For the first time since 1914, the U.S. was now in a position where it had to borrow money from abroad to pay for its imports. In 1980, despite the economic recession and inflationary pressures the U.S. had still kept up a trade surplus of about $166 billion; by 1987 Americans owed foreigners $340 billion. The new trade imbalances were, in part, the product of "neo-liberal" policies that rewarded companies that outsourced production to low-wage countries as well as an increase in oil imports.

By the middle of the decade, President Reagan had succeeded in realigning the economic debate away from a positive opinion of the role of government and toward a culture that valued deregulation, "free markets," and more business-friendly policies. In 1987, he appointed Alan Greenspan to chair the Federal Reserve Board, which was a post he held for the next 18 years, thereby institutionalizing many of the tenets of Reaganomics. Deregulation, along with "free trade" and cutting welfare spending, became bipartisan orthodoxy in Washington as Reagan shifted domestic policy definitively in the Republicans' direction.

THE ENVIRONMENT

From the time Richard Nixon signed the landmark legislation that founded the EPA, in addition to the Clean Air Act, the Clean Water Act, and the Endangered Species Act, there had been a bipartisan consensus for protecting America's land, air, and water. Jimmy Carter might have had his share of problems as president, but his energy and environmental policies were forward looking. He witnessed firsthand how the price of oil could wreak havoc with the U.S. economy. Oil prices rose from $4 per barrel to over $30 per barrel between 1973 and 1980, and even reliable allies like the shah of Iran had pushed the Organization of Petroleum Exporting Countries (OPEC) to raise prices through restricting output. In response, Carter searched for ways to reduce the nation's dependency on foreign petroleum by exploring alternative energy and conservation.

Carter had solar panels installed on the roof of the White House to heat water and generate electricity, and he used the "bully pulpit" to exhort Americans to conserve energy. He started the first federal agency dedicated to developing solar power, the Solar Energy Research Institute (SERI), and appointed the environmental activist and Earth Day cofounder, Denis Hayes, as its director. Carter increased SERI's budget annually and wanted Americans to view his solar energy program with the same sense of national commitment as they had shown toward the Apollo space mission.

President Reagan wasted little time in changing the direction of the nation's energy and environmental policies. According to SERI Director Hayes, administration officials "fired almost half our staff" and "reduced our $135 million budget by $100 million." They also "terminated all our contracts with universities—including two Nobel Prize winners—in one afternoon." In what would become a recurring theme in Reagan's handling of government programs he didn't like, he first starved SERI's operating budget, which forced drastic cuts in researchers and staff, and then folded it into an existing agency inside the Department of Energy. Reagan then ordered the solar panels taken down from the White House roof, thereby quashing even Carter's symbolic effort to sponsor alternative energy.

But the new administration's policy reversals were not limited to alternative energy. Reagan appointed Robert Burford, a Colorado rancher who had been cited for illegally grazing his livestock on federal lands, to head the Bureau of Land Management. John Crowell, a former timber corporation lawyer, became assistant secretary of the Interior for natural resources. Secretary of Transportation Andrew "Drew" Lewis Jr. rolled back regulations that improved the fuel efficiency of cars and trucks. Secretary of Energy Donald Hodel suggested that the best way to address the problem of ozone depletion was to urge people to apply stronger suntan lotion. For the first time, people who had been for years either fighting against or harshly criticizing federal environmental agencies now found themselves running these agencies. As top appointments went to people with little expertise in environmental policy, a wave of career regulators resigned in protest. The earlier bipartisan consensus on the environment had been shattered.

Some of Reagan's top environment officials had been part of the so-called Sagebrush Rebellion, which was a movement spearheaded by western logging, mining, and ranching interests that lobbied for privatizing public lands. Extractive industry corporations had spent lavishly to pump up the political clout of the "Sagebrush Rebels," and given their strength in the West and their donations to his

1980 campaign, Reagan needed little prodding to shift his environmental priorities in their direction. Their views on land and water management fit nicely with Reagan's own deeply held philosophical commitment to *laissez-faire* economics. If government really was "the problem" and "not the solution of our problems," as Reagan said in his first inaugural address, then environmental regulations were nothing more than a burdensome intrusion into the workings of the economy.

Yet public support for preserving the environment did not evaporate after Reagan's inauguration. Polls consistently showed that government efforts to ensure a healthy environment were still very popular. To take one example, during Reagan's first term a Harris poll found that 86 percent of those surveyed supported the Clean Air Act. Despite Reagan's electoral victory there was little evidence that the public was clamoring to grant greater freedom to corporations to befoul the nation's air, land, and water. Environmental activism continued, particularly in the acid rain-ravaged Northeast, and on the West Coast, where any local politician who supported offshore drilling or the logging of old-growth forests could be very quickly tossed out of office.

According to his biographer, Lou Canon, Reagan had an aesthetic appreciation of nature and loved the outdoors. He was an avid horseman and enjoyed nothing more than staying at his sprawling California ranch. During his presidency, Reagan spent almost a full year (345 days) at Rancho del Cielo, perched at 2,250 feet in the Santa Ynez Mountains northwest of Santa Barbara. But Canon also points out that Reagan had little use for conservationism or other efforts to safeguard the environment. He tells the story of exasperated EPA officials trying to explain to Reagan, without success, the seriousness of acid rain, which destroyed fish and plant life in thousands of lakes in the United States and Canada. In the late-1970s, acid rain, which was mostly the by-product of sulfur and nitrogen oxides from the smokestacks of the Rust Belt, had become such a problem that Carter had reached an agreement with Canadian Prime Minister Pierre Trudeau to reduce emissions. In contrast, Reagan shelved Carter's deal with Canada and even questioned the scientific evidence that industrial pollutants caused acid rain. Amidst the faltering economy he simply had no interest in imposing additional regulations on business. In 1990, Congress ended up successfully passing restrictions similar to those Carter had proposed, but not before hundreds of lakes and streams had been adversely affected.

To head the EPA, Reagan chose a Colorado state legislator, Ann Gorsuch-Burford, with no background as an environmental manager, and she wasted no time in starving the EPA's operating budget by $200 million and firing nearly one-fourth of its staff. Experienced professionals left the agency while those who remained became increasingly demoralized. Gorsuch-Burford, along with one of her top assistants, Rita Lavelle, soon found themselves at the center of the first major scandal of the Reagan presidency. Since 1980, polluting industries had been paying into a $1.8 billion "Superfund" that was targeted to clean up toxic waste sites across the United States. The General Accounting Office had identified more than 378,000 dumpsites that needed to be decontaminated, and the EPA listed 850 as top priorities. (As of 1985, only six had been cleaned, and even those were not done adequately.)

The press and congressional investigators uncovered a series of sweetheart deals the EPA had brokered with corporate polluters in managing the Superfund program. Before becoming director of the EPA's hazardous waste program, Rita Lavelle had been a public relations executive for the Cordova Chemical Company, a subsidiary of Aerojet

General Corp. that had an abysmal environmental record in California. She refused to give Congress subpoenaed documents and lied during her testimony about the Superfund deals. Lavelle was later convicted of obstruction of justice and perjury, fined $10,000, and served three months in federal prison. EPA Director Gorsuch-Burford was cited for contempt of Congress for stonewalling the investigation.

The president believed that the media had subjected Gorsuch-Burford and Lavelle to a "lynching," but the EPA scandal became a huge embarrassment. In August 1984, a report from the House Energy and Commerce Oversight Committee summarized: "Top-level officials of the Environmental Protection Agency violated their public trust by disregarding the public health and the environment, manipulating the Superfund program for political purposes, engaging in unethical conduct, and participating in other abuses." Reagan had appointed industry hacks to key environmental posts at a time when new and complicated problems, including toxic waste, acid rain, and dioxins, were testing the government's ability to respond.

Reagan's political aide, Richard Wirthlin, became concerned that the administration's environmental record could become a political liability as Reagan prepared for his reelection in 1984. He prevailed upon the president to replace the disgraced EPA chief with William Ruckelshaus, who was a well-respected Washington insider who had been the agency's first director under President Nixon. "By the time I got back," Ruckelshaus said, "the agency was in such a state of turmoil that the main thing that needed to be done was to calm it down and put it back to work." Had Reagan simply maintained the bipartisan policy trajectory at the EPA, no matter how tepidly, he could have avoided what became the biggest domestic policy scandal of his first term.

But no official personified the Reagan administration's new direction on the environment more than the Secretary of Interior James Watt. Watt was a "Sagebrush Rebel" who was originally from the tiny town of Lusk, Wyoming. He became a leading lawyer for the Mountain States Legal Foundation where he fought the government in court on behalf of mining, timber, and agricultural interests. Secretary Watt advocated drilling for oil off California's pristine stretch of coastline at Big Sur and referred to a river rafting trip he took in the Grand Canyon as "tedious." "We will mine more, drill more, cut more timber," he promised, while pushing ahead to open 80 million acres of federally protected wilderness to private developers. Watt was a far cry from previous secretaries of the Interior, such as Stewart Udall who served under Kennedy and Johnson, who were more often than not dedicated conservationists.

During Watt's confirmation hearing when answering questions about how he would administer public lands he told a stunned congressional panel that the "Scriptures" would be his guide, "which call upon us to occupy the land until Jesus returns." For many members of Congress, Watt's apocalyptic worldview did not bode well for someone presiding over 740 millions acres of America's wilderness and national parks. Watt wanted to privatize as much federal land as he could get away with and succeeded in opening up formerly protected wilderness and wetlands to private developers. A *Time* magazine cover story in 1982 labeled it the "Land Sale of the Century." So reckless were many of Watt's federal oil leases that they were subsequently thrown out in court. Within a year of his appointment environmentalists organized a full-fledged Dump Watt movement that gathered over a million signatures on petitions nationwide.

Watt even got into trouble with First Lady Nancy Reagan after he banned a performance by the Beach Boys, a surf rock band of the 1960s. They were scheduled to play at a July 4th celebration at the National Mall. Watt believed the Beach Boys would attract an unsavory crowd to the nation's capital. Unbeknownst to the secretary was the fact that Nancy Reagan was a huge Beach Boys fan and she made sure his decision was revoked. But it was Watt's penchant for impolitic remarks that ultimately did him in. He publicly boasted about a special advisory panel he was forming in the Department of Interior that liberals should love because, as Watt put it: "I have a black, I have a woman, two Jews, and a cripple." The congressional uproar following this statement forced his resignation in September 1983. As with the case of the EPA's Gorsuch-Burford, Reagan saw Watt as "the victim of a two-and-a-half year lynching." Years after he left office Reagan still persisted that Watt had done "a darn good" job. But Watt's legacy lived on in the form of the Minerals Management Service (MMS), which he created in 1982 by secretarial order, not legislation. The MMS allowed oil and mining corporations to manage billions of dollars in royalties they paid to the U.S. government that were earmarked for regulating them. For decades after Watt's departure the MMS had a troubled history of corruption and coziness with the industry it was supposed to oversee.

In the 1980s, the environmental movement confronted the administration by shifting its focus toward Washington-centered advocacy instead of local community organizing. Their membership went up during the decade, but the mainline environmental organizations, such as the Sierra Club and the National Wildlife Federation, relied more heavily on computerized mailing lists, fundraising, and ties to specific Washington lawmakers. Lobbyists and lawyers often became more vital to the movement than the activists who fought local battles on behalf of America's wilderness.

During Reagan's second term, environmentalists had some success in reasserting their influence. In 1986, Congress reauthorized the Safe Drinking Water Act, and also passed the Emergency Planning and Community Right-to-Know Act, which required industries to report releases of toxins and assisted communities in planning for chemical emergencies. Congress also thwarted efforts to open the Arctic National Wildlife Refuge (ANWR) in Alaska to oil and gas exploration. The Reagan administration overreached in rolling back environmental regulations and was caught off guard by the public's strongly negative reaction. As he was known to do with other policies, Reagan veered in the direction of public opinion. Throughout his second term, he largely bequeathed to Congress leadership on environmental issues.

The importance of the government's role as environmental watchdog was driven home on March 24, 1989, when the worst environmental catastrophe to hit the United States in decades occurred off Prince William Sound, Alaska. Early in the presidency of George Herbert Walker Bush, an oil tanker, the *Exxon Valdez*, ran aground spilling over 11.5 million gallons of oil and damaging 1,300 miles of coastline. The Federal Emergency Management Agency (FEMA), along with the EPA, the Department of Interior, and other federal agencies had little choice but to coordinate their efforts to deal with the environmental crisis that killed at least 200,000 birds, 2,800 sea otters, 250 eagles, 22 killer whales, and caused the collapse of the herring population in the region. Investigators uncovered evidence that Exxon had been negligent in not properly maintaining the radar equipment on the vessel and vetting personnel. The *Exxon Valdez* spill led to the passage of the Oil Pollution Act of 1990. Among the new law's provisions was a requirement for double hulls on all oil tankers serving U.S. ports and new rules relating to crew safety, licensing, and working conditions.

REVIEW QUESTIONS

1. What role (if any) did the March 1981 assassination attempt against President Reagan play in setting the tone for his administration's relationship with the press and the Congress early in his presidency?

2. What were the key changes in U.S. domestic policy that the Reagan administration sought during the first few years?

3. What were the key components of what became known as "Reaganomics?" How did these new budgetary and spending priorities reflect Reagan's worldview? What was Reagan's view of the role of the federal government in American society?

4. How did the new administration address the issue of poverty in America in a period of economic recession? What was the new administration's view on labor unions, social programs, and government regulations? How was Reagan able to pass much of his agenda even when the opposition party controlled the House of Representatives?

5. In what ways did the Reagan administration alter the bipartisan consensus on environmental protection that had characterized the previous decade? What do Reagan's appointments of personnel to key posts in his government tell us about his views on conservationism and protecting the environment?

mysearchlab CONNECTIONS SOURCES ONLINE

READ AND REVIEW

Review this chapter by using the study aids and these related documents available on MySearchLab.

Study Plan
Chapter Test
Essay Test

Documents
Health Study on Reye's Syndrome Deaths (1992)
Health study on the deaths of over 1,400 children from Reye's Syndrome.

Ronald Reagan, the Air Traffic Controllers Strike (1981)
President Reagan's remarks about the striking air traffic controllers of PATCO.

Exxon Valdez (1989)
Environmental Protection Agency (EPA) summary of EPA's efforts to deal with the Exxon Valdez oil spill.

Paul Craig Roberts, The Supply-Side Revolution (1984)
Roberts discusses the debate over Keynesian economic theory and the effects of deficit spending.

RESEARCH AND EXPLORE
Use the databases available within MySearchLab to find additional primary and secondary sources the topics within this chapter.

Video
Ronald Reagan on the Wisdom of Tax Cuts

UNITED STATES

2

Foreign Policy in Reagan's First Term

CHAPTER OUTLINE

Foreign Policy

Central America

Nuclear Freeze/Strategic Defense
Initiative

Lebanon

Grenada

FOREIGN POLICY

President Reagan signaled a shift in the orientation of U.S. foreign policy by appointing Army General Alexander M. Haig Jr. to be his Secretary of State, and the hard-line academic, Jeane Kirkpatrick, to be his United Nations Ambassador. Reagan's choices stood in stark contrast to the liberals, Cyrus Vance and Warren Christopher, who headed the State Department under President Carter, and the civil rights leader and confidante of Martin Luther King Jr., Andrew Young, who served as United Nations ambassador.

Early on, Secretary Haig tried to carve out a role for himself as the chief architect of American foreign policy. He was a four-star general whose rise through the ranks was among the swiftest of any officer in U.S. history. He completed a combat tour in Vietnam as a lieutenant colonel before becoming the top military adviser to Nixon and his assistant for national security affairs Henry Kissinger. In August 1974, Haig was the White House

President Reagan appointed the Georgetown University academic, Jeane Kirkpatrick, to be the U.S. Ambassador to the United Nations. A 1979 *Commentary* article Kirkpatrick had written that distinguished between "authoritarian" and "totalitarian" regimes had caught Reagan's eye. Fiercely anti-communist, she became one of the most well-known and hawkish members of Reagan's foreign policy team during his first term.

Four-star Army General Alexander M. Haig Jr. was Reagan's choice for Secretary of State. He, along with Kirkpatrick, called for a more aggressive posture toward the Soviet Union than had characterized the previous administration. Among Reagan's closest advisers, Haig quickly earned a reputation as a loose canon. His bellicosity played a role in Reagan's decision to sideline him after he served only 18 months in favor of the more diplomatic and conciliatory George Shultz.

chief of staff at the time of Nixon's resignation, and President Gerald Ford appointed him Supreme Allied Commander of NATO. He then passed through the "revolving door" to become president and chief operating officer of United Technologies Corporation, a major defense contractor. When Reagan asked Haig to be his Secretary of State he was already well-known in Washington and had earned his share of enemies.

Kirkpatrick was a Georgetown University professor with expertise in Latin America who had been part of an influential Washington think tank, the "Committee on the Present Danger," which lobbied for a tougher U.S. national security posture. She caught Reagan's attention when an article of hers appeared in the November 1979 issue of *Commentary* magazine where she drew a qualitative distinction between "authoritarian" and "totalitarian" governments. "Authoritarian" regimes, Kirkpatrick argued, might censor the press, crack down on civic organizations, and jail or even torture political opponents, but they did so while preserving cultural traditions and retaining key components of the private economy. They were therefore open to future reform. "Totalitarian" regimes, on the other hand (those under Soviet dominance), upended property relations with a "command economy" that trampled the underlying culture. According to Kirkpatrick, these types of regimes, even in tiny Nicaragua, were nearly impossible to dislodge once they took root.

Upon assuming the post, Ambassador Kirkpatrick toured six Latin American nations and when she returned she pushed for closer ties with the anti-communist military juntas of Uruguay, Argentina, and Chile. While visiting Santiago, she met with General Augusto Pinochet who had ruled Chile for eight years after shooting his way into power as the head of a military cabal. Pinochet's CIA-backed coup of September 11, 1973, had torn down one of Latin America's longest standing democracies and replaced it with one of its most durable dictatorships. In the late 1970s, the regime's human rights abuses became such an embarrassment to the United States that Congress cut off U.S. weapons sales. Kirkpatrick wanted to reverse this policy and "normalize completely relations with Chile, in order to work together in a pleasant way." Two days after she left Santiago, the Pinochet government expelled four well-known activists, among them the president of the Chilean Commission on Human Rights, who had tried to meet with the ambassador. Kirkpatrick believed the socialist Sandinista government in Nicaragua and the revolutionary movements in El Salvador and Guatemala had shaped the conditions where the United States could no longer shun its "authoritarian" friends.

Secretary Haig's State Department backed multilateral bank loans and arms sales to governments whose human rights records had earlier roused Carter and the Congress to shut off the spigots of American aid. Since Reagan was known to delegate tasks liberally among his senior advisers and cabinet secretaries, Haig believed he had a free hand to formulate the administration's foreign policy. He had been a driving force in ratcheting up tensions with Libyan leader Colonel Muammar Gaddafi over the status of the Gulf of Sidra. (American warplanes shot down two Libyan MIG fighter jets over the disputed area in March 1981.) He was the most hawkish cabinet official and his bellicosity behind closed doors sometimes unnerved Reagan's close political advisers. Haig's brusque style and impolitic public remarks (such as when he declared he was "in control" following the assassination attempt against Reagan) gave headaches to Michael Deaver, the president's top public relations aide, who was always protective of Reagan's image. It quickly reached a point where Deaver and others around Reagan longed to see Haig's power diminished.

The Reagan administration's response to the Soviet Union's more robust ties to certain Central American and Caribbean nations was to buttress leaders who were willing to crush internal subversion and protect U.S. interests in the Hemisphere. Kirkpatrick's "authoritarian"/"totalitarian" dichotomy, along with Haig's martial diplomatic style, fit in well with this new direction in foreign affairs. It was also a departure from both Nixon's more conciliatory policy of détente and Carter's putative emphasis on human rights.

After the Soviet Union invaded Afghanistan in December 1979, Carter rallied the United Nations against the intervention, added billions of dollars to the U.S. defense budget, and enforced an embargo on American grain sales to the U.S.S.R. (which had been a component of détente). He also ordered an American boycott of the 1980 Olympic Games in Moscow and reinstituted the Selective Service law requiring young men to register for the military draft. Cold War tensions had been rising steadily before Reagan took office and his National Security Council (NSC) suspected a Soviet hand wherever violent uprisings occurred. "Let's not delude ourselves," Reagan said in 1980, "the Soviet Union underlies all the unrest that is going on. If they weren't engaged in this game of dominoes, there wouldn't be any hot spots in the world."

Further complicating U.S.–Soviet relations during Reagan's first years in office was the illness and death of several top Soviet leaders. Premier Leonid Brezhnev, who had been in power since 1964, died in November 1982, and his death marked a period of uncertainty in the Kremlin. Brezhnev had managed a long period of expansion of Soviet strength in the world and the end of his regime brought forth an unpredictable interregnum. Western "Sovietologists" busied themselves trying to make sense out of the arcane procedures that governed successions in Russian leadership. Brezhnev's death came at a time when the Soviet Union was undergoing immense challenges. In Poland, workers of the "Solidarity" labor movement, headed by Lech Walesa, were weakening the Soviet-backed government in Warsaw with general strikes and the periodic shutdown of the

Gdansk shipyards; in Afghanistan, Russian troops were bogged down in a debilitating guerrilla war that was growing more unpopular each day.

After Brezhnev's death the mantle of Soviet leadership fell upon the former KGB chief Yuri Andropov, who was an elderly veteran of the politburo and widely seen as a hard-liner. Andropov served only about eight months as the General Secretary before he died and bequeathed the premiership to yet another old guard Kremlin leader, Konstantin Chernenko. Chernenko in turn was premier for about a year before he died. When Reagan was accused of putting a chill on U.S.–Soviet relations he said that he'd love to have better relations with Russian leaders but "they keep dying on me." The transition in Moscow set the stage for a stagnant period in Soviet diplomacy. The occupation of Afghanistan was becoming a costly fiasco, especially with the United States aiding the Afghan guerrillas and Arab volunteers of the Mujahideen who were fighting the Soviets, and most U.S. experts on Russia postulated that the ailing old men in power were unlikely to pursue new adventures despite the administration's fiery rhetoric to the contrary.

CENTRAL AMERICA

In July 1979, barely six months after the Iranian Revolution, the United States lost another important ally, this time in Nicaragua. As was the case in Iran, a succession of U.S. administrations had propped up a family dynasty in Nicaragua whose latest steward was the notoriously corrupt strongman, Anastasio Somoza. A worker and peasant rebellion had been brewing in Nicaragua for decades. Finally, a leftist coalition, the *Frente Sandinista de Liberacion Nacional* or FSLN (Sandinista National Liberation Front) named after Augusto Sandino, the nationalist leader who battled U.S. Marines in the 1920s, ousted the Somoza dictatorship. Once in power, the Sandinistas put in place a new social contract that combined socialist development models with a commitment to Catholic concepts of liberation theology and social justice. A segment of the church had played a role in helping the revolution and several priests became high-ranking Sandinista officials. At first, President Carter thought he could work with the new government in Managua and continued the Somoza-era economic assistance. But as uprisings engulfed other countries in Central America, most notably El Salvador, Carter and the Congress cut off most aid to Nicaragua.

In early 1981, the State Department published a White Paper titled "Communist Interference in El Salvador," outlining an elaborate Soviet conspiracy behind the insurgencies in Central America. Most specialists who knew the region saw the uprisings as the result of the crushing poverty of workers and peasants alongside decades of authoritarian rule from local oligarchies. The White Paper, which was an official report that Secretary Haig himself brought to Congress and testified on behalf of the administration, was reminiscent of an earlier foreign policy document during the presidency of Lyndon Johnson that was used to justify the Vietnam War. Filled with anti-communist hyperbole, it painted a picture of the civil unrest in El Salvador as evidence of Soviet treachery and framed the conflicts in Central America in East-West terms.

By the end of 1982, El Salvador—a small, densely populated country of less than 5 million people—became one of the single largest recipients of U.S. aid in all of Latin America. Skeptical members of Congress had difficulty understanding why the Salvadoran Army with its 17,000 soldiers and allied paramilitaries could not suppress a rebel force that was estimated to be about one-fourth its size. The administration argued it was because of outside (Soviet) interference, and began looking for ways to "interdict" arms going to the Salvadoran rebels of the Faribundo Marti National Liberation Front (FMLN). In November 1981, Reagan signed a National Security Decision Directive (NSDD 17), which supplied $19 million in covert U.S. aid to train and equip Nicaraguan exiles who were amassed along the Honduran border. The administration avowed that U.S. support for the "contras" (shorthand for "counter-revolutionaries") was conceived to "interdict" arms flowing from the Sandinistas to the FMLN guerrillas in El Salvador, and not to overthrow the government in Managua. The contras staged hit-and-run operations from base camps across the Honduran border, and its command structure and rank-and-file soldiers came almost entirely from Somoza's National Guard. At the same time, the Reagan administration cut off all U.S. assistance to Nicaragua, including wheat exports, which caused breadlines throughout the country.

Although Nicaragua does not share a border with El Salvador, the administration stood by its assertion that the purpose of the contras was solely to stop the alleged arms traffic. The FMLN, like the Sandinistas, derived its name from a martyred nationalist leader, and it functioned as a militia arm of an umbrella organization representing the political left: the *Frente Democratico Revolucionario* (FDR). Many members of Congress had serious doubts that former soldiers of Somoza's fiercely anti-Sandinista National Guard, including Colonel Enrique Bermudez who had been Somoza's military attaché who became a contra leader, would risk their lives just to keep weapons from going to rebels in a third country. The administration held to this argument but never extinguished congressional suspicions. The veteran Massachusetts representative, Edward Boland, who chaired the House Intelligence Committee, questioned the contra operation from the start. He was a popular figure who had a 96 percent approval rating in his home district. (He spent only $47 on his 1982 campaign.)

In October 1982, after a rash of press leaks about the contra project, such as a *Newsweek* cover story that exposed the CIA's use of Argentine agents and Somoza National Guardsmen to wage a secret war against the government in Managua, Boland amended a defense appropriations bill. The "Boland Amendment" forbade any department or agency of the U.S. government to arm the contras "for the purpose of overthrowing the government of Nicaragua." Money for the "interdiction" of arms could continue. The House passed the legislation, with Boland's amendment, by a vote of 411 to 0. This subtle change in the law grabbed little media attention at the time, but would play a central role in the most serious crisis of Reagan's presidency. In early 1983, Reagan told a joint session of Congress: "El Salvador is nearer to Texas than Texas is to Massachusetts [and] Nicaragua is just as close to Miami, San Antonio, San Diego, and Tucson as those cities are to Washington," implying that geographical proximity could determine the power of Central American nations vis-à-vis the United States. The president further warned that if the United States could not defend its interests in Central America, "we cannot expect to prevail elsewhere. Our credibility would collapse, our alliances would crumble and the safety of our homeland would be put in jeopardy." Yet Boland and others on Capitol Hill remained leery that the national security of the United States depended on events that unfolded in Managua, San Salvador, or Tegucigalpa.

Initially, Western European nations looked positively upon the Sandinista revolution in Nicaragua mainly because the Somoza regime had been so discredited. They assisted the new government in its education and health care programs and largely opposed U.S. efforts to undermine a government that clearly had popular support. But the administration pressed America's allies to cut off aid to Nicaragua, claiming that the country's

2.5 million inhabitants, like Fidel Castro's Cuba, had succumbed to communist power. Without help from Europe and with the mounting contra raids, the Nicaragua government had little choice but to turn to Cuba and the Soviet Union for help. Ideologically, the Sandinistas had far more in common with Cuba than they did with any of the U.S.-backed governments in the region. The administration argued the only way to resist communist interference in the Western Hemisphere was to bulk up the pro-U.S. regimes in El Salvador, Guatemala, and Honduras, and a greater amount of U.S. economic and military assistance poured into Central America in a three-year period than had gone to the region over the previous 30 years. Ambassador Kirkpatrick told a group of fundraisers that Central America had become "the most important place in the world for us."

Long festering social and economic injustices had cultivated the conditions for the popular rebellions in Central America. For decades the concentration of wealth and land ownership, coexisting alongside pervasive rural poverty, had scarred these societies. In Guatemala, for example, the top quarter of the population earned 67 percent of the nation's wealth while the bottom quarter accounted for only 7 percent, and less than ten percent of farm workers owned any land. In El Salvador, the concentration of wealth was even more pronounced with two percent of the population owning 60 percent of the arable land and controlling a third of the nation's income.

Reagan's Director of Central Intelligence, William Casey, who had been his campaign manager in 1980 and whose espionage experience dated back to the Office of Strategic Services during World War II, beefed up the contras' strategic position along the Honduran-Nicaraguan border. He later established a second, smaller anti-Sandinista front on Nicaragua's southern border with Costa Rica. Throughout Reagan's first term Casey and the CIA enlarged the contra operation with the president's enthusiastic support. Most of the rest of the world, including the World Court that ruled against the CIA operation in 1986, viewed the contras as little more than mercenaries and terrorists.

In March 1983, the administration was saddled with its first serious public relations disaster relating to Nicaragua when the press reported that the CIA had mined Nicaragua's harbors. A Soviet tanker had struck one of the mines and the incident contradicted the President's public assurances that his administration was not trying to topple the Nicaraguan government. Reagan had secretly approved the mining operation as part of a wider war of sabotage against Nicaragua, but Director Casey did not notify the Intelligence Committees in the House and Senate, and keeping Congress in the dark outraged lawmakers from both political parties. Senator Edward Kennedy sponsored a resolution that condemned the covert action. In the House, there was a vote strengthening the earlier Boland Amendment to cut off U.S. aid to the contras. Reagan assured Congress that he was "complying fully" with both Boland Amendments, which restricted funding to "humanitarian" aid and restated the limited goal of interdicting arms going to El Salvador. "We're not doing anything to try and overthrow the Nicaraguan government," Reagan said.

The Salvadoran military, like Somoza's National Guard, had a longstanding reputation for brutality. El Salvador's notorious "death squads" were mostly gangs of heavily armed men with ties to the security services who roamed the countryside in pickup trucks terrorizing peasants who joined labor unions or cooperatives on the country's coffee and cotton plantations. Local diocese of the Catholic Church often sided with the Salvadoran agricultural workers in their struggle, which incited the death squads to target priests and nuns for retribution. The March 1980 murder of Archbishop Oscar Romero and the rape and murder of four American churchwomen in December 1980 drove home the dangers among

Catholic missionaries who assisted El Salvador's peasants. President Carter's ambassador to El Salvador, Robert White, called the men among the government-backed paramilitaries: "pathological killers." The Reagan administration, with the help of conservative think tanks and cold warriors from both parties in Congress, consistently questioned the nature of the repression in El Salvador. They argued it was uncertain which elements of Salvadoran society were responsible for the spike in violence. The dominant narrative that arose was that the government in San Salvador was steering a "centrist" path while "extremists" from both the "Left" (the FMLN) and the "Right" (the death squads) battled it out. The mounting civilian death toll was the unfortunate outcome of being "caught in the crossfire."

In March 1982, El Salvador held national elections lauded by the U.S. as "free and fair." Some international observers, however, were less persuaded because the FDR had been effectively barred from participating. The elections gave the center-right government of President Jose Napoleon Duarte of the Christian Democratic Party renewed legitimacy in the eyes of Congress and bipartisan votes followed to turn on the taps of more U.S. military and economic aid. Military assistance to El Salvador went from $5.9 million in fiscal year 1980 to $35.5 million in 1981, to $82 million the following year. During this same period, economic assistance rose from $58.3 million in 1980 to $114 million in 1981, to $182.2 million in 1982.

By the end of its first 18 months in office, the Reagan administration's efforts in framing the conflicts in Central America as part of the East-West struggle were largely successful and had won over many congressional Democrats. Even liberal members of Congress viewed the Sandinista government with suspicion, especially after it became clear that Havana and Moscow were aiding it. Lawmakers generally didn't think much of the contras either, but saw them as the "lesser of two evils." The administration censured the lack of democratic freedoms in Nicaragua under the Sandinistas while it armed and equipped the remnants of Somoza's National Guard. The contras were never powerful enough to overthrow the government, but their hit-and-run tactics, sabotage of economic targets (coordinated with the U.S. sanctions), and acts of terror compelled the Sandinistas to divert scarce resources away from badly needed social programs and toward security.

In Guatemala, the same month as the elections in El Salvador, General Efrain Rios Montt came to power in a military coup. The most populated of the Central American states, Guatemala, with just under 7 million people in 1982, had also experienced a historic upswing in armed resistance to oligarchic rule. General Montt sought to stymie the insurgency's base by wiping out as many as 400 Mayan villages in the country's highlands and relocating people to areas of greater government control. Montt's "Victory 82" scorched-earth campaign precipitated a refugee crisis that international human rights organizations condemned. Amnesty International had ranked Guatemala as one of the world's worst human rights violators. Reagan told the press he thought critics of the regime had given Montt "a bum rap."

In Honduras, the U.S. sustained a thinly veiled dictatorship under General Gustavo Alvarez who drew up a new constitution for the country in 1982. Honduras became the key staging ground for the contra war. Reagan appointed the career diplomat, John Negroponte, who had extensive counterinsurgency experience in Southeast Asia during the Vietnam War, to be his ambassador in Tegucigalpa. General Alvarez worked closely with Ambassador Negroponte, and was dedicated to insuring that Honduras did not follow Nicaragua's socialist path. Alvarez, like Montt, had received his officer's training from the "School of the Americas" (renamed "the Western Hemispheric Institute for Security

Cooperation"), which remains the United States' preeminent institution for instructing Latin American military personnel. Honduras also was the recipient of American military aid, including expensive fighter jets that many observers saw as an extravagance for an impoverished agricultural country of about 4 million people.

Inside the United States, the administration's new emphasis on cracking down on its enemies in Central America galvanized opposition. The Committee in Solidarity with the People of El Salvador (CISPES) came forward in 1981 as an organization representing peace activists, clergy, and other groups that worked with refugees who were fleeing the violence. CISPES held candlelight vigils on the anniversaries of the slaying of Archbishop Romero (the first was held on March 24, 1981), and of the murder of the four American churchwomen. CISPES also organized large protests, including a May 1981 demonstration in Washington DC, which drew nearly 100,000 people; and another in March 1982 where about 60,000 people turned out. On the West Coast, CISPES activists put up a temporary "blockade" of the naval facility at Port Chicago in Oakland, which was a point of departure for shipping U.S. weapons to El Salvador. There were regional and local actions in San Francisco, Los Angeles, and New York, all cities that had large numbers of Salvadoran and Guatemalan immigrants.

Five Catholic churches in Tucson, Los Angeles, San Francisco, Washington, and Long Island declared themselves "sanctuaries" for refugees escaping the wars in Central America. In 1982, as the violence in Guatemala escalated, the Quiche Indian human rights activist, Rigoberta Menchu, visited nearly a hundred U.S. cities to educate Americans about the U.S. role. (Ten years later, she won the Nobel Peace Prize.) When the number of contra attacks grew in intensity along the Honduran-Nicaraguan border, a small contingent of American Vietnam War veterans camped there to use their presence and the media attention it drew to shield civilians from the fighting.

The U.S. role in the civil wars in Central America, most notably the contra war in Nicaragua, strained U.S. relations with some of the bigger countries in the hemisphere, especially its neighbor to the south. In Mexico, President Lopez Portillo tried to play the role of peacemaker by initiating what became known as the "Contadora peace process." He joined with the heads of state of Venezuela, Costa Rica, and Panama to construct a multilateral framework to resolve the wars through negotiations. But the key sticking point was the participation of the Sandinista government, which the Reagan administration vehemently opposed. The U.S. enlisted its allies in El Salvador, Guatemala, and Honduras to block any possibility of Contadora's success.

NUCLEAR FREEZE/STRATEGIC DEFENSE INITIATIVE

In the field of nuclear weaponry, Reagan asked Congress to fund a new generation of intercontinental ballistic missiles (ICBMs), including 100 MX missiles. The MX missiles were equipped with the latest computer technology and could be transported to avoid detection. The administration also requested more D-5 submarine-launched ballistic missiles (SLBMs), which were mounted on nuclear-powered Trident submarines. To replace aging B-52 jet bombers, the administration revived the B-1 bomber that Carter had canceled, and threw more resources behind the B-2 "stealth" bomber. These new bat-winged warplanes were invented to evade enemy radar and penetrate deep into Soviet territory. The production of computerized cruise missiles was also stepped up, which could fly at tree top level and be fired from ships, planes, and trucks.

The administration also revived the long dormant concept of "civil defense" as part of its wider strategy to insulate Americans from the effects of nuclear war. Despite luke-warm support for the idea from the Joint Chiefs of Staff and the Office of Management and Budget (OMB), Reagan's first budget asked Congress to double spending for civil defense to $252 million. The Federal Emergency Management Agency (FEMA), which co-ordinated relief efforts during natural disasters, drew up a seven-year $4.2 billion plan for building bomb shelters. FEMA estimated that building permanent shelters for the entire U.S. population would cost $70 billion.

In late 1981, Deputy Undersecretary of Defense T. K. Jones told the *Los Angeles Times* journalist Robert Scheer that with proper preparation Americans could withstand a nuclear attack: "Dig a hole, cover it with a couple of doors, and then throw three feet of dirt on top. It's the dirt that does it. If there are enough shovels to go around, everybody's going to make it." Scheer wrote a book about the new administration's attitude toward civil defense titled *With Enough Shovels*. Another Reagan official assured Congress that the U.S. Postal Service would continue to deliver mail in the event of a nuclear war "even if the survivors ran out of stamps," leading one incredulous lawmaker to ask: "How can you deliver mail when there are no homes or addresses?"

A few private corporations, such as AT&T, followed the government's lead and built their own bomb shelters for top executives. Federal agencies published instructional pam-phlets for keeping the economy going in the aftermath of a nuclear exchange. "Victory in a nuclear war will belong to the country that recovers first," a Federal Reserve booklet proclaimed. The Federal Reserve also agreed to clear all checks, "including those drawn from destroyed banks" and guaranteed "credit cards would be honored in a post-attack economy." The Yale psychiatrist, Robert J. Lifton, denounced such plans as "the logic of madness," and Representative Edward Markey (Democrat of Massachusetts) characterized the civil defense regimen as "a band-aid over the holocaust."

In March 1981, the Reverend Jerry Falwell predicted there soon would be nuclear Armageddon: "We believe that Russia, because of her need for oil—and she's running out now—is going to move in the Middle East and particularly Israel because of their hatred of the Jew and that it is at that time when all hell will break out. And it is at that time when I believe there will be some nuclear holocaust on this earth." (Russia was nowhere near "running out" of oil.) Falwell's political action committee, the Moral Majority, distrib-uted its own pamphlets titled "Nuclear War and the Second Coming" and "Armageddon and the Coming War with Russia." In June 1982, when Israel invaded Lebanon, true adherents to conservative evangelical Christian eschatology saw it as a sign of the begin-ning of the "End Times." The Reverend Pat Robertson, a colleague of Falwell's, believed the Israeli invasion was "the beginning of the longed-for end." He announced on his Christian Broadcasting Network: "The whole thing is in place now, it can happen at any time." The public discussions about Armageddon by some of Reagan's high-profile reli-gious supporters, who sometimes visited the White House, along with the resurrection of civil defense, heightened many people's fears of nuclear war.

For decades the Soviet Union had been playing catch up to the United States in the research, development, and deployment of nuclear weapons and delivery systems. The Soviets could not keep pace with the technological innovations that had been a key feature of the American military since World War II, but by the 1980s they had reached a level of "parity" in terms of "throw weights," "yields," and the ability to wage nuclear war. Across the Atlantic, however, the nuclear balance appeared to favor the Soviet Union when in the late-1970s it deployed medium-range SS-20 missiles, which could annihilate cities through-out Western Europe. In an attempt to counter the perceived Russian advantage, the Reagan administration placed its own Pershing II intermediate-range missiles in West Germany capable of hitting Soviet cities in about the same time the SS-20s could strike Europe.

New leaps forward in computerized telemetry and the targeting accuracy of American missiles allowed Pentagon planners to adopt a new strategy called "counter-force." No longer would the American nuclear arsenal act only as a "deterrent" taking aim at cities along the lines of "mutual assured destruction" (MAD); American missiles now had the capacity to knock out enemy missiles in their silos before they were launched. Since the Soviets were far more dependent on land-based ICBMs than the U.S.'s "strategic triad" of bombers, ICBMs, and SLBMs, "counterforce" theories had an added plausibility. Critics were quick to point out that "counterforce" made nuclear warfare more "thinkable" by putting both countries on hair triggers and might even engender a "first strike" mental-ity of "use them or lose them." It was these kinds of considerations Soviet military officers had in mind when they tried to make sense out of the intentions of a joint U.S.-NATO war game, "Able Archer," in late 1983, that provoked them to put their nuclear forces on their highest alert. (The Soviets' panicky reaction to Able Archer compelled Reagan to send a private message to Soviet Premier Yuri Andropov to reassure him that the United States had no intention of attacking the Soviet Union.)

The U.S. decision to deploy Pershing II missiles in West Europe inspired a wave of popular resistance in Germany and other countries allied with the United States. The Nuclear Freeze movement, whose strategy was to apply grassroots pressure for a bilateral moratorium on the production, testing, and deployment of nuclear weapons, grew in re-sponse to the ratcheted up nuclear tensions. In the United States, even elite voices such as former Defense Secretary Robert McNamara and the Cold War foreign policy sage, George Kennan, spoke out in favor of freezing nuclear weapons.

The rapid mobilization of anti-nuclear protest in Europe and in the United States caught the Reagan administration by surprise. On October 10, 1981, over 250,000 protesters gathered in Bonn, West Germany, to voice their opposition to the renewed arms race (and the Federal Republic's role in it). Two weeks later, some 200,000 people demonstrated in Brussels, and the following month there was an anti-nuclear rally of over 400,000 people in Amsterdam. On June 12, 1982, in New York City's Central Park, an estimated 750,000 to 1 million people participated in a nuclear freeze demonstration making it one of the largest single protests in American history. By the end of 1983, about 5 million people had taken part in active resistance to the deployment of the Pershing II "Euro Missiles" or in support of a freeze. After a series of local referenda calling for a freeze were passed (mostly in New England towns), Senators Edward Kennedy, Mark Hatfield of Oregon, and 17 of their col-leagues cosponsored a nuclear freeze resolution in the U.S. Senate; 122 members of the House put forth their own resolution. A CBS/*New York Times* poll taken in the spring of 1982 showed that 72 percent of Americans supported a bilateral nuclear weapons freeze.

In October 1982, at a time when 8 states were about to hold voter initiatives en-dorsing the freeze, Reagan told a gathering of military veterans that those who petitioned for the ballot measures "want the weakening of America." He also suggested "foreign agents" had instigated the anti-nuclear movement and that its supporters were "carrying water" for the Russians. Five months later, the president told a gathering of the National Association of Evangelicals in Orlando, Florida: "A freeze would reward the Soviet Union for its enormous and unparalleled military buildup. It would prevent the essential and long overdue modernization of United States and allied defenses and would leave our aging forces increasingly vulnerable." In the same speech, he famously labeled the Soviet Union "an evil empire," and quoted a young man who said: "I would rather see my little girls die now, still believing in God, than have them grow up under communism and one day die no longer believing in God."

During this heated debate about nuclear weapons and rising U.S.-Soviet antipathy, ABC television aired a made-for-TV movie, *The Day After,* which graphically depicted the hellish effects of thermonuclear war. On November 20, 1983, about 100 million television viewers watched *The Day After,* which still stands as a record audience for a made-for-TV movie. It's a classic disaster genre movie where the main characters in Lawrence, Kansas, catch snippets of news flashes over their televisions and radios about a military confrontation in Berlin between the United States and the Soviet Union. "News bulletins" announce that tactical nuclear bombs have been detonated over the heads of advancing troops. In the context of the early 1980s, *The Day After* was a horrifying film precisely because the scenario it portrayed was so plausible.

When conservatives attacked *The Day After*—the antifeminist author, Phyllis Schlafly, said, "This film was made by people who want to disarm the country"—the president of ABC Motion Pictures claimed he never intended the movie to be a political statement. But the political implications were clear. The White House Office of Communications hastily drew up talking points for administration officials to blunt the controversy by underscoring the logic of "deterrence" and the wisdom of the nuclear buildup. Representative Edward Markey, who was an original sponsor of the freeze resolution in Congress, said *The Day After* "put the lie to the whole notion of 'limited nuclear war.'" The fictionalized TV drama was the perfect medium to reach not only the American people, but also the president himself. Given Reagan's long career in front of the camera and his love of movies he understood the potency of well-produced visual narratives. After watching a video of the movie that was sent to him prior to its broadcast, Reagan wrote in his diary: "It is powerfully done, all $7 million worth. It's very effective and left me greatly depressed."

In March 1983, Reagan introduced a new element into the strategic nuclear mix: a theoretical space-based antiballistic missile system called the "Strategic Defense Initiative" (SDI). In a primetime address, Reagan laid out his vision for a battery of antiballistic missiles (ABMs) that would form a "protective shield" over the continental United States. Reagan called upon "the scientific community who gave us nuclear weapons" to go back to the drawing board and "turn their great talents to the cause of mankind and world peace: to give us the means of rendering these nuclear weapons impotent and obsolete." The press dubbed SDI "Star Wars" because it imagined a central computer coordinating X-ray lasers, electromagnetic rail guns, subatomic particle beams, and other exotic high technology to shoot down Soviet missiles before they could reach their targets. Reagan also conveyed the possibility of sharing this futuristic U.S. missile defense system with the Soviet Union. It was a public relations masterstroke that co-opted the language of the nuclear freeze and diluted the criticisms of the anti-nuclear movement. The White House now had its own "initiative" filled with the rhetoric of peaceful coexistence and the longing to rid the world of these pernicious weapons.

Critics of "Star Wars" questioned the concept behind SDI as technologically far-fetched, prohibitively expensive, and a violation of the 1972 Anti-Ballistic Missile (ABM) Treaty, which explicitly outlawed militarizing outer space. Soviet leaders castigated SDI for not only undermining the ABM Treaty, but also in the context of Reagan's arms buildup as yet another piece in a comprehensive strategy to obtain U.S. nuclear superiority. Undaunted, Reagan pushed ahead with Star Wars and in the mid-eighties authorized the "Strategic Defense Initiative Organization" to coordinate the procurement effort with Congress. His decision to add a new ABM system complicated negotiations to diminish the superpowers' nuclear arsenals. Hard-liners among Reagan's national security staff welcomed SDI as a bargaining chip and an opportunity to scuttle existing nuclear arms control agreements they never supported.

In September 1983, when the Soviet Air Force mistakenly shot down a Korean Air Lines plane (KAL-007), U.S.-Soviet hostility reached an alarming new high. The Boeing 747 had veered off course over Soviet airspace and Russian military officers, thinking it was an American RS-135 spy plane they had detected earlier in the area, fired on the aircraft killing 269 people, with 62 among them being Americans. Reagan reproached it as if it had been a premeditated attack. "It was an act of barbarism," he said. "There is no way a pilot could mistake this for anything other than a civilian airliner." The incident, Reagan added, was "born of a society which wantonly disregards individual rights and the value of human life and seeks constantly to expand and dominate other nations." Some American talk-radio DJs hosted call-in debates about whether the United States should "nuke" the Soviet Union for shooting down the Korean plane. The nuclear freeze movement had gathered momentum not only in response to Reagan's decision to expand the U.S. arsenal and sponsor civil defense, but also to the more confrontational tone his rhetoric was bringing to East-West relations. In January 1984, the *Bulletin of the Atomic Scientists*, which had displayed a "Doomsday Clock" on the cover of its journal beginning in 1947 to gauge the danger of nuclear war, had moved its minute hand from seven minutes to "midnight" to just three.

LEBANON

In the early 1980s, the Israeli-Palestinian conflict had reached one of its periodic boiling points. The Palestine Liberation Organization (PLO), under the leadership of Yasser Arafat, in its ongoing resistance to the Israeli occupation of Palestinian territories, had been using southern Lebanon as a staging ground for attacks against northern Israel. Israeli Prime Minister Menachem Begin wanted to push the PLO out of its sanctuaries in southern Lebanon as well as its headquarters in West Beirut. In June 1982, the Israel Defense Forces (IDF) began bombing and shelling Lebanon from the air and from sea. Targets included apartment buildings in the civilian neighborhoods of West Beirut and other areas where the PLO freely operated. CNN's live broadcasts of the IDF's assault added a new element of immediacy to the Arab-Israeli conflict. One of the goals of the invasion was to carve out a 25-mile "buffer zone" in southern Lebanon to stifle the threat to Israel's northern border. The Israelis had willing allies among a few of the Lebanese factions that had been embroiled in their own civil war since 1975, most notably the small but powerful Maronite Christian minority that possessed its own "Phalangist" militia.

Secretary of State Haig was the most enthusiastic supporter inside Reagan's cabinet for the IDF operation and shared Israeli General Ariel Sharon's determination to degrade the PLO's strength in Lebanon. Sharon, Haig, and others, framed the military action as an effort to diminish Russian influence in the Middle East, and pointed to the Soviet arms going to Syria as evidence of outside interference. But they had difficulty fitting the complex religious, sectarian, and civil clashes in Lebanon into the wider East-West rivalry. After weeks of violent images and civilian casualties being shown nonstop on CNN, Reagan's top political aide, Michael Deaver, as well as his national security adviser, William P. Clark Jr., both objected to the IDF assault. Deaver even threatened to resign if the administration did not press Israel to end its siege.

Secretary Haig appeared to have offered his unconditional support for Israel's military intervention in Lebanon and his stand unnerved some among Reagan's inner circle who preferred to proceed more cautiously in that volatile part of the world. It was at that time, in July 1982, when the president agreed to ease Haig out and he was maneuvered into proffering his resignation. In what was the first major change in Reagan's cabinet the president replaced Haig with George P. Shultz who had served as Nixon's treasury secretary and had been a senior executive at the San Francisco based Bechtel Corporation. Shultz was known to have a far cooler head than Haig and he fit in better with the more cautious foreign policy goals those closest to Reagan hoped to pursue.

For three months, the Reagan administration did nothing to stop the IDF offensive in Lebanon. Then in August 1982, bowing to pressure from its Arab allies, the United States finally asked Israel for a cease-fire. Secretary of State Shultz believed that a U.S. troop presence could be a stabilizing force and he supported sending U.S. marines as part of a multinational peacekeeping force. Reagan decided to send in 800 marines to arrange security for an intricately negotiated settlement whereby thousands of Palestinian fighters agreed to leave Lebanon.

In mid-September, when Muslim fighters assassinated the Maronite Lebanese President-elect, Bashir Gemayel, the Phalangist militias tied to his political party vowed revenge. Two days later, operating in a part of Beirut under IDF control, Gemayel's militiamen slaughtered several hundred Palestinian men, women, and children at the Shabra and Shatilla refugee camps. News of the massacre triggered protests in Europe, the United States, Israel, and the Palestinian territories. At that point, Reagan doubled the number of American marines in Lebanon to avert more civilian massacres. The American troops attempted to wedge themselves between Lebanon's warring factions. The U.S. now had 1,600 marines in Lebanon with no clearly defined mission other than "peace keeping." In the chaos of the multisided and vicious civil war, with regional actors Syria and Israel escalating the violence (each armed by opposing superpowers), the goals of the U.S. operation were murky. Lacking a "front line" in the battlefield, American soldiers spent days and weeks billeted near the Beirut airport where they sustained continual sniper fire.

Given that the small marine presence was not enough to tip the balance in favor of any one faction in Lebanon's ethnic and sectarian hostilities, Reagan's gesture of committing troops was widely interpreted to be symbolic. It was an indication to the Soviets that the United States was monitoring the situation in favor of Western interests; therefore the objective was more diplomatic than military. It was also the first significant deployment of U.S. troops since the Vietnam War. One of Reagan's objectives might have been to cross that line in order to give him more flexibility in pursuing military options elsewhere in the world. The American marines found themselves sitting on the sidelines of a multidimensional civil conflict. Even the limited objective of "peacekeeping" proved impossible in the cantonized and unstable atmosphere of Lebanon in the early 1980s. Worse still, Lebanese Muslims condemned the American presence as nothing more than a U.S.-Israeli attempt to prop up the Maronite Christian minority. That concern had been on the minds of some of Reagan's top advisers, including Defense Secretary Casper Weinberger, who advised against intervening directly with U.S. troops. They believed the U.S. forces could not for long remain "neutral" and would be swept into the factional and sectarian battles raging in Lebanon, which is exactly what happened.

It was in this context when, on April 18, 1983, a small team of Muslim fighters on a suicide mission assaulted the American embassy in Beirut resulting in the deaths of 63 people, including 17 Americans. In "retaliation," the USS *New Jersey*, which was patrolling off Lebanon's coast, adopted the Israeli Navy's tactic of shelling Druse and Shia militia positions from sea. The American military response antagonized the Muslim factions who staged their own "retaliation." Lebanon's Shias, especially in the south, had a sizeable political and military organization in Hezbollah (the Party of God), which the Islamic Republic of Iran under Ayatollah Khomeini armed and financed. Because of the long-standing alliance between the U.S. and Israel and the IDF's use of American weaponry, Hezbollah made no distinction between the two countries. In addition to car bombs and sniper fire targeting U.S. personnel, Hezbollah and other anti-U.S. groups began kid-napping American diplomats and private citizens, which made Reagan's already messy Lebanon policy even messier.

The taking of American hostages as bargaining chips by Shia militants had a fright-ening precedent with the 444-day Iranian hostage ordeal that brought down the Carter presidency. The last thing Reagan wanted, with his reelection pending, was to be saddled with his own hostage crisis in Lebanon. His past criticisms of Carter's handling of the Iranian debacle could come back to haunt him. Reagan was also genuinely concerned about the fate of the Americans in enemy hands. Then, on October 23, 1983, a large Mercedes-Benz delivery truck filled with 12,000 pounds of explosives and two Hezbollah suicide bombers rammed through the barriers of the U.S. marine barracks near the air-port. The gigantic blast killed 241 U.S. military personnel and it was the largest number of marines murdered in a single day since the Vietnam War.

After the marine barracks bombing Reagan reaffirmed Lebanon as being "central to our credibility on a global scale." Vice President Bush, touring the blown out facil-ity, promised that the administration was "not going to let a bunch of insidious terrorist cowards shape the foreign policy of the United States," and Secretary Shultz explained to reporters: "We are in Lebanon because the outcome will affect our whole position in the Middle East. To ask why Lebanon is important is to ask why the Middle East is important." Over the weeks and months that followed Reagan restated his resolve to stay in Lebanon to "finish the job." In early February 1984, he criticized House Speaker Tip O'Neill for opposing his Lebanon policy, saying O'Neill "may be ready to surrender, but I am not." Yet later that month, with little fanfare, he ordered a "phased redeploy-ment" of American soldiers out of Lebanon, and by April the last of the U.S. troops had departed.

Reagan's decision to pull the marines out of Lebanon, however, did not stop Hezbollah and other militant groups from abducting Americans in Beirut. In March 1984, the Lebanese terrorist organization, Islamic Jihad, kidnapped an American official, William Buckley, who became the fourth American hostage taken in the country since 1982. Buckley was the CIA's Chief of Station in Beirut and his colleagues in Washington assumed he would be tortured to coerce him to disclose the names of other agents work-ing in the region. Since he later died in the hands of his captors this bleak assessment was probably correct. As long as CIA Director Casey believed Buckley was still alive, he did everything within his power, with the President's support, to try to free his high-ranking envoy as well as the other Americans held captive.

Politically, Reagan's decision to withdraw U.S. forces from Lebanon was a wise one because staying there, especially after the marine barracks bombing, was growing more unpopular each day. The American people had little appetite for open-ended military commitments in foreign lands after experiencing the bitter divisions of the Vietnam era. Had Jimmy Carter reversed himself on such a high-profile troop deployment that cost over 200 Americans their lives, there is little doubt Reagan would have criticized him for "cutting and running." But the entire episode would be quickly knocked off the front pages of newspapers and dumped from the 24-hour news cycle after the President embarked on his second military intervention that, unlike Lebanon, could be nothing but a sure winner.

GRENADA

Since 1979 a popular leftist leader, Maurice Bishop, had ruled the Caribbean island of Grenada, a former British colony with a population of about 110,000. Bishop, who headed the "New Jewel" movement, had come to power in a nearly bloodless coup against a corrupt and authoritarian ruling clique. Bishop's government, the Marxist People's Revolutionary Government (PRG), sought closer ties to Fidel Castro in Cuba and the Sandinistas in Nicaragua. After Castro began sending doctors, teachers, and construction workers to Grenada Bishop came under greater U.S. scrutiny. One of Bishop's goals was to expand the runways of Grenada's only airport to accommodate larger planes to attract European tourists. The new airport became a symbol of Grenadian sovereignty and the U.S. government's objections to it on the grounds that it could accommodate Soviet aircraft only strengthened Bishop's nationalist credentials. The idea that Grenada constituted a "threat" to the United States, with or without a new airport, was widely questioned.

In mid-October 1983, events in Grenada took a grave turn when an aggressive faction of Bishop's former New Jewel allies overthrew his government and killed him. Although the U.S. State Department had refused to recognize Bishop's government his ouster and murder set off alarm bells throughout the Caribbean. Members of the U.S.-backed Organization of Eastern Caribbean States (OECS) suspected a Cuban hand behind the coup and beseeched the United States to intervene. Reagan referred to those who ousted Bishop as a "brutal gang of thugs," which was not an inaccurate description. The gang that shot its way into power was illegitimate in the eyes of most Grenadians.

The administration professed that the unrest endangered the lives of several hundred American students who were attending St. George's School of Medicine on the island and that they might be taken hostage. On October 25, barely 48 hours after the marine barracks bombing outside Beirut, 7,000 American marines along with navy seals descended on Grenada to "liberate" the island. The invading soldiers, in what the Pentagon labeled "Operation Urgent Fury," met only scattered resistance from a small security detail that had been weakened by the internal violence. The military engagement was mainly directed against a contingent of about 650 lightly armed Cubans who were members of a construction corps. The U.S. bombed a psychiatric hospital by accident, which accounted for about half of the several dozen civilian deaths among Grenadians. After nine days of fighting, 19 American soldiers had been killed and 116 wounded. The Cubans counted 71 dead and 59 wounded, while the toll among Grenadians was 110 killed and 337 wounded.

The American troops had a ten-to-one advantage over the Grenadian and Cuban defenders, and it was later learned that "friendly fire" or mishaps accounted for over half of the American casualties. The Pentagon, believing that open media access during the

Vietnam War had abetted the defeat, excluded the press from covering the operation by simply barring reporters' access to the island. "We got there just in time," Reagan told the American people in a nationally televised address two days after the invasion began. He also affirmed that the crisis in Grenada was "clearly related" to the wider struggle between the United States and the Soviet Union.

Grenada was not only the first application of U.S. armed combat of its kind by the all-volunteer military in the post-Vietnam War era, but it was also the first unambiguous U.S. military triumph since Vietnam. Administration spokespeople underscored that the Grenada mission was necessary to save the lives of American medical students after political violence had engulfed the island. They also said they wanted to roll back Cuban expansionism and defend the neighboring governments of the OECS that solicited the U.S. action.

White House Press Secretary Larry Speakes later admitted that no one among Reagan's top advisers really believed the American medical students were in danger. The plight of the students, he recalled, played only a minor role in Reagan's decision to invade the island. Still, the television images of young Americans greeting their loved ones and kissing the ground at the tarmac when they arrived home were politically advantageous and Americans rallied behind the military effort. Some of the scenes were reminiscent of Reagan's inauguration day when the American hostages in Iran returned home safely. Lost in the flag-waving celebrations, however, were the public statements from the director of St. George's School of Medicine saying that the physical safety of the students had never been in question.

Thrusting Grenada to the center of the Cold War rivalry did not win many converts internationally. The U.S. faced criticism for violating the treaty of the Organization of American States (OAS) as well as the U.N. Charter, and the U.N. General Assembly voted to "deplore" the U.S. invasion by a vote of 122 to 9 (with 27 abstentions). Seven members of the House of Representatives tried to start impeachment proceedings against the president for ordering the invasion without congressional authorization. Yet these aspersions seemed to matter little. Reagan's approval rating shot up to 63 percent, the highest rate he enjoyed since April 1981 when he was recovering from the assassination attempt. The U.S. military gave out nearly 9,000 medals to the personnel who participated in "Operation Urgent Fury." The U.S. Army alone (not including the Navy, Marines, and Air Force) awarded more medals than there had been combatants on the other side. During Reagan's entire two-term presidency, Grenada was the only time the U.S. military engaged in such an armed invasion, which demonstrates his high degree of caution toward the use of military force. The national jubilation was a collective tonic for the string of military failures that had plagued the United States during the 1970s.

REVIEW QUESTIONS

1. How did President Reagan's National Security Council (NSC) differ from previous administrations in its outlook toward the rest of the world and toward the Soviet Union? Was the Reagan Administration's foreign policy team successful in realigning U.S. relations with the nations of Latin America?

2. Why did the Reagan administration believe that Central America was so vital to U.S. "national security?" Was arming the Nicaraguan counter-revolutionaries ("contras") a necessary action in order to neutralize the growing "communist" threat in the Western Hemisphere as the administration claimed? Why or why not?

3. Why did the Reagan administration believe it was necessary for the United States to embark on a buildup of nuclear warheads and delivery systems? Was the "Nuclear Freeze" movement a response to this buildup? How does Reagan's "Strategic Defense Initiative" fit into the nuclear arms race of the early 1980s?

4. What were the U.S.'s goals in deploying troops to Lebanon in 1982? What was President Reagan's response to the October 1983 Marine barracks bombing?

5. Why did President Reagan order the invasion of the island of Grenada? Did the political unrest and turmoil in Grenada really threaten U.S. "national security?" Why or why not?

mysearchlab CONNECTIONS SOURCES ONLINE

READ AND REVIEW

Review this chapter by using the study aids and these related documents available on MySearchLab.

Study Plan
Chapter Test
Essay Test

Documents
Jeane Kirkpatrick, Dictatorships and Double Standards (1979)
Kirkpatrick on the Carter Administration's foreign policy failures.

Ronald Reagan, National Security Decision Directive (NSDD-17) (1981)
This directive authorized aid to the Nicaraguan contras.

Boland Amendments (1982 and 1984)
Text of amendments that banned funds from the budget being used by the federal government to aid the contras.

Ronald Reagan, Speech to the House of Commons (1982)
Reagan proclaims the failure of communism.

Bill Chappell, Speech to the American Security Council Foundation (1985)
Chappell explains the SDI concept to the Security Council Foundation.

RESEARCH AND EXPLORE

Use the databases available within MySearchLab to find additional primary and secondary sources the topics within this chapter.

Map Discovery
The Cold War Military Stand-off

3

Rainbow Politics and Social Movements

CHAPTER OUTLINE

THE OPPOSITION IN 1984

In June 1984, a Republican strategy memo was circulated among Reagan's top political advisers that laid out a simple goal for the campaign: "Paint Ronald Reagan as the personification of all that is right with, or heroized by, America," and compose a narrative "where an attack on Reagan is tantamount to an attack on America's idealized image of itself—*where a vote against Reagan is, in some subliminal sense, a vote against a mythic 'America.'*" [Original Emphasis] The campaign assembled a crack team of Madison Avenue advertising specialists to handle television commercials and to implant in the public's consciousness the "heroized" America the memo envisioned. These public relations experts were from powerhouse New York advertising firms that normally would be competing against each other. One of the team's creative directors,

---

Reverend Jesse Jackson, who ran for president in the 1984 and 1988 Democratic primaries, was instrumental in freeing a downed American Navy flier, Lt. Robert Goodman Jr., from captivity in Syria after the plane in which he was the navigator was shot down. Jackson organized an entourage of religious leaders to travel to Syria to press Syrian president, Hafez al-Assad, to release Lt. Goodman. President Reagan is pictured here in the Rose Garden honoring Jackson and Goodman and praising the success of the mission (January 1984).

Phil Dusenberry, was famous in the industry for his exquisitely edited TV commercials for Pepsi Cola and other corporate giants. Called the "Tuesday Team" (because they met on Tuesdays), these highly skilled publicity agents set to work with access to a vast assortment of patriotic images of the president culled from events throughout his first term.

When it came to Reagan's public persona, Michael Deaver and the rest of the White House communications office were ahead of their time. In one noteworthy case, the CBS journalist, Leslie Stahl, had run a short news segment contrasting Reagan's appearance at what was then called the "Handicapped Olympics" with the fact that his administration had pressed Congress to reduce funding for programs for the disabled. Not long after the story aired, the White House's Richard Darman thanked Stahl for the "great piece," referring to it as a "five-minute commercial" for Reagan. "Didn't you hear what I said?" Stahl asked incredulously. "Nobody heard what you said," retorted Darman. "They just saw the five minutes of beautiful pictures of Ronald Reagan. They saw balloons. They saw the flags. They saw the red, white, and blue. Haven't you people figured out yet that the picture always overrides what you say?" Darman's response to the stunned TV reporter summed up the Reagan-Bush campaign's understanding of the power of well-crafted visuals to evoke desired political effects.

With skills honed from running elections in the "media state" of California, Reagan's reelection outfit knew how to put together an effective public relations strategy. They had amassed hours of footage for use during the campaign, which included scenes of Reagan at the demilitarized zone in Korea donning a flak jacket and spying through field glasses toward the communist north, his greeting the heroes of the 1984 Los Angeles Olympic Games, and the spectacular outdoor setting of his June 6, 1984, speech at the Pointe du Hoc memorial in France on the 40th anniversary of D-Day. For all the shrieking about the "Hollywood elite" that came from a vocal segment of social conservatives there was no shying away from the fact that Reagan himself was a product of Tinsel Town. No president in U.S. history had a better grasp of the power of theatrics and message discipline to reach the American people, which had earned him the moniker: "the Great Communicator." The campaign combined savvy Madison Avenue advertising techniques with the slick production values of the movie business.

The campaign produced a number of campaign commercials the Tuesday Team called "feel-good ads." They were constructed to evoke patriotic themes befitting a Norman Rockwell painting. One of these advertisements (ads), titled "Morning Again in America," opens with panoramic shots of a family farmhouse and segues to scenes of a wedding party and then to an elderly man raising Old Glory up a flagpole in front of a group of enraptured schoolchildren. The flag fills the screen, gently waving in the wind, the emotive music swells and a male narrator speaks about young couples getting married and buying homes, lower inflation, and greater opportunity in a country that is "stronger, prouder, and better" than it was four years earlier.

Reagan showed keen interest in the aesthetics of his campaign commercials and had a sixth sense to gauge their emotional impact. At the first White House meeting of the Tuesday Team, he briefly stopped by the room where the conference was being held, opened the door and said: "Since you're the ones who are selling the soap, I thought you'd like to see the bar." He lent his own narrator's voice, polished since his days announcing baseball games on radio in the 1930s, for a voice-over of one of the "feel-good" commercials. Titled "America Is Back," the ad targeted an electorate that had for years grown familiar with Reagan's soothing voice, making it one of the campaign's more persuasive efforts.

Throughout the 1984 election season, the mainstream news media were awestruck with Reagan and his campaign's central slogan: "Leadership That's Working." Echoing the Republican strategy memo of June 1984, *Newsweek* magazine repeated nearly verbatim its goals, stating that Reagan represented "America as it imagined itself to be—the bearer of the traditional Main Street values of family and neighborhood, of thrift, industry and charity instead of government intervention where self-reliance failed." The advertising acumen of the Tuesday Team would have been formidable enough, but with *Newsweek*, *Time*, and *U.S. News and World Report* strumming similar chords a sympathetic press amplified the messaging tenfold. As Leslie Stahl had discovered, even critical examinations of Reagan's policies mattered little so long as the visuals were flattering.

During Reagan's first term, the leaders of the Democratic National Committee (DNC) had changed the rules governing the nominating procedures to favor "insider" candidates. They cleaved off a new category of party officials, called "super-delegates," who were mostly from the congressional delegations, but also could accommodate other Washington power brokers. The DNC also jumbled together primaries and caucuses and scheduled them on fewer days to give an edge to the candidate who could most quickly amass PAC money and endorsements from the largest special interest groups. Although the DNC's rule changes made conventional political sense, their effect was to throw a wet blanket over the grassroots energy of local organizers. The "super-delegates" and front-loaded primaries and caucuses guaranteed that any insurgency could be snuffed out. Compared to Reagan's ideologically driven and spirited partisans, the Democratic effort in 1984 lacked enthusiasm and looked more like a loose collection of liberal special interest groups than a political movement.

The only "outsider" candidate in the 1984 Democratic primaries was Reverend Jesse Jackson who had sent a detailed letter to DNC Chair Charles Manatt deploring the new nominating rules. Jackson made the convincing case that the nominating reforms had the effect of locking out African Americans, Latinos, women, and other nontraditional candidates like himself. Jackson singled out the so-called threshold rule as being unfair because candidates who didn't win 20 percent of the vote in the primaries were completely cut out of the delegate race. The DNC chair assured Jackson and his supporters during a joint press conference that the Reverend's concerns would be considered, but southern Democrats blocked his attempt to repeal the "threshold rule."

JESSE JACKSON'S RAINBOW COALITION

Jesse Louis Jackson was born in 1941 in Greenville, South Carolina. Growing up in the South, he bore the hardships and humiliations of the Jim Crow system of racial segregation. In his segregated high school he showed promise as an athlete and eventually parlayed his athletic skills into a college scholarship to the all-black North Carolina Agricultural and Technical State University in Greensboro. There he distinguished himself as student body president and as a civil rights leader. After graduating college he threw himself into civil rights activism and by 1966 he had become one of the youngest organizers in the highest echelons of Martin Luther King Jr.'s Southern Christian Leadership Conference (SCLC). King appointed Jackson to be an executive director of the SCLC in Chicago, which became Jackson's new hometown. Two years later the Chicago

Theological Seminary ordained Jackson a Baptist minister. He was instrumental in starting up the organization: "People United to Save Humanity" (PUSH), later renamed "People United to Serve Humanity." The overriding themes of the movement were black economic empowerment and the electoral mobilization of minorities and the poor to give them a greater voice in local and regional politics.

On November 3, 1983, Jackson announced he was entering the Democratic presidential primaries. His reputation as one of King's lieutenants who had been with the legendary leader in Memphis at the time he was killed, gave Jackson the opportunity to come off as a kind of successor to King in American politics. When he declared his candidacy the press parsed the minutiae of Jackson's relationship with King to the point of casting doubts on some of his claims. The television news outlets never seemed entirely comfortable covering Jackson in 1984 given his progressivism, unapologetic censure of Reagan, and emphasis on black community organizing. Even though Jackson worked hard to mobilize the Democratic base and went on to win 12 percent of the delegates at the national convention in San Francisco, journalists omitted him from the dominant "horse-race" coverage, instead fixating on his personality and character traits to fill columns inches and television news segments. In general, the news media gave the Jackson campaign a fair shake despite the fact he had little realistic chance of winning the nomination. But he was five times more likely than any other Democratic candidate to have his personality or background dissected in a news story.

Jackson built a groundswell of opposition to Reagan's budget priorities, the proxy wars in Central America, the nuclear buildup, and the administration's "constructive engagement" policies toward the apartheid regime of South Africa. At a time when the Democratic leadership was swimming with the conservative tide in Washington, Jackson's campaign let the country know that the progressive base of the party still had a pulse. Jackson's support among white voters generally came from environmentalists, peace activists, and advocates for the homeless as well as gays and lesbians who felt disfranchised with the ascendance of the social conservatives and who believed not enough was being done to combat the HIV/AIDS epidemic. Jackson's "Rainbow Coalition" tried to use the primaries to galvanize the Left. The attitude of DNC leaders toward Jackson's candidacy was one of benign opportunism. They wanted his advocacy of traditionally liberal positions to "bring home" core Democratic voters, but they preferred he didn't pull the party in his direction.

The press coverage of Jackson's successful effort to secure the release of a U.S. Navy flier who was being held in Syria is illustrative of the general tone the media had toward his candidacy. On December 4, 1983, Lieutenant Robert O. Goodman Jr. was shot down while flying a "retaliatory" bombing sortie against Syria. The previous day Syrian antiaircraft guns had fired on American reconnaissance planes over Lebanon, and the United States dispatched 28 carrier-based planes to knock out Syrian positions in the mountains east of Beirut. The Navy's two-man jet crashed into a mountainside that the Syrians controlled. The 26-year-old pilot, Lt. Mark Lange of Fraser, Michigan, was killed, while 27-year-old Lt. Goodman of Portsmouth, New Hampshire, the bombardier-navigator, ejected before the plane went down. Suffering from broken ribs and other injuries, Goodman was taken to a military prison in Damascus.

After Jackson sent a telegram to Syrian President Hafez Al-Assad, with whom he had met two years earlier, urging him to release Goodman on "humanitarian" grounds, the government invited Jackson to come to Damascus to meet with the prisoner. Dan

Rather of CBS News reported the story this way: "He's bound for Syria tonight on a self-appointed mission to try to gain the release of captured U.S. Navy flier Robert Goodman Jr. Jackson calls it a 'mission of hope'; some others are calling it 'mission impossible'—even a 'grand-standing ego trip.'" The press generally recounted Jackson's efforts to free the American officer as little more than an "election stunt." Since Goodman was from New Hampshire, the site of the first primary, some commentators presumed he was just trying to gain votes. Others saw Jackson's efforts as racially motivated since the young officer was African American. A CBS News tag line from the Middle East when Jackson's entourage arrived in Syria reported: "Getting here got Jesse Jackson a lot of ink and air time, but now the burden has shifted to him to show that everything here that smacks of campaigns will help and not hinder getting Lieutenant Goodman out."

Behind the scenes, Jackson pulled together a delegation of ecumenical religious leaders that included some highly skilled negotiators, and he coordinated his efforts with the U.S. State Department. His moral appeals had weight in Syria and beyond, in part, because he had brought with him some American Muslim leaders, including Louis Farrakhan of the Nation of Islam. When Jackson's efforts to win the freedom of Lt. Goodman proved successful on the morning of January 3, 1984, President Reagan ordered a U.S. government plane to fly the delegation to Andrews Air Force Base outside of Washington. The next morning Reagan welcomed Goodman home with a joyful ceremony in the Rose Garden where he praised Jackson as a true American patriot.

Jackson's triumphant mission to Syria and his reception at the White House earned him some favorable publicity, but among many Jewish Americans his role in national politics was met with far less enthusiasm. A significant number of politically active Jewish Democrats believed Jackson was cultivating ties to Israel's enemies at a time when the IDF was waging war against Arab militants in Lebanon. Jackson's criticisms of Israel's treatment of the Palestinians and his 1979 meeting with Yasser Arafat of the Palestine Liberation Organization (PLO) also cost him Jewish support. Prominent Democrats circulated photos of Jackson with Arafat in an attempt to derail his candidacy. Jackson's close relationship with the Chicago-based Farrakhan also hindered his outreach to Jewish voters. Farrakhan had played a role in helping Jackson free Lt. Goodman, even leading an Arabic prayer before one of the meetings, but he was also known for his anti-Semitic rhetorical blasts. Jackson's already strained relations with American Jews set the stage for what became a major gaffe on his part that effectively ended his campaign.

Not long after his return from Syria, Jackson confided to an African-American *Washington Post* reporter, Milton Coleman, while on a flight to New York City, that he was traveling to "Hymietown" where the only topic of interest was "Hymie." Coleman publicized Jackson's use of the ethnic slur, and Jackson's handling of the episode only made matters worse. First, he denied having used the term; then he said he didn't remember using it. Within days he changed his story and formally apologized in a New Hampshire synagogue on the night before the primary. Full-page ads appeared in the *New York Times* asking: "Why would any Jew vote for Jesse Jackson? Why would any decent American?" The incident torpedoed Jackson's candidacy and brought widespread condemnation not only from Jews, but also from civil libertarians who were watchful of the rights of religious minorities as well as those who were concerned about his character because he apparently lied about the episode.

WALTER MONDALE AND GERALDINE FERRARO

During the Korean War, Walter "Fritz" Mondale had been a corporal in the U.S. Army and subsequently earned a law degree from the University of Minnesota Law School. He distinguished himself as a lawyer in Minnesota and rose through the ranks of the state's Democratic politics during its liberal heyday. A protégé of Senator Hubert Humphrey (who lost his bid for the presidency to Nixon in 1968), Mondale had served from 1960 to 1964 as Minnesota's Attorney General where he cut his teeth at a time when the Great Society and other liberal causes dominated American politics. In December 1964, when President Lyndon Johnson named Humphrey to be his vice president, the Minnesota governor appointed Mondale to fill his seat in the Senate. Mondale then went on to win two terms in his own right. Sometimes called "Fighting Fritz," Mondale was known to be an excellent debater who had a firm grasp of domestic and foreign policy. In 1976, Jimmy Carter asked him to be his running mate in his successful presidential bid. As Mondale prepared to run against Reagan in 1984, a key disadvantage that clung to the former vice president was his identification with the economic recession of Carter's final years.

Mondale spent little time reaching out to the grassroots activists of the party, which resulted in a campaign that lacked enthusiasm and momentum. Out on the stump, he repeatedly warned voters about Reagan's looming budget deficits and promised to take the unpopular action of raising taxes to address the fiscal crisis. Reagan, whose supporters fondly called him "the Gipper," took to calling Mondale "Coach Tax Hike." The Mondale campaign played on people's concerns about nuclear war with an array of ads criticizing Reagan's "Star Wars" missile defense system. But by 1984 Reagan had largely mollified people's fears by repeatedly stating that a "nuclear war can never be won, and must never be fought."

Attempting to give his lackluster campaign a shot in the arm, Mondale made a bold move in naming New York Representative Geraldine Ferraro to be his running mate. He would take advantage of what polls indicated to be a growing "gender gap" between Republicans and Democrats. Ferraro became the first ever woman to be on the ticket of a major American political party as well as the first Italian American. Ferraro was popular among her constituents of the Ninth Congressional District in Queens, and she had served in a leadership role in the House Democratic Caucus as well as on the Budget Committee. But she was little known outside her district and she had never run for statewide office. She couldn't guarantee a *bloc* of electoral votes as a governor or Senator might be able to do, and her lack of name recognition gave the Reagan-Bush campaign an opening to define her in the minds of voters. Despite Ferraro's credentials that clearly qualified her for the job, the choice took on the air of "identity politics" and the GOP exploited this perception.

With a woman running for the second highest office in the land gender politics introduced a new dynamic to the 1984 presidential race. During Reagan's first term, the women's movement had been stunned by the defeat of the Equal Rights Amendment (ERA) and the ferocity of the antifeminist backlash. As Representative Ferraro and Vice President Bush prepared for their sole debate, news reports surfaced that Barbara Bush, the vice president's wife, called Ferraro: "A four million dollar—I can't say it—but it rhymes with rich." Shortly thereafter, Bush's press secretary, Peter Teeley, floated the same gender-loaded term when he confided to reporters that "some people" saw Ferraro's mannerisms as "bitchy." When Ferraro heard about Mrs. Bush's remark she asked an aide: "Why is that nice old lady calling me a bitch?" Involving the wife of the

New York Representative Geraldine Ferraro became the first woman ever on the presidential ticket of a major American political party when former Vice President Walter Mondale chose her to be his running mate in 1984. Ferraro's role in the campaign and her contentious debate with Vice President George Herbert Walker Bush brought to light a new gender dynamic in presidential politics. Although Mondale would be defeated in a lopsided rout, Ferraro's nomination symbolized the opportunities opening up for women in politics even in the "conservative" 1980s.

Republican candidate neutralized the gender component by turning voters' attention to a public fight between two women representing the opposing political parties. Bush's strategists apparently saw some advantage in ginning up pre-debate controversy with a gender-specific barb pointed at the first female vice presidential candidate.

On October 11, 1984, the first-ever American vice presidential debate between a woman and a man took place. Midway through the encounter Ferraro pointedly pushed back against what she believed was Bush's condescending attitude toward her. Vice President Bush, who had served in many high-powered Washington posts, including chairman of the Republican National Committee (RNC) and CIA Director, at times had taken on the paternalistic air of an educator saying more than once to Ferraro: "Let me help you." His tone induced steely stares from his opponent who said: "I almost resent, Vice President Bush, your patronizing attitude." The moment became a "zinger" that received a lot of TV airplay. But political commentators generally declared Bush the victor, and most opinion polls agreed.

The press later fact-checked some of Bush's assertions during the debate and found them wanting. Bush's press secretary explained: "You can say anything you want in a debate, and 80 million people hear it. If reporters then document that a candidate spoke untruthfully, so what? Maybe 200 people read it, or 2,000 or 20,000." In any event, the vast majority of voters had already solidified their feelings toward the candidates and probably weren't going to switch their votes from Reagan to Mondale (or vice versa) based on something their running mates said in a debate.

In his two debates with Reagan, Mondale evinced his skills as a politician and even managed to flummox the president on a few occasions, which prompted a few news stories about Reagan's advanced age. But the "centrist" political strategy of the Mondale-Ferraro campaign, with its top-down endorsements, identity politics, and assurances of tax hikes, was a failure by almost any measure. Mondale lost 49 states and only squeaked out a victory in his home state of Minnesota. His only other victory was in the District of Columbia. Reagan won 525 electoral votes to 10 for Mondale giving the incumbent president the largest electoral-vote landslide in U.S. history. Even appointing the first woman running mate failed to stop Reagan from winning a bigger share of the female electorate than Mondale. Fifty-four percent of women voters chose Reagan, which was a 7 percent gain over 1980.

Reagan won 62 percent of male voters, 63 percent of white voters, and increased his tally among Latino voters by seven points from his 1980 margin. Three out of five first-time voters also cast their ballots for Reagan. According to a CBS/*New York Times* poll taken in December 1984, people who used computers favored Reagan over Mondale by wide margins, meaning the 73-year-old president was popular with younger voters. Overall, Reagan won 59 percent of the popular vote (53,428,357 to Mondale's 36,930,923 votes). Mondale had won nine out of ten African-American voters, but Jesse Jackson's work registering new voters bore little fruit in swelling black turnout in the general election.

It wasn't all bad news for the Democrats. Although the Republicans won seventeen seats in the House of Representatives, they didn't come close to offsetting the Democratic gains of 1982. Democrats still enjoyed a 70-seat majority, and in the Senate they picked up two seats. Despite Reagan's landslide victory his coattails in 1984 were not as impressive as they had been in 1980. Still, after the election, House Democrats of the Ninety-seventh Congress grew even more deferential to Reagan and drifted further to the right. "In my fifty years in public life," House Speaker Tip O'Neill told Reagan, "I've never seen a man more popular than you with the American people."

Reagan's 1984 reelection was all the more impressive because it followed four presidencies that fell short of serving out two full terms. After the November 1963 assassination of President John F. Kennedy, his successor, Lyndon Johnson, by March 1968, had to withdraw from his party's nominating process mostly in recognition of his failed Vietnam policies. Nixon became the only president to resign the office after he was implicated in the Watergate scandal. And Gerald Ford was largely seen as a caretaker president who leapfrogged from the House right into the presidency after a brief stint as vice president without ever having to face a national electorate. Jimmy Carter was a one-term president who by the time he left office had an approval rating as low as Nixon's at the height of Watergate. The nation seemed to want a successful two-term president. And with the economy on the mend and Reagan's political skills on full display, 1984 became a watershed year not only for Reagan and the conservative agenda, but also for the presidency itself.

RACE RELATIONS

Martin Luther King Jr.'s organizing efforts, his dedication to nonviolence, and his extraordinary leadership contributed mightily to bringing down the Jim Crow system of racial segregation in the American South. King had been instrumental in winning passage of the landmark civil rights and voting rights acts and had become an inspirational figure to millions of people around the world. His assassination on April 4, 1968, in Memphis, Tennessee, at the age of 39, led to a protracted national discussion about the meaning of his life's work. The idea of a federal holiday honoring Dr. King had been a rallying cry in African-American communities since the time of his death. By the early 1980s, the political pressure had built to the point where enacting a holiday for King could no longer be resisted even by a popular conservative president.

Reagan opposed a Martin Luther King Jr. Day, not only because he saw it as a waste of tax dollars, but also because he believed King's radical views and associations during the course of his career made him a poor choice for the honor. The civil rights battles of the previous decades were still fresh in people's memories and the African-American contingent in Congress, most notably the Black Caucus in the House of Representatives, had a morally persuasive voice in lobbying for the King holiday and rallying public support. Beginning in 1979, Representatives John Conyers (Democrat of Michigan) and Shirley Chisholm (Democrat of New York) submitted and resubmitted the King Day legislation in every new session of Congress. In late 1983, Reagan relented after the House voted 338 to 90, and the Senate 78 to 22 in favor of the holiday, indicating that there were enough votes to override a presidential veto.

The president held a signing ceremony with King's widow, Coretta Scott King, by his side, and spoke fondly of King's role in making the United States a freer and more just nation. The event coincided with the administration's rolling back of affirmative action and weakening both the Equal Employment Opportunity Commission (EEOC) and the Civil Rights Division of the Department of Justice. Still, Reagan proved he could be accommodating even when he had reservations. Since the Congress already passed the measure with veto-proof majorities, he had little to lose. In what would become a recurring theme of Reagan's style of governance, he would resist measures he didn't like until the political costs became too great and then adopt them as his own. Ideological purity could always be bent to fit political reality. The King holiday is a good example of how Reagan reaped benefits from displaying flexibility even though in other areas affecting the black community his administration was pushing in a direction that King surely would have opposed.

The recession of the early 1980s hit African-American communities hard. By the beginning of 1983, black unemployment had reached 21 percent and the unemployment rate for African-American teens was a staggering 52 percent. Federal social programs that assisted the poor and legal safeguards against racial discrimination in hiring were needed more than ever in the context of the battered U.S. economy. But the Reagan administration was going in the opposite direction on all of these fronts. In 1981, Reagan named Clarence "Penny" Pendleton Jr. as the chair of the U.S. Commission on Civil Rights. The commission was one of the federal government's preeminent bodies dedicated to fighting racial prejudice in the workplace. Pendleton had switched to the Republican Party in 1980 after saying he had had enough of "bleeding-heart liberalism," and his appointment signaled a shift in the federal government's attitude toward the enforcement of civil rights statutes. Pendleton derogated affirmative action and believed in only "color-blind" policies. He became one of the more high-profile black conservatives in the 1980s until he died of a heart attack in 1988 at the age of 57.

Reagan elevated a handful of black officials who went on to have significant public careers. In 1982, he appointed Clarence Thomas to head the EEOC, which made him, along with Housing and Urban Development (HUD) chair Samuel Pierce, one of the highest-ranking blacks in the administration. The permanent EEOC dated back to the Civil Rights Act of 1964 and coordinated federal efforts against racial discrimination in the private sector. Thomas had served on the staff of Republican Senator John Danforth of Missouri and came with Danforth to Washington in 1979 as a young lawyer fresh out of Yale Law School. He was a staunch conservative who, like Penny Pendleton, opposed affirmative action and any other federal program that used race as a basis for formulating policy (even though he had benefited from affirmative action himself). At the EEOC, Thomas oversaw 3,100 employees working out of 48 field offices.

Thomas dismissed the use of statistics in calculating the effects of racial inequality in American society. Testifying to Congress in 1984, he pointed to the example of the all-black Georgetown University basketball team, which represented a predominantly white school, as evidence that standard measurements of racial discrimination could not be trusted. In the same testimony, he ripped into African-American leaders for "disenfranchising blacks." "Blacks don't have clout in the Democratic Party," he said. "And the black leaders have alienated blacks so badly from Reagan and the Republican Party—made him into an evil person—that there is no chance at this point for blacks to discuss the Republicans as an alternative to the Democratic Party." Thomas's position at the EEOC became a key steppingstone in his fast-track legal career that culminated in his 1991 appointment to the U.S. Supreme Court to succeed the retiring civil rights legend Thurgood Marshall.

The Department of Labor held in abeyance affirmative action rules in awarding contracts to minority-owned businesses, and the Department of Justice, under Attorneys General William French Smith and Edwin Meese III, discontinued the practice of requiring employers to maintain race and gender-based hiring goals. The Department of Justice also stopped enforcing court-mandated busing of children as a means to counteract the effects of de facto racial segregation in public schools, calling it "ineffective and unfair." By the late 1970s, school busing had become so unpopular in some cities, particularly Boston, that it pushed significant numbers of white working-class voters to abandon their traditional allegiance to the Democratic Party to become "Reagan Democrats." In a period of high unemployment, Republican politicians became adept at denouncing mythical "quotas" and "set-asides" to turn white working-class voters against the Democrats.

Despite the shift in priorities of the federal government there were noteworthy gains by African-American politicians who won elective office. In 1982, Andrew Young, the veteran civil rights leader and Carter's ambassador to the United Nations, was victorious in the Atlanta mayoral race. The following year, in a political triumph of grassroots organizing, Harold Washington was elected the first African-American mayor of Chicago. Mayor Coleman Young of Detroit also became a high-profile black mayor, and Wilson Goode, who, like Harold Washington, was able to build a coalition of diverse ethnic groups, became the first black mayor of Philadelphia. These elections proved that marshalling black voters at the municipal level could be a pathway to local power. In 1982, Los Angeles Mayor Tom Bradley nearly won the California governorship. After leading in the polls against his Republican opponent, George Deukmejian, Bradley lost in a close race. (Political commentators chalked up his defeat to "the Bradley Effect," the concept that white voters tell pollsters they're willing to vote for a black candidate only to change their minds inside the privacy of the voting booth.) In the early 1980s, the civil rights activist John Lewis was elected to the Atlanta City Council and later to the U.S. Congress, and in 1984, Jesse Jackson made his presidential run that mobilized the party's base. Jackson's national grassroots organization, the Rainbow Coalition, built an ethnically diverse network of community organizers in cities across the United States.

In addition to successes in the electoral arena, African Americans in the 1980s made historic gains in advancing all fields of American society and culture. A new generation of talented young black writers and scholars exemplified the new opportunities the civil rights movement had opened up for them. African-American literature saw a resurgence that affected the nation's collective imagination. In 1982, Alice Walker published *The Color Purple* that won the Pulitzer Prize for Fiction the following year, and in 1985 the director Steven Spielberg adapted it to film, which boosted the careers of two young black women who played starring roles, Whoopi Goldberg and Oprah Winfrey. Later in the decade, Tony Morrison's *Beloved* became part of the American literary canon. *Beloved*, which follows the experiences of a mother and daughter who escaped slavery, won the Pulitzer Prize in 1988 and propelled Morrison toward winning the Nobel Prize for Literature in 1993.

In the 1980s, a new generation of black scholars carved out careers in academia. Henry Louis Gates Jr., who taught at Yale and Cornell, founded the "Black Periodical Literature Project" that republished Harriet Wilson's 1859 book, *Our Nig*, the first novel printed in the United States by a black author. Other young African-American academics built impressive careers, including the sociologist William Julius Wilson, the theologian Cornell West, the historian Nell Irvin Painter, the singer and composer Bernice Johnson Reagon, and many others. The struggles on college campuses of the 1960s and 1970s over the creation of Black Studies departments paid off in the 1980s by nurturing an immensely gifted cohort of young black intellectuals.

In the movie industry there remained a paucity of African-American filmmakers with the rare exception of the director Spike Lee who, along with Martin Scorcese, became one of the most famous graduates of New York University's film school. Lee's style had a real-world aesthetic that grappled with complex racial and social issues. His NYU thesis film, *Joe's Bed-Stuy Barbershop: We Cut Heads* (1982) gained critical notoriety after it was chosen for a Museum of Modern Art New Directors/New Films exhibition. Lee's skewering of racial attitudes and his use of drastic shifts in orientation and Brechtian devices—such as having performers speak directly to the camera—set him apart from other young filmmakers. His debut feature film, *She's Gotta Have It* (1986), displayed his breadth in taking on comedic and sexual subject matter. Lee's *Do the Right Thing* (1989) was among the best pictures of the 1980s in its nuanced portrayal of the complexities of race relations in a Brooklyn neighborhood. Lee's career, begun in the 1980s, flourished in later decades making documentaries and feature films and attaining a place in the front rank of American filmmakers.

In May 1984, President Reagan paid tribute to the pop music mega-star Michael Jackson in a weird Rose Garden ceremony where the president thanked Jackson for donating his song "Beat It" to an antidrunk driving campaign. At the event, Jackson wore his signature pseudomilitary costume complete with epaulets and faux medals. With the release of his 1982 *Thriller* album, which music industry publications named one of the greatest records of all time, Jackson was the biggest African-American entertainer in the 1980s. *Thriller* went "multiplatinum" selling 29 million copies. The "King of Pop's" appearance with the conservative president came at a time when the black population was coalescing into an anti-Reagan *bloc*. Some of Jackson's critics saw his visit as a tacit endorsement of the administration's policies toward civil rights and poverty that were deeply unpopular in the black community.

Between 1985 and 1990, the most watched television show in America by both blacks and whites was *The Cosby Show*. This situation comedy had been the vision of the actor and comedian, Bill Cosby, who played a successful gynecologist on the show and head of the Huxtable family. The female lead, performed by Phylicia Rashad, was a high-powered lawyer. The Huxtables brought into Americans' living rooms a close-knit black family that supremely valued higher education. (One Huxtable daughter went to Princeton while the other attended a prestigious all-black college.) With a jazz soundtrack and African art in the home *The Cosby Show* expressed an understated racial pride. For half an hour every week in primetime, this show presented a picture of a super-functional upper-middle class black family. Although racial issues were unavoidable, the characters, comedy, and plot lines looked past the controversies of racism and inequality that had been on the front burner of American politics for nearly two decades. The success of *The Cosby Show* among white audiences might have had something to do with the essentially conservative values the show projected. Cosby's vision of a charming, family-centered sit-com broke from the dominant themes that had boxed in African-American television characters. Part of the show's genius can be found in its forthright yet nuanced counterpoint to the black stereotypes that permeate American entertainment culture.

In January 1985, the Chicago talk-show host, Oprah Winfrey, made her national television debut with a slot on NBC's *The Tonight Show*. Later that year, Quincy Jones, the African-American musician, arranger, and producer of Michael Jackson's *Thriller* album, recruited Winfrey to play the leading role of Sofia in the movie production of *The Color Purple*. By the end of the decade, Winfrey not only had her own phenomenally successful TV talk show but her own production company. Her mass following, consisting primarily of women of all ages, classes, and ethnicities, catapulted Winfrey to becoming the most successful and influential black businesswoman in America.

Americans had long been familiar with the phenomenon known as "white flight" as white people fled the cities for the suburbs, but in the 1980s, this trend was followed by "black flight" as middle-class African Americans, who were poised to take advantage of the new opportunities, followed a similar pattern. The social consequences of this process, which William Julius Wilson describes in *The Truly Disadvantaged* (1987), resulted in a bifurcated black community and the further impoverishment of many African-American urban areas. Wilson follows the rise of a black "underclass" left behind by those who vacated the inner cities in search of greater economic opportunities and higher property values. "Black flight" and its attendant social dislocations were the result of a segment of the African-American population building careers in academia, the professions, and in the business world on a scale that would have been impossible just twenty years earlier.

There were other social forces at work in the 1980s that adversely affected African-American communities. In 1985, with the invention of "crack" cocaine, low-income people living in economically depressed areas had access to the drug as never before. Pharmacologically identical to the powder variety, crack could be packaged and sold in small quantities, or "rocks," suitable for smoking. This far cheaper version of coke became an inner city currency as well as a business outlet for thousands of small-time dealers. Its sale and distribution intensified gang activity and within a year the public perception of crack was keenly associated with the black underclass. Crack also became the largest single contributing factor to the spike in the incarceration rate of young black men.

By the summer of 1986, news accounts flooded the airwaves and print media about the new "epidemic" of drug abuse in America. Some journalistic accounts defined "crack whores" and "crack babies" in terms that matched the stereotypes of "welfare queens." Congress appropriated $2 billion for the drug war and passed the Anti-Drug Abuse Act of 1986. Federal prison sentences for drug offenders shot up and there were more severe penalties for selling crack cocaine than powder. Since it was more likely that blacks would be convicted for possessing crack than whites, it put in place sentencing guidelines that could be racially discriminatory. In 1980, African Americans, who were roughly 12 percent of the population, comprised 23 percent of those arrested for drug crimes, and by the end of the decade that number jumped to 40 percent. Clearly, there was still a long way to go in the struggle for racial equality, but African Americans had entered an era that transcended many of the older civil rights struggles despite the rise of new and unforeseen challenges.

THE ERA, FEMINISM, AND BACKLASH

In 1972, Congress passed the Equal Rights Amendment, which dated back to the early twentieth century and whose operative clause read simply: "Equality of rights under the law shall not be denied or abridged by the United States or by any state on account of sex." Twenty-two state legislatures quickly ratified the constitutional amendment, and in 1976 both the Democratic and Republican Party platforms endorsed it. The Republican First Lady, Betty Ford, campaigned for it. Most observers at that time believed the ERA's passage was nearly guaranteed. But the momentum slowed in the late 1970s, and after Indiana became the 35th and final state to ratify it in 1977, the measure languished falling just short of the necessary 38. In the summer of 1978, the National Organization for Women (NOW) and other ERA advocacy groups organized a march of 100,000 supporters in Washington DC and successfully lobbied Congress to extend the deadline for ratification to June 30, 1982. Thereafter came an acrimonious battle that revealed some of the new complexities the feminist movement faced in the 1980s.

Phyllis Schlafly, who headed an organization called the "Eagle Forum/STOP ERA," along with Concerned Women for America, and other mostly religious-based anti-ERA groups, evoked many of the old fears that had fomented female opposition to women's suffrage back when the Nineteenth Amendment was being ratified. Anti-ERA organizers claimed the amendment would deny women the right to spousal support, overturn privacy laws, send women into combat, and enshrine abortion and gay rights in the Constitution. In 1980, the Republican Party struck the ERA from its platform thereby freeing the Reagan-Bush campaign to harness the grassroots energy of the social conservatives who fought against the amendment. Pro-ERA women's groups were caught off guard but continued to lobby Congress and state legislatures, and to facilitate petition drives, walkathons, and fundraisers. Some women adopted the tactics of their radical sisters from the suffrage era such as hunger strikes, picketing the White House, and civil disobedience. But they were fighting an uphill battle in a period of rising conservative strength. The Christian evangelical wing of the Reagan coalition deplored not only the ERA, but also the Supreme Court's 1973 ruling, *Roe v. Wade*, which constitutionally protected abortion rights.

The ERA dispute also brought to the fore some old divisions inside the women's movement. Spirited debates broke out around the concepts of "equality" and "difference,"

Conservative Christian activist Phyllis Schlafly led the charge against the Equal Rights Amendment (ERA) to the U.S. Constitution that sought to codify equal treatment for women. Schlafly's "Eagle Forum" played a pivotal role in defeating the ERA by lobbying states to block its ratification. Her highly successful antifeminist organizing efforts not only illustrated the divisions among women, but also the extent of the antifeminist "backlash" against the women's movement that enveloped the 1980s.

the meaning of "human nature," and the role of religion in society. In June 1982, after the ERA went down in flames a network of 200 nonpartisan women's groups formed the National Conference of Women's Organizations, with 10 million members that pressed Congress to reintroduce the ERA in every new session. Supporters of the ERA pointed to the irony that it was the feminist movement that opened up the space for anti-ERA women's groups to be effective in the public arena. Susan Faludi, whose 1991 book *Backlash* captures the ennui of gender relations in the 1980s, describes this contradiction: "The activists of Concerned Women for America could report to their offices in their suits, issue press releases demanding that women return to the home, and never see a contradiction. By divorcing their personal liberation from their public stands on sexual politics, they could privately take advantage of feminism while publicly deploring its influence. They could indeed 'have it all'—by working to prevent all other women from having that same opportunity." The divisive battles over the ERA and the amendment's ultimate failure marked an end point of a period in the 1970s when women's reproductive and workplace rights stood on solid ground in mainstream American politics.

Aside from Reagan's high-profile appointment of Sandra Day O'Connor in September 1981 to be the first woman Justice of the U.S. Supreme Court, his record on elevating women to high government positions was unimpressive. He appointed roughly half the number of women to posts that required Senate confirmation than his predecessor making him the first president in over a decade to move backward on this front. The number of women of the White House staff dropped from 123 in 1980 to sixty-two in 1981. Reports of sex discrimination and sexual harassment were on the rise, but Reagan's EEOC under Clarence Thomas, which was charged with pursuing legal remedies, slowed its activities to a crawl while its public relations office, often contradicting its own figures, asserted that sexual harassment was on the decline. The White House also eliminated the Coalition of Women's Appointments and the Working Group on Women.

A class action lawsuit brought by women who worked for the retail giant Sears, Roebuck & Company, the largest private employer of women in the U.S. at the time, illustrates the government's lagging attitude toward sex discrimination in the 1980s. The original lawsuit stemmed from hundreds of complaints by female employees that the company was tracking them into sales positions where their pay was substantially lower than their male counterparts doing identical retail work. On average, American saleswomen earned 51 to 53 cents to a man's dollar. There was a degree of optimism that the EEOC would help the plaintiffs in the Sears case because it had mandated other companies, including AT&T, General Motors, and General Electric, to pay compensation to settle similar sex discrimination suits.

The trial lasted 10 months through 1984 and 1985, with Sears' lawyers arguing that the company was not guilty of discrimination because women "naturally" gravitated toward sales in departments that brought lower commissions. They cleverly played on the age-old dichotomy between "equality" and "difference" and found an expert witness, Rosalind Rosenberg, a Barnard College women's history professor, who was willing to argue that women "naturally" desired not to sacrifice family obligations to enhance their incomes. Sears was not guilty of "discriminating" against female employees, Rosenberg claimed, since the women themselves chose to earn less than the men based on their innate dispositions.

Another argument the Sears attorneys pursued was that these saleswomen were augmenting their husbands' incomes and therefore didn't need opportunities for advancement. Making hash out of this assertion was the fact that many of these working-class women were single mothers or widows who cared for one or more children (some of them had as many as five children), and they had quite loudly expressed their ambition to grab any chance to upgrade their incomes (hence the lawsuit). Even the married women had little incentive (natural or otherwise) to pass up additional income because, contradicting Professor Rosenberg's testimony, about one-fourth of the women who worked at Sears had husbands who were unemployed, and another fourth had husbands who earned only $15,000 a year.

The Sears legal team divined a conspiracy where "a female underground within EEOC" was biasing the commission with "feminist" assumptions. The Sears attorneys required thirty EEOC employees to file depositions outlining their ties with outside women's rights groups or feminist leaders. They were trying to prove there was a "conflict of interest" within the EEOC because the federal agency was tainted by its feminist associations. It was an odd angle to take since Reagan's EEOC was hardly being aggressive and was seeking ways to settle the case. The presiding Judge, John A. Nordberg, a Reagan appointee, questioned whether American women suffered discrimination in the workplace at all and ordered the EEOC to prove it. Predictably, Judge Norberg ruled in Sears' favor, thereby validating the argument that women naturally preferred lower-paying jobs. The Sears case was a setback for women's pay equity and it added to the sense that in the conservative 1980s American women were in for some tough battles over rights they thought they had already won.

In 1981, Betty Friedan, the feminist icon and author of the 1963 book, *The Feminine Mystique*, published *The Second Stage* where she criticized the women's movement for what she believed was its knee-jerk radicalism. Friedan argued that women were spending too much time blaming men or the government for their own failings. The emphasis on sexual politics, she alleged, had brought about a "feminist mystique," which discredited feminism in the eyes of Middle America. On the other end of the spectrum, feminist author Barbara Ehrenreich identified, in the 1980s, divisions "between the 'bourgeois' feminists who wanted to scale the occupational hierarchy created by men and the radical feminists who wanted to level it." Friedan's book whipped up criticism from those who believed she had overlooked the role of radical feminists in helping thousands of women fight against domestic violence and sexual harassment in the workplace. For these women "the second stage" of feminism, which Friedan described, had not yet arrived because the struggles of the "first stage" were not over.

There were other conflicts that divided the women's movement such as the role of pornography in society and the status of sex workers. Feminist activist Andrea Dworkin, and the Canadian law Professor Catherine MacKinnon, advocated stricter censorship laws on the sale and distribution of pornographic materials. Their concerns coincided with the explosion of sexually explicit images that the mass marketing of videocassettes and VCRs had made possible. Dworkin and MacKinnon's legal proposition was that pornography was a civil offense against the rights of women to lead secure lives and it was the basis for antiporn ordinances in Minneapolis and Indianapolis passed in 1983. Dworkin and MacKinnon's antiporn crusade, which underlined the abundance of violent and degrading images of women, as well as the exploitation of women's bodies by male profiteers, propelled them into tactical alliances with some of the most puritanical, antifeminist elements of the Republican Christian Right. This bizarre confederacy in support of censorship divided the women's movement. The scholars Ellen Carol DuBois and Linda Gordon pointed out that the "feminist attack on pornography and sexual 'perversion' . . . fails to distinguish its politics from a conservative and antifeminist version of social purity, the Moral Majority and [the] 'family protection movement.'"

In 1984, the Reagan administration entered the porn debate with the appointment of Attorney General Edwin Meese III to head a commission to look into pornography's harmful social effects and how the federal government might respond. Among the commissioners was the ultra-conservative Christian radio host and head of "Focus on the Family," James Dobson. The Meese Commission enlisted the help of the Dworkin/MacKinnon-aligned group, Women Against Pornography, which brought forth witnesses to testify about the damage caused by porn and its attendant violations of public decency. From June 1985 to January 1986, the commission held hearings in several cities and published its nearly 2,000-page report in mid-1986, known as the "Meese Report." Dworkin and MacKinnon praised the law enforcement provisions the commission recommended and adjured their implementation. The Meese report's findings culminated in the formation of a National Obscenity Enforcement Unit, which was a team of federal prosecutors that assisted local law enforcement authorities in shutting down pornographers. Many veterans of the feminist movement deplored what they saw as a violation of First Amendment guarantees of free speech and criticized the restrictions on women's choices as well as the paternalism of the Meese Commission "protecting" women from sex-related work. But the most stinging rebuke pointed to the bizarre political alliances that had been forged between radical feminists and right-wing religious groups that also opposed women's reproductive rights.

It was in this environment of "feminist" antiporn crusades when a new AM radio phenomenon took off that exulted in male chauvinism. One example was the popularity of the Howard Stern and Don Imus radio shows, which were dominated by locker room humor free of any semblance of treating women as equals. Radio's "bad boys" (as they were called) achieved high ratings by articulating male frustrations with the post-Second Wave culture. The call-in radio format found a market in giving men permission to be immature, bawdy, sexist, and uncharitable toward women and minorities. In addition, right-wing talk shows proliferated at the same time, hosted by men, such as Rush Limbaugh, who were also overtly chauvinistic. "Conservative" radio fit in perfectly with the Reagan administration's attacks on affirmative action, "welfare queens," and liberals in general. Limbaugh became well-known for his vivid depictions of feminists as jackbooted thugs, which he called "feminazis." These new attacks on women in the media as either sex objects or fascists stemmed not only from feelings of insecurity among millions of men regarding the new gender roles, but also from the fact that women in the 1980s, despite the backlash, were making tangible gains in the business world and professions.

Business schools were graduating more women with MBAs than ever before and by the end of the decade women were roughly 30 percent of managerial employees. Women were entering the white-collar workforce in large numbers and finding new opportunities that an earlier generation of feminists had opened for them. A significant percentage of the approximately 17 million new jobs that were added to the American economy during the 1980s went to women who had become second earners in households struggling to maintain their standard of living. Magazines geared toward career women such as *Savvy* and *Working Woman* offered women advice about how to succeed in the business world that was often contradictory, superficial, and counterproductive. They typify the confusing signals women were receiving as they built professional careers. Some books advised women that the key to success was being more like men and squashing any impulse that might be construed as "feminine." Charlene Mitchell and Thomas Burdick's *The Right Moves* (1985), for example, told career women they should "eliminate the notion that the people with whom you work are your friends." Whereas other books gave the opposite advice, such as Marilyn Loden's *Feminine Leadership* (1985), which roused women to embrace their nurturing and intuitive sides.

There were books that counseled women to neuter their sexuality and avoid workplace romances, while others, such as Leslie Aldridge Westoff's *Corporate Romance* (1985), suggested that women should focus their "energy that derives from sexual excitement" to be "more productive on the job." Still other books were filled with tips for proper behavior, such as Letitia Baldrige's *Complete Guide to Executive Manners* (1985), which prescribed how female executives should comport themselves in public spaces: "Enter the bar with a briefcase or some files. . . . Hold your head high, with a pleasant expression on your face. . . . After you have ordered your drink, shuffle through a paper or two, to further establish yourself." What was often ignored in the prescriptive literature was that women might be better served by equal pay and antidiscrimination laws, access to flexible work schedules, quality child care, and other reforms that feminists had long advocated. Instead, these books generally advised women to endure the hardships of the corporate workplace as isolated individuals fretting about how best to fit into a system that was slanted against them.

But nothing cut to the core of women's rights in the 1980s more than the conflicts over abortion. No amount of advice literature for women could adequately prepare them for the fierce backlash against *Roe v. Wade* that erupted in antiabortion protests from an ascendant religious Right. In 1983, at a prayer meeting in Binghamton, New York, a 24-year-old Christian activist, Randall Terry, conceived "Operation Rescue." Terry and Operation Rescue became famous for organizing hundreds of protests at women's clinics across the country. Operation Rescue activists became well-known for blockading women's health clinics and harassing patients often by shoving giant photographs of aborted fetuses in their faces. They glued shut clinic doorknobs and dogged employees as they made their way to and from work. At one point Operation Rescue militants occupied a clinic in Binghamton, ripped out the phone lines, smashed furniture, and barricaded themselves in the building until the police broke down the doors and arrested them.

During the 1988 Democratic National Convention in Atlanta, Operation Rescue gleaned its most extensive national media coverage when its activists descended on the city for a week of antiabortion protests. By the time the convention was over 134 protesters had been arrested. Terry became a regular guest on the *Morton Downey Jr. Show* and other television and radio talk shows. In 1992, he made headlines again after he was sentenced to five months in prison for trying to send a dead fetus to President Bill Clinton. Terry and Operation Rescue failed to roll back abortion rights but their extremism, militant tactics, and direct confrontations at women's clinics nurtured an environment that was hospitable to the idea of intimidating doctors who performed abortions.

The defeat of the ERA, the Sears case, and Operation Rescue were all evidence of a well-organized "backlash" in the 1980s against the earlier gains of the second wave feminist movement. The loud protests from antichoice women like Phyllis Schlafly and others who were identified with the religious Right, coupled with a socially conservative ethos emanating from Washington, bred the very real fear that women were losing the political ground they had won in the 1960s and 1970s. The Canadian author, Margaret Atwood, caught this sentiment in her 1986 dystopian novel, *The Handmaid's Tale*, which became a bestseller and depicts a society where women live as second-class citizens under a right-wing Christian theocracy. In a sense, the feminist project in the 1980s encountered a set of changing circumstances similar to those that the African-American civil rights movement faced. Like blacks, the social advances of women of the previous two decades had fashioned new challenges that arose from their past successes. Women were still entering politics, the professions, and the business world in large numbers. Despite the rise of social conservatives and the vigorous counterattack against feminism, turning back the cultural clock to a time of more rigid gender roles had little chance of success.

HIV/AIDS

In the summer of 1981, a growing number of patients began showing up at San Francisco hospitals and clinics with an unidentified disease. The variety of symptoms meant that tracing its origins was difficult but since it only seemed to afflict gay men doctors and clinicians called the new disease GRID: "Gay Related Immune Deficiency." In 1982, when the Centers for Disease Control (CDC) in Atlanta learned that heroin addicts, heterosexual women, newborn babies, and people who had undergone blood transfusions also showed signs of the disease, it lost its "gay" distinction and was seen as a generalized public health emergency. (Six months earlier, the Reagan administration had slashed the CDC's budget as part of its ongoing effort to reduce government waste.) In 1981, there had been 243 known deaths attributable to the disease, which was now called AIDS (Acquired Immune Deficiency Syndrome), but the yearly death toll would rise to 5,386 by 1985. It was not until 1986 when scientists first detected a link between HIV (Human Immunodeficiency Virus) and AIDS.

Going back to the June 1969 Stonewall Inn riots in Greenwich Village, gay men had been involved in a long-term struggle for civil rights and political recognition. Throughout the 1970s, they gained greater social acceptance and found their independent political voice, manifested most notably by the election of Harvey Milk to the San Francisco Board of Supervisors in 1976. But in the 1980s, it was within the crucible of the life-and-death battles surrounding HIV/AIDS where the gay community gained a new cohesion, solidarity, and strength. At the local level, gay activists took charge of the crisis exhorting condom use and mobilizing for greater public and private resources to fight the spread of the disease.

The AIDS epidemic of the 1980s tested American society's ability to respond humanely to a complex configuration of problems. Not everyone was ready to acknowledge the true dimensions of the crisis that had broken out at a time when social conservatives had attained a new level of power. The emergence of AIDS presented those opposed to homosexuality with opportunities to pass moral judgment. "The sexual revolution has begun to devour its children," Patrick Buchanan of the White House communications office declared. "And among the vanguard, the Gay Rights activists, the mortality rate is highest and climbing. The poor homosexuals. They have declared war upon nature, and now nature is exacting an awful retribution." The Reagan administration, reflecting its intrinsic conservatism, was slow to respond to the AIDS crisis. It wasn't until 1987 that Reagan first spoke publicly about AIDS, even though by then 20,000 people had died from the disease worldwide.

In 1982, the New York writer, Larry Kramer, pulled together a spirited brigade of gay rights activists and founded a new organization called "Gay Men's Health Crisis" (GMHC). The group coordinated its efforts from headquarters in New York and San Francisco and raised over $150,000 in the first year. The "Silence=Death" campaign followed, which overtly connected the struggle of HIV/AIDS with the wider movement for lesbian, gay, bisexual, and transgender (LGBT) rights. The "Silence=Death Project" used as its logo the pink triangle that the Nazis had forced homosexuals to wear in the concentration camps. When the group's militant tactics succeeded in bringing attention to the crisis some of its founders formed the "AIDS Coalition to Unleash Power" (ACT UP). Established in 1987, ACT UP engaged in acts of civil disobedience to demand government assistance in combating AIDS. ACT UP also fought to bring local control to the organizations that sustained people living with AIDS and defied the power of "AIDS experts" inside the medical and government bureaucracies. These public battles around AIDS constituted a powerful subtext that shaped American society's changing views of sexual identity.

It wasn't until the film and television star Rock Hudson died of AIDS in October 1985 that the disease began to garner the mainstream attention it deserved. Hudson was a cultural icon, life-long Republican, and a friend of the Reagans. Most of his fans didn't know he was gay. His death from the disease allowed newspapers, magazines, and even the tabloids to begin to discuss AIDS in a more serious way. "Hudson's death gave AIDS a face," said the actress Morgan Fairchild, who costarred with Hudson in the television show *Dynasty*. Other celebrities and entertainers began taking public stands and drumming up more resources for fighting the disease, which was taking its toll in the theater and dance communities. In 1985, the legendary film actress, Elizabeth Taylor, entered the fray when she became the founding national chairperson of the American Foundation for AIDS Research (amfAR). Taylor used her friendship with Nancy Reagan to press the president behind the scenes to come out for greater resources for AIDS research. She testified before Congress, appeared in several public service announcements, and worked tirelessly as a fundraiser and public advocate for victims of the disease.

Later in the decade, the AIDS movement found another effective mainstream spokesperson in a young Indiana boy, Ryan White, who contracted the disease while receiving a blood transfusion to treat his hemophilia. White presented the nation with an innocent victim of AIDS free of the burdensome stereotypes that heterosexual society held about gay men. His fight against the myth that AIDS could be spread through casual contact gained national attention as White's family wrestled with various school officials who wanted to bar him from enrolling. He appeared regularly on television news and talk shows until he died of AIDS at the age of 18. In 1989, ABC aired a television movie dramatizing his life, *The Ryan White Story*. White's efforts pushed the nation in the direction of greater acceptance and sympathy toward those who suffered from HIV/AIDS.

In 1988, the literary critic and author, Susan Sontag, wrote an essay titled "AIDS and Its Metaphors," which touched a sensitive nerve among the educated public and sparked enormous criticism. In it, Sontag linked racist assumptions in American society with a wider interpretation of the cultural meaning of the AIDS crisis. "Illustrating the classic script for plague," she wrote, "AIDS is thought to have started in the 'dark continent,' then spread to Haiti then to the United States and Europe. It is understood as a tropical disease: another infestation from the so-called third world. . . . The subliminal connections made to notions of a primitive past and the many hypotheses that have been fielded about possible transmission from animals (a disease of green monkeys? African swine fever?) cannot help but activate a familiar set of stereotypes about animality, sexual license, and blacks." Sontag's deconstruction of the mainstream discourse about AIDS stirred a fierce debate among intellectuals because she had used the dominant view of AIDS to unpack what she believed were some unpleasant and deep-seated prejudices of American culture.

As AIDS began to infect more heterosexuals the idea that sexual activity could result in death spread fear and anxiety. Parents and school boards added the threat of acquiring AIDS to their warnings to teenagers against experimenting with sex. The young people who entered adolescence during the 1980s, sometimes called "Generation X," became the first modern generation to come to terms with the idea that having sex could kill them. To counter this narrative ACT-UP deployed clever media techniques to bring a "sex positive" message to the fight for greater funding of AIDS research, and reached out to young people with the advertising campaign: "Kissing Doesn't Kill." Later in the decade ACT-UP also organized a nonviolent direct action at St. Patrick's Cathedral in New York City to protest Cardinal John O'Connor and the Church's ban on contraception, which gay activists saw as a death sentence for thousands of sexually active young people. The event drew over 4,000 demonstrators and ended in 111 arrests. But by disrupting a Sunday Mass ACT-UP's organizers had walked straight into a public relations buzz saw. The action became fodder for ridicule in the press that galvanized their nemeses among the Religious Right while annoying allies that often worked in coalition with gay organizations.

By the end of the decade state and local governments, along with nongovernmental organizations, were pitching "safe sex" campaigns with public service announcements that underscored condom use and other safeguards that gay organizations had been advocating for years. All of the open talk about sexuality and homosexuality, especially targeting younger people, did not blend well with the more puritanical undercurrents of American culture as well as the social conservatives who preferred not to discuss sex at all.

REVIEW QUESTIONS

1. What were some of the main issues facing the United States as Reagan sought re-election in 1984? What does the 1984 presidential race teach us about gender and race relations during the eighties?

2. How successful was Jesse Jackson in mobilizing the Democratic Party's base leading up to the 1984 elections? What structural changes had taken place in the selection process of each party's nominees?
3. What were the major trends and changes that took place among African Americans during the eighties? How did African-American politicians, scholars, artists, professionals, and civil rights organizers transform American society in this period?
4. What does the struggle over the passage of the Equal Rights Amendment (ERA), the Sears Case, and Operation Rescue teach us about gender roles and feminism in the 1980s? Why were American women so divided on the ERA?
5. When the HIV/AIDS epidemic broke out what was the response of the federal government? In what new ways did the LGBT community organize itself to counter the societal effects of the AIDS epidemic and to further its goals of equality and civil rights? What were the limitations of some of the more militant protest tactics?

---

mysearchlab CONNECTIONS SOURCES ONLINE

READ AND REVIEW

Review this chapter by using the study aids and these related documents available on MySearchLab.

Study Plan
Chapter Test
Essay Test

Documents
Operation P.U.S.H. Platform (1971)
This document outlines the founding goals of Jesse Jackson's organization.

The Bush-Ferraro Vice-Presidential Debate (1984)
Debate between vice presidential candidate Geraldine Ferraro and Vice-President George H. W. Bush.

Roe v. Wade (1973)
Text of the landmark decision on women's right to abortion.

The Equal Rights Amendment
Amendments affirming that women and men have equal rights under the law.

RESEARCH AND EXPLORE

Use the databases available within MySearchLab to find additional primary and secondary sources the topics within this chapter.

Video
Ronald Reagan Presidential Campaign

4

Popular Culture and the Culture Wars

CHAPTER OUTLINE

TECHNOLOGY AND POPULAR CULTURE

Few decades can top the 1980s in the changes that took place in the field of consumer electronics and popular culture. Astonishing new devices transformed the way people related to television, music, movies, and their workplaces. The mass marketing of videocassette recorders (VCRs) permanently altered the intimate bond between Americans and their television sets. Popular music was mass-produced in new formats and consumed on new devices. There was the Hollywood debut of "high-concept" movies and new sound and image technologies. And Americans were being introduced to personal computers

---

It was during the 1980s when the "blockbuster" Hollywood movie was institutionalized complete with "synergies" connected to sound tracks and merchandise. The filmmaker and producer, George Lucas, revolutionized the experience of moviegoers with technological breakthroughs in sound and visuals from his state-of-the-art California studio, Lucasfilm. In the early 1980s, his *Star Wars* epic amassed an audience that would have been unimaginable in size just a few years earlier. Lucas's mythological tale set in outer space, which draws upon themes from Joseph Campbell's *The Hero with a Thousand Faces,* became one of the transformative popular culture events of the decade.

for the first time, which revolutionized the way people processed information for work and for play.

With the advent of the VCR, for the first time, television viewers were no longer beholden to the three networks' broadcast schedules and could record shows and watch them at their convenience. In 1980, 1.9 million U.S. households owned VCRs, but by the end of the decade, the number had grown to 62.3 million, or about two-thirds of all households. At first Hollywood film corporations fought the new VCR technology fearing it would cost them revenues as people taped movies instead of paying to see them in theaters. They also presumed they would lose control over duplicated movies. The Hollywood powerhouse, Universal Studios, fearing widespread copyright infringement, filed a lawsuit against Sony for marketing the device. By the time the Supreme Court settled in Sony's favor in 1984, the extensive marketing and distribution of VCRs had become a *fait accompli*. Movie companies that had contested the new technology later became its chief beneficiaries after it opened up new secondary markets for them to sell their films in video format. Once entertainment corporations lowered the retail price of videos they discovered there was a new demand as consumers assembled their own libraries of their favorite movies. Video sales turned out to be extremely profitable. The widespread distribution of VCRs also made room for a new small business sector as video rental shops sprang up in neighborhoods across the country. The market value derived from the sales of home videos leapt from $280 million in 1980 to an astounding $5.1 billion by 1989.

Another unexpected outcome of the widespread distribution of VCRs was the boost they gave to the pornography industry. For the first time, pornography could be consumed discreetly without involving seedy urban sex shops. Upstanding suburbanites, even those living in socially conservative areas, could now more readily rent or purchase pornographic materials. By the mid-1980s, pornography companies were releasing a thousand new titles each year and earning annual revenues through the sale of videotapes of over $400 million. The lucrative market in buying and selling sexually explicit images, the fruit of the capitalist free market, tended to work against the social conservatives' calls for a return to "family values."

In August 1981, Warner Communications launched Music Television (MTV), which was the first cable TV channel dedicated solely to popular music. The first video played on the station was fittingly "Video Killed the Radio Star" by the British pop band The Buggles. The videos on early MTV play lists christened a new era where visual representations of popular music became just as important as the music itself. There was an emphasis on how a song "looked" on MTV, which affected popular tastes. Producers began rearranging their artists' music to fit the demands of MTV, and it gave performers a new pathway to advertise their records and start careers. Within a few years, MTV had 24.2 million viewers and was shaping the sensibilities of millions of young people as they looked to the station for cues about the latest fashions and dance tunes.

For media conglomerates, MTV played a significant role in developing "synergies" for marketing music and other cultural products as well. For example, the MTV video of the theme song for the movie *Top Gun*, "Take Your Breath Away" by the band Berlin, featured long sequences of images of fighter jets and characters from the film in a pastiche that looked like a lengthy commercial. Video sales of *Top Gun* sold 2.5 million copies in the first week. Similarly, producers of the movie *Flashdance* broadcast an MTV video that catapulted its theme song to being a hit even before the film was released. The director of *Flashdance* edited four music videos using shots from the film that ran on MTV. In less than three weeks the picture grossed over $20 million and the sound-track sold a million copies. *Flashdance* and *Top Gun,* both produced by the Paramount "high-concept" team of Don Simpson and Jerry Bruckheimer, fostered a "synergy" with record sales. In the 1980s, media companies were constantly seeking new ways to sell movies, soundtracks, even lifestyles, and MTV gave them another means to exploit the lucrative youth market.

Also revamping the way Americans consumed music was the colossal success of Sony's "Walkman" and its imitators. Portable audio cassette players with stripped down earphones freed people from fixed music systems as they listened to music while jogging (part of a fitness fad of the 1980s), riding a bike, or taking public transit. The Walkman became a craze in the United States as millions of Americans "cocooned" themselves in public spaces while "privately" enjoying music. This highly individualized technology fit in well with American culture. By 1983, propelled in part by the popularity of the Walkman, music cassettes for the first time outsold vinyl records.

In addition to MTV, cable television companies introduced major programming changes that left an enduring imprint on American popular culture. Not only did CNN and other 24-hour news channels alter the way Americans tuned into news and politics, but Home Box Office (HBO) also afforded another opportunity to profit by re-airing movies that people might have missed in theaters as well as producing its own content. HBO and other "pay per view" stations offered new revenue streams for entertainment companies as well as new "synergies." The Home Shopping Network, which allowed people to purchase products after viewing them on TV with an immediacy that was novel, modified consumption habits and was an early precursor to shopping via computer. The 24-hour sports network, ESPN, changed the way fans consumed sports entertainment and imparted new opportunities for athletes to become major celebrities.

In June 1986, as part of an agreement with the Federal Communications Commission (FCC), cable television networks began 24-hour live coverage of deliberations on the floor of the House of Representatives and the U.S. Senate. The Cable-Satellite Public Affairs Network (C-SPAN) became a new publicity vehicle for airing partisan debates from inside Congress in real time. Soon backbenchers from both major parties were going live on C-SPAN to push their agendas as well as their own personal careers.

The 1980s was also the decade when the "blockbuster" movie came to the fore. Entertainment industry executives stumbled upon mass marketing principles that squeezed every dime out of their films with video tie-ins, soundtrack albums, toys, and advertising partnerships with fast food chains. Given the expense of so-called saturation releases, blockbuster movies like *The Empire Strikes Back* (1980), *E.T.* (1982), *Return of the Jedi* (1983) *Ghostbusters* (1984) and *Batman* (1989), each came with bigger and more elaborate promotional blitzes. With the enormous profits at stake media conglomerates sought new ways to repeat this formula. The Walt Disney Company pioneered new promotional methods that targeted children to press their parents not only to see movies, but also to purchase related merchandise.

Throughout the decade the fantasy and science fiction genre was the biggest moneymaker for Hollywood, and it was directly linked to the revolutionary innovations in sound systems and computerized effects. George Lucas, the originator of the *Star Wars* epic, along with his engineering team at Lucasfilm, were at the cutting edge in researching and developing new sound and visual technologies. Sound systems in movie theaters across the country underwent digital overhauls with Lucasfilm's THX auditory technology. The movie *Star Trek: The Wrath of Khan* (1982) contains a minute-long special effects sequence of a barren planet being brought to life (produced by Lucasfilm) that was Hollywood's first foray into computer-generated images (CGI). Thereafter digitally based filmmaking and the ability to jump convincingly from CGI to live-action, along with the new sound technologies, revolutionized the American movie industry.

Large media corporations took advantage of the "synergizing" of the cultural marketplace to become more consolidated. In the 1980s, with the exception of banking, acquisitions and mergers in the media sector outnumbered all others, totaling $89.2 billion. In 1984, the Australian media mogul, Rupert Murdoch, owner of News Corporation, added Twentieth Century-Fox to his extensive holdings of newspapers, book publishing, and television stations. The concentration of ownership continued until only a handful of conglomerates dominated global media: Bertelsmann, General Electric, News Corporation, Seagram, Sony, Time Warner, The Times Group, Viacom, and the Walt Disney Company. Mark Fowler, who was Reagan's chair of the FCC from 1981 to 1987, was a gung ho proponent of deregulating the industry and saw no downside to the trend toward oligopoly. "It's time to move away from thinking of broadcasters as trustees," he said, "and time to treat them the way that everyone else in this society does, that is, as a business. Television is just another appliance. It's a toaster with pictures." In 1987, the FCC also jettisoned the "Fairness Doctrine" that had governed the public airwaves for decades, particularly in relation to radio, that had previously tied media company leases to having ideologically balanced programming that served the public interest. Absent the Fairness Doctrine mandating pluralism on the airwaves highly partisan right-wing radio shows came to dominate the primetime line up on AM radio.

Personal computers (PCs) were still in their infancy, but there were early marketing successes as more businesses recognized the potential of computers to increase efficiency and fatten their bottom lines. One of the more striking aspects of the development of PCs was that so few people at the time predicted the radical alteration of society they were about to bring. When businesses first began using computers they were normally in a centralized location with workers sharing time on a "main frame." It didn't take long, however, for executives to realize that by distributing computer terminals to each employee's workstation they could boost productivity. For the business world, PCs were the most earth shaking development since the invention of the typewriter. Companies, including Apple, Compaq, Commodore, IBM, Sperry, Wang, and many others competed fiercely for market share.

More affordable computers opened up new opportunities for the mass marketing of video games. Arcade games that were once only the preserve of amusement parks became widely available for home use. Japanese and U.S. companies took the lead in the new gaming technology. In 1978, the Japanese Taito Corporation and its publisher, American Midway Games (the company that licensed Pac-Man in 1980), distributed "Space Invaders" in a profit-sharing arrangement. The demand for new games drove innovations. In 1987, gaming took a huge leap forward when Nintendo presented a new generation of games with its Entertainment System and Sega's Master System. A multibillion-dollar industry was born.

On October 13, 1983, another milestone was reached in the new communications environment when journalists, TV crews, and several hundred curious onlookers assembled at Soldier Field in Chicago for an exposition of the cellular telephone. The regional phone company, Ameritech, sponsored the event where one of its executives demonstrated the new device with a call to Germany while sitting in the driver's seat of a

Chrysler convertible. On the other end of the line was a great-grandson of Alexander Graham Bell, inventor of the telephone. Some commentators compared the new wireless telephone to the moon landing. There was now a product that gave people the freedom to place a phone call from anywhere, without wires, that portended a revolution in the telecommunications industry.

Music companies began marketing digital Compact Disks (CDs) for the first time and the new format for storing music data at first was seen as a high-end complement to vinyl and cassette tapes. Compact disk production accelerated when the British company, Phillips, along with Sony (developer of the VCR), yielded a set of technical specifications for all CD formats called the "Red Book," which gave CDs greater mass appeal because they could be played on devices manufactured by many different companies. The development of CDs did for music what VCRs did for movies: supply new revenue streams for entertainment companies by giving them the opportunity to rerelease back catalogues in a new format. Baby boomers, who grew up with vinyl (whose collections were degrading due to wear and tear) could now purchase the same music in digital form. Music companies (and the artists) had the potential to profit twice on the sales of the same music. In 1984, Sony mass produced the first portable CD player, which rapidly replaced the Walkman in popularity. Although CDs were still seen as exotic and the first CD players were clunky and expensive, by the end of the decade CD sales began to outpace vinyl and tape. The economies of scale necessary for the mass production and distribution of CDs were instrumental in bringing society into the "digital age," and laid the foundation for subsequent breakthroughs in digitizing and streaming audio and visual information. It was the digital revolution of the 1980s that made possible the Internet revolution of the 1990s.

THE PARENTS MUSIC RESOURCE COUNCIL

Following President Reagan's landslide reelection victory social conservatives had reached a new level of authority not only inside the administration, but also in the culture at large. A handful of self-appointed guardians of public decency began policing the boundaries of what was acceptable in American popular culture. One example of this renewed societal concern was the Parents Music Resource Council (PMRC) that bounded onto the scene in early 1985. Mary Elizabeth "Tipper" Gore, the wife of Tennessee Senator Albert Gore Jr., cofounded the PMRC along with other Washington spouses after she purchased for her 8-year-old daughter a copy of Prince's *Purple Rain* album. She was horrified by the lyrics of the song, "Darling Nikki," which broaches the topic of female masturbation. When Tipper Gore heard "Darling Nikki" in December 1984 it inadvertently touched off what became one of the more publicized "culture wars" of the decade.

Prince Rogers Nelson was a hugely successful pop star in the 1980s whose songs were often crossover hits in the rock and R&B worlds. He produced his own records from his home in Minneapolis, starred in his own feature film, *Purple Rain* (1984), and exhibited his talents in dizzying live performances. The movie *Purple Rain* had an "R" rating so its sexual content was well-known. But that didn't stop Ms. Gore from being alarmed at the lyrics, which motivated her to lead the effort with other like-minded parents to call for warning labels on popular music albums. "We are not censors," Tipper explained to *Rolling Stone* magazine. "What we are talking about is a sick new strain of rock music glorifying everything from forced sex to bondage to rape." The only thing the PMRC wanted, she insisted, was "a tool from the industry that is peddling this stuff to children, a consumer tool with which parents can make an informed decision on what to buy."

The PMRC, in addition to Tipper, had as original members Susan Baker (the wife of Treasury Secretary James Baker III), Pam Howar and Sally Nevius (the wives of Washington businessmen), and the spouses of nine other U.S. senators. They compiled a list of songs, the "Filthy Fifteen," which they believed to be the most egregious pop music offenders. The "Filthy Fifteen" included, in addition to "Darling Nikki," Sheena Easton's "Sugar Walls" (written and produced by Prince); *Judas Priest's* "Eat Me Alive"; *AC/DC's* "Let Me Put My Love Into You"; and *W.A.S.P.'s* "Animal (Fuck Like a Beast)." The PMRC subsequently broadened its definition of "obscene" by adding to the list the relatively tame fare of "I'm on Fire" by Bruce Springsteen, "Do That to Me One More Time" by the Captain and Tennille, and "Torture" by the Jacksons. The group allied itself with the National Parents and Teachers Association (PTA) and urged people to monitor the play lists on local radio stations. It wasn't long before President Reagan chimed in saying popular music was espousing "the glorification of drugs and violence and perversity."

In the spring of 1985, the PMRC sent an open letter to Stanley Gortikov, the president of the Recording Industry Association of America (RIAA), requesting the music business to attach the following rating labels to albums: "X" for "profane or sexually explicit"; "O" for "occult"; "D/A" for "drugs or alcohol"; and "V" for "violence." Gortikov rejected the PMRC's code, but hinted he was open to some kind of parental warning. Legislation favorable to the recording industry was pending before Congress that if enacted would slap a new tax on blank cassette tapes to "recover" costs from consumers who reproduced copyrighted music. At stake was a potential revenue stream for the record companies that could be as high as a quarter of a billion dollars. Al Gore was a cosponsor of the Senate version of the bill.

This new public battle over rock 'n' roll lyrics came at a time when Reverend Jerry Falwell's "Moral Majority," Phyllis Schlafly's Eagle Forum, and the televangelist empires of Jimmy Swaggart, Jim and Tammy Faye Bakker, and Pat Robertson (who would run for president in the 1988 Republican primaries) were more politically influential than ever before. These standard-bearers of the religious Right postulated that voters in 1984 had given their brand of social conservatism a mandate. After Jimmy Swaggart accused rock music of breeding "adultery, alcoholism, drug abuse, necrophilia, bestiality and you name it," Walmart began removing dozens of "offensive" albums and magazines from its racks including *Rolling Stone*. (The record labeling controversy coincided with a similar, though less acrimonious, battle over the new "PG-13" rating on gory Hollywood movies that was also thrust on the entertainment industry by outside advocacy groups.)

The composer and touring rock musician, Frank Zappa, became the chief public foil to the PMRC after he penned a letter that appeared in the music industry magazine *Cashbox*, titled "Extortion, Pure and Simple." In it, Zappa argued that the record industry was so set on getting its corporate-friendly tax legislation through Congress it was willing to squash First Amendment free speech rights. "The RIAA must tap-dance for these Washington wives or the industry's bill will feel the wrath of their famous husbands," Zappa wrote. For nearly two years Zappa traveled the television and radio circuit deploring the PMRC even though the organization had not targeted his catalog of music. Zappa also criticized Prince for remaining silent amidst the PMRC's calumny since it was the lyrics of his "Darling Nikki" that ignited the controversy.

Since the 1960s Frank Zappa had been a fierce detractor of the recording industry's power to dictate the tastes and sensibilities of the music-consuming public. Zappa had writ-

Rock musician, satirist, and composer Frank Zappa became the most outspoken public foil to the efforts of the Parents Music Resource Council (PMRC), which sought to require warning labels on all mass-produced popular music alerting parents of lyrical content that glorified sex, drugs, or violence. Zappa sparred with PMRC representatives on television and radio shows, including Tipper Gore, the wife of Tennessee Senator Al Gore. In September 1985, he testified against the proposed labeling requirement before the Senate Committee on Commerce, Science, and Transportation where he denounced the PMRC's efforts as "fundamentalist frogwash" and an attack on the First Amendment protections of free speech.

ten and produced over 60 albums, including the 1982 song, "Valley Girl," which became an accidental hit. "Valley Girl" was a satirical pop tune that contained the authentic teenage argot of Zappa's 15-year-old daughter, Moon Unit, who imitated the slang of her privileged girlfriends who combed the shopping malls of the San Fernando Valley. It became an instant pop cultural sensation. Soon, there were "Valley Girl" lunchboxes, *The Official Valley Girl Coloring Book* (a Zappa father-daughter effort), a "Valley Girl" doll, and a hastily shot film of the same title starring Nicholas Cage in his first movie role. "Sociologically," Zappa said, it was "the most important record of 1982 in the United States."

Zappa had supporters in the music industry who also opposed the PMRC. Punk rockers, such as Jello Biafra of the *Dead Kennedys*, were up in arms, and even some clean-cut musicians, such as Donny Osmond and John Denver, became unlikely allies in fighting the PMRC. What concerned Osmond was that parental warning labels might compel him to "dirty up" his lyrics to earn a more restrictive rating because the kids buying his albums would assume that anything winning their parents' seal of approval wasn't "cool." He believed labeling would therefore lead to more obscene content, not less. Osmond appeared with Zappa on Ted Koppel's *Nightline*, and in September 1985 John Denver testified with Zappa before the Senate Committee on Commerce, Science, and Transportation. Five of the committee members had wives on the PMRC.

"The PMRC's case is totally without merit," Zappa said in his testimony, "based on a hodge-podge of fundamentalist frogwash and illogical conclusions." To the elected officials "who sit idly by while their wives run rabid," Zappa pointed out, "Ronald Reagan came to office with the proclaimed intention of getting the federal government off our backs." The PMRC's mission, however, was "to force certain people to wear it like a lampshade at a DC Tupperware party." The titillating nature of the controversy bred great public interest. When Zappa came to Congress, in addition to C-SPAN, jammed into the hearing room were 35 live television feeds and over 50 still photographers.

On *Nightline* and elsewhere Zappa suggested that parents take the initiative and introduce their children to classical music and jazz, which are instrumental and therefore had no offensive lyrics. "Children in the 'vulnerable' age bracket have a natural love for music," he said. "If, as a parent, you believe they should be exposed to something more uplifting than 'Sugar Walls,' support music appreciation programs in schools. . . . Your children have a right to know that something besides pop music exists." The PMRC's representatives who made the TV rounds laying out the case for the warning labels often blurred the lines between the images in MTV videos, photographs and art layouts on record packaging, and racy live performances. Yet it was the words to which they objected. The middle-age women who defended the PMRC on TV often read lengthy snippets of the lyrics they found objectionable. They seemed to be unaware that they were giving the songs greater public exposure by reciting the material. Television news shows couldn't resist running sexy clips of MTV visuals (like Madonna) whenever guests debated the PMRC. In fact, the British pop singer, George Michaels, said that the PMRC's harping about his song "Sex" from his *Faith* album helped the single sell 3 million copies.

In November 1985, Zappa released *Frank Zappa Meets the Mothers of Prevention;* the final cut, "Porn Wars," loops together sound bites from the senators who had grilled him at the hearing two months earlier. Tucked in the barrage of electronic sounds are Senator Paula Hawkins of Florida talking about "fire and chains and other objectionable tools of gratification," and Senator Slade Gorton of Washington reproaching Zappa as "boorish" and questioning whether or not he was even capable of understanding the U.S. Constitution. No other American musician possessed the skills, imagination, and sociological understanding to pull together this kind of fusion of music and social commentary. But it was all for naught. The same month Zappa's spoof of the PMRC was available in record stores the RIAA capitulated to the organization's pressure and began placing "parental advisory labels" on records, tapes, and CDs.

MADONNA AND SPRINGSTEEN

One song that made it onto the PMRC's "Filthy Fifteen" was "Dress You Up" by a young entertainer from Detroit who became a pop culture icon in the 1980s. Born in 1958 and raised in an Italian-American/French-Canadian Catholic family, Louise Veronica Ciccone (Madonna) began her career in 1977 when she relocated to New York to study ballet with Alvin Ailey. She ended up joining several Greenwich Village repertory dance companies before signing a deal with Sire Records as a solo performer. She was known for her formidable work ethic and spent years performing in clubs and hustling her recordings.

Madonna was a perfect match for the MTV era because her visuals, choreography, and fashion template were integral to the music itself. In March 1984, the song "Borderline," from her eponymously titled first album, broke into the Top Ten. What followed was a string of 17 Top Ten hits, a record for a female solo artist. Madonna's dance moves drew heavily from themes circulating through the New York gay nightclub scene, and she was an outspoken proponent of LGBT rights and greater funding for HIV/AIDS research. She also single-handily crafted a new "guttersnipe" chic in the world of young women's fashion. Leather jackets, lingerie, lace gloves, mismatched earrings, and high-heeled boots were all part of Madonna's ever-changing persona. Her overt displays of female sexuality elicited condemnation from social conservatives and often thrust her to the center of the culture wars of the period.

The video for her 1984 song, "Like a Virgin," drew upon Catholic iconography and the controversy surrounding her use of religious signifiers unleashed a torrent of free publicity. Her decision to don wedding attire in the MTV video incited attacks from the religious Right as a defilement of marriage, as did a highly sexual live performance of the song at the MTV Music Awards. The video for "Material Girl," from the same album, appropriated a Marilyn Monroe mystique that mimicked the musical number, "Diamonds Are a Girl's Best Friend." Some critics saw it as nothing more than glorifying the eighties' values of instant gratification and conspicuous consumption, while others applauded its portrait of a sexually empowered woman. Later in the decade, Pepsi-Cola Company dropped a multimillion-dollar contract backing one of Madonna's tours after Christian conservatives mobilized against her not just for her licentiousness, but because the video for the song "Like A Prayer" (1989) starred an African-American Christ character.

Students of American popular culture have commented widely on Madonna's carefully scripted public image as a prodigious work of performance art. With her use of iconic imagery and her deliberate shift of the "gaze" in her videos, she presented herself not just as an object of male sexual desire, but also as a desiring female subject. Her video, "Express Yourself," subverted the male-centeredness of MTV and was also noteworthy for its delineation of the male body. Madonna's aesthetic as well as her role in the pop culture of the 1980s has become the subject matter for a spate of books, articles, and even Ph.D. dissertations. Nearly everything Madonna stood for can be judged as a pop cultural counterweight to the thriving political power of the decade's social conservatives and their often-callous prejudices.

Yet a pop artist didn't have to be as sexually adventurous and flamboyant as Madonna to earn a spot on the PMRC's "Filthy Fifteen." Bruce Springsteen, the all-American working-class hero from Asbury Park, New Jersey, found himself in the PMRC's crosshairs for his song, "I'm on Fire," from his 1984 album *Born in the USA*. The lyrics of "I'm on Fire" are relatively benign musings about sexual longing and the MTV video had little overt sexual imagery. But that didn't stop the PMRC from attacking it. The rest of *Born in the USA* is noteworthy for its portrayal of a declining America where Rust Belt towns succumbed to the loss of manufacturing jobs. The title cut critiques the shoddy treatment received by Vietnam veterans who had been cast aside when their service was over. The record sold over 20 million copies and opened a world tour that lasted two years. The booming, anthemic chorus of "Born in the USA," which echoed the "USA! USA!" chant during the 1984 Olympics, caused some confusion. To Springsteen's chagrin, the 1984 Reagan-Bush campaign blared the song at its rallies. The campaign only ceased playing it when Springsteen's lawyers threatened to sue the Republican National Committee. (*Born in the USA* later had the distinction of becoming the first commercial compact disc pressed in the United States.)

HIP-HOP AND JAZZ

The PMRC had concentrated on the musical tastes of youngsters mostly from the white suburbs, but rising out of Brooklyn and Los Angeles in the 1980s was a genre that would have a permanent effect on popular music. The gritty neighborhoods of the decaying inner cities originated a new kind of young African-American artist. The after-hours scene on the East Coast found MCs (Masters of Ceremonies) and DJs (disc jockeys) spinning multiple turntables, rapping, and syncing up beats in all-night dance parties. MTV eschewed these artists and although their lyrical content was often far more harsh than most of the material on the "Filthy Fifteen," their music had not yet reached a wide enough audience to make it on the PMRC's radar.

In the 1970s, the Barbados born "Grand Master Flash" (Joseph Saddler) brought to the Bronx Caribbean-style rap and DJ techniques while performing with Kurtis Blow and Lovebug Starski. In 1980, he signed with Sugar Hill Records after joining forces with five other MCs in a band named Grandmaster Flash & the Furious Five. The band let loose a series of seminal hip-hop tracks: "Freedom" (1980); "The Adventures of Grandmaster Flash on the Wheels of Steel" (1981); "The Message" (1982); and "White Lines" (1983). The record industry saw hip-hop as a passing trend, but the new musical form surpassed all expectations in sales and popularity. The genre took off in 1984 when two New York musician/producers, Rick Rubin and Russell Simmons, formed Def Jam records. It was the first significant label dedicated to hip-hop. LL Cool J, the Beastie Boys, and Run DMC came out with albums on the Def Jam label. Run DMC's 1986 record, *Raising Hell,* bolstered hip-hop's status as a crossover rock genre. The band's rendition of *Aerosmith's* "Walk This Way," along with the accompanying MTV video, became a runaway hit.

Later in the decade a hip-hop sub-genre, "gangsta rap," connoted the world and attitudes of the inner city where violence and drugs were a normal part of the social landscape. With the advent of gangsta rap hip-hop ceased being predominantly an East Coast phenomenon. Ice T (Tracy Marrow) who was originally from Newark, New Jersey but grew up in Los Angeles, released *Rhyme Pays*, which was the first hip-hop album that sold enough to carry a PMRC-style parental advisory label. Another group of gangsta rappers from Los Angeles (Ice Cube, Dr. Dre, Eazy-E and MC Ren) formed N.W.A. (Niggaz Wit Attitude), and their second album, *Straight Outta Compton* (1988), defined the new genre. The record is part political tract, part withering condemnation of American racism and police brutality. The most famous song, "Fuck the Police," turns the tables on the LAPD by putting it on trial in a mock courtroom. The music that caught the tenor of black urban life became increasingly popular among white suburban youth. In the 1980s, hip-hop joined the blues, soul, and jazz as a popular African-American musical idiom with worldwide appeal.

In contrast to the African-American pop music of the 1960s and 1970s, aggressive hip-hop and gangsta rap marked a shift away from civil rights oriented themes. One exception was the New York band *Public Enemy*. The band's three core members—MCs Chuck D and Flavor Flav along with DJ Terminator X—rose out of Roosevelt, Long Island, and all attended Adelphi University. Public Enemy became known for an aesthetic that blends the familiar signifiers of cars, sex, money, and guns, with a post–civil rights critique of American racism. These rappers appropriated the stereotypes of gang violence to sell records but turned them on their head by giving listeners a more politically engaged set of ideas and possibilities.

The 1980s was also a period when pop musicians labored to advance a number of worthy social causes. One example was the January 1985 performance of "We Are the

World." Written by Michael Jackson and Lionel Ritchie and produced by Quincy Jones, the song raised money for famine relief in Ethiopia. Years of drought and warfare in East Africa had claimed the lives of over a million people. Jones, Jackson, and Ritchie brought together music industry heavyweights to sing on the video. Among the musicians were Bruce Springsteen, Mick Jagger, Stevie Wonder, Cyndi Lauper, Ray Charles, Billy Joel, Diana Ross, Smokey Robinson, and many others. "We Are the World" became the biggest-selling single of all time and solicited millions of dollars in donations for food aid for Africa. The express political purpose of the project, along with its international distribution, unearthed the power of pop artists to bring attention to international causes.

After the success of "We Are the World" promoters in England repeated the effort with a benefit concert, "Live Aid," that was held simultaneously at Wembley Stadium in London and JFK Stadium in Philadelphia. British pop star and producer, Bob Geldof, had coordinated two prior events in England that raised nearly $16 million for the victims of the Ethiopian famine. The July 13, 1985 "Live Aid" concert included Elton John, Madonna, Sting, U2, Eric Clapton, The Four Tops, Run DMC, David Bowie, and Tina Turner. Phil Collins, who was a huge concert draw in the 1980s, performed in London in the morning (with Prince Charles and Lady Diana in the audience), and then hopped on the Concorde to Philadelphia to play with Sting and Eric Clapton that evening. MTV and CNN carried the event all day on live television. The concerts and related sales of merchandise amassed another $80 million for famine relief. Following "Live Aid," the country music legend, Willie Nelson, organized several "Farm Aid" concerts to pool money for America's ailing farmers who suffered hard times as mechanized agribusiness and globalization took their toll on family farms.

The decade also saw an efflorescence of modern jazz. Many of the most important innovators of the 1950s and 1960s were attaining new peaks in their mature years, blending jazz with other genres, touring, and nurturing a new generation of extremely talented young musicians. Jazz education became institutionalized in the 1980s as jazz programs and big bands became fully integrated into the curricula of many of the nation's colleges and universities. A dedicated cadre of educators drilled young musicians in the canon of American jazz. The legendary jazz drummers Buddy Rich, Art Blakey, Max Roach, Billy Cobham, Tony Williams, Jack DeJohnette, and many other soloists, including Miles Davis, Sonny Rollins, Freddy Hubbard, Ron Carter, Sarah Vaughn, Dizzy Gillespie, Herbie Hancock, Chic Corea, and Dave Brubeck, were tireless performers throughout the decade. The deaths of Buddy Rich in 1987 and Miles Davis in 1991 marked a kind of turning point as the old guard passed the torch to a new generation.

The 1980s gave rise to a cohort of young jazz artists who would have a far-reaching effect on jazz music and education, among them Wynton and Bradford Marsalis. The Marsalises got their start as sidemen for Art Blakey's "Jazz Messengers." In 1987, Wynton Marsalis cofounded a jazz program at Lincoln Center, which went a long way toward bringing jazz its due as a major American art form. At the same time as purists were canonizing jazz, rock instrumentation and electronic instruments, especially the new digital keyboards and MIDI (Musical Instrument Digital Interface), opened a "cross-over" space for jazz artists. The legendary bassist, Jaco Pastorious, personified this new aesthetic by redefining what was possible on the electric bass and inspiring a generation of young imitators before his untimely death in 1987 at the age of 35. The electric jazz innovators of the period broke new ground for musicians across the spectrum who specialized in other genres, such as rock, funk, and hip-hop.

In addition to famine relief for Ethiopia, American and British pop musicians worked to heighten awareness of the racial injustices going on inside South Africa where a small white minority dominated a large black majority. In late 1985, an antiapartheid album, *Sun City,* was released after a member of Bruce Springsteen's E Street Band, Steven Van Zandt, along with a group called "Artists United Against Apartheid," recruited an all-star cast of musicians. Included among them were Bob Dylan, George Clinton, Gil Scot-Heron, and many others, who used the title song and album to orchestrate a musicians' boycott against performing at the Sun City resort located in a white enclave about a two hour drive from Johannesburg.

THE ARTS AND CULTURE WARS

By the mid-1980s, the self-congratulatory ethos of Wall Street had crept into the New York art world as Yuppies, foreign investors, and even investment banks and corporations snapped up expensive works of art as symbols of status and success. Wealthy individuals and institutions began trading in Van Goghs, Cezannes, and Gaugins as if they were shares of common stock and the intense speculation pumped up an "art bubble." At the beginning of the decade, the highest prices paid for paintings at a public auction were $6.4 million for Turner's *Juliet and Her Nurse* and $5.4 million for Velazquez's *Portrait of Juan de Pareja*. By 1988, these prices would be looked at as bargains after Picasso's *Yo Picasso* sold for $47 million and Van Gogh's *Irises* for $53.9 million.

In this super-charged art world, with over 90,000 artists working in New York City alone, even so-called underground artists could become commercial successes. Jeff Koons, for example, a former commodities trader, attained instant fame for his ceramic sculptures of Michael Jackson and his pet chimpanzee. Though he never claimed any special meaning to his work, Koons grasped the superficiality of mass-produced celebrity in the '80s and his *Michael Jackson with Bubbles* (1988) sold for $5.6 million. He became a powerful player in the art scene with a reputation for fiercely defending his copyrights (even while freely appropriating ideas from other artists). In 1988, the same year his *Pink Panther* ceramic made a splash, a photographer sued Koons for stealing subject matter for another sculpture, *String of Puppies*; (a three-judge panel ordered Koons to pay an undisclosed settlement.)

One New York artist whose meteoric rise elucidates the way artists could be hyped and marketed in the 1980s was Jean-Michel Basquiat. Born in Brooklyn to a middle-class Haitian and Puerto Rican family, Basquiat gained notoriety as a graffiti artist with the tagline "Samo" whose anarchistic drawings questioned definitions of "public art." At the age of 18, he had been sleeping on friends' couches only to find himself a few years later selling his paintings for as much as $50,000. His neo-expressionist use of color, text, and African-American themes differed markedly from the minimalist orientation of New York artists in the 1970s. Basquiat had no formal training but was well-versed in art history and had grown up immersed in the world of New York's museums. Fluent in French, Spanish, and English he was able to absorb a diverse canon while never straying far from his urban roots.

In 1984, Basquiat had his first major show at the Mary Boone Gallery where he unveiled some paintings of African storytellers, or *griots*, which fit in well with the emergent hip-hop culture. The renowned pop artist, Andy Warhol, mentored Basquiat through the Manhattan publicity machine and collaborated with him on a few projects. The Whitney Museum procured some of his paintings and there were exhibitions of his work from the Ivory Coast to Germany and France. A 1985 cover story in the *New York Times Magazine* lauded Basquiat's talents, but also concluded that "the nature and rapidity of his climb" would be "unimaginable in another era." Surrounded by sycophants and bearing the pressures of fame, he periodically left New York to spend time in Los Angeles and

The sudden rise of the former graffiti artist Jean-Michel Basquiat illustrated the super-charged (and super-hyped) nature of the New York art world in the eighties. His death in 1988, at the age of 27, from a heroin overdose was a tragic testimony to his succumbing to the pressures of 1980s celebrity.

Hawaii. He died of a heroin overdose on August 12, 1988, at the age of 27. Basquiat's swift ascent and early death were intricately linked to the highly commercialized art world of the 1980s.

Amidst the mushrooming art trade, where artists like Koons and Basquiat could become media stars overnight, there was also a backlash against "objectionable art" animated by a powerful assemblage of social conservatives. Social conservatives attacked the National Endowment for the Humanities (NEH) and the National Endowment for the Arts (NEA) because of their funding of controversial artists and exhibits. Republican senator from North Carolina, Jesse Helms, demanded deep cuts in both agencies' budgets. Bashing the NEH and the NEA could pay political dividends by fueling what became known as the "culture wars" and putting liberals on the defensive. Inserted into the middle of this conflict was an unlikely antagonist in the form of a little-known artist of Honduran and Cuban ancestry named Andres Serrano. In 1988, Serrano became the focal point of heated attacks after the Southeastern Center for Contemporary Art gave him a visual arts award for a work titled *Piss-Christ*. Composed a year earlier, *Piss-Christ* is a cibachrome photograph of a white plastic crucifix submerged in a glass of Serrano's urine. The artist said he never intended to denigrate Christianity but only wished to affirm the common attributes that Christ shared with the rest of humanity. When Senator Helms caught wind that Serrano had gotten a portion of a $15,000 honorarium that included NEA money he used the photograph as a rallying cry to cut off all public financing of "offensive" art. A bipartisan group of senators signed an open letter excoriating Serrano's photographs.

Serrano's inspiration was similar to that of the motion picture *The Last Temptation of Christ* (1988), which also aroused the enmity of religious conservatives. Based on Níkos Kazantzákis's novel, Martin Scorcese directed the movie that delves into Christ's human qualities, exploring his doubts and biological urges. Even before the film was finished the Christian Right had targeted for protest Scorcese, Universal/MCA (the movie's distributor) as well as specific theaters. The Reverends Jerry Falwell, R. L. Haymers (of the Fundamentalist Baptist Tabernacle), and Donald Wildman (of the American Family Association) vowed to boycott MCA if the movie were released. The Campus Crusade for Christ founder, Bill Bright, offered to pay Universal $10 million for the prints so he could burn them. Some more extreme religious groups accused the heads of Universal and MCA, Sidney Scheinberg and Lew Wasserman, of being part of a Jewish conspiracy to slander Christianity.

While the debate was still simmering around Serrano's *Piss-Christ* and Scorcese's *The Last Temptation,* another target in the culture war arose: the gay visual artist Robert Mapplethorpe. The artist's photographs celebrated a pre-AIDS aesthetic that was playful and unapologetically homoerotic. When an exhibition of his work, titled *The Perfect Moment,* was planned for the Corcoran Gallery in Washington DC, the American Family Association, Senators Helms and Alfonse D'Amato (Republican of New York), and Representative Dick Armey (Republican of Texas), petitioned for its cancellation. Helms and his colleagues were on a mission to restrict NEA funding for what they judged to be "shocking, abhorrent and completely undeserving art." By June 1989, they succeeded in pressing Corcoran to abandon its showing of *The Perfect Moment.* (In protest, some of Mapplethorpe's supporters held an outdoor event where they projected giant images of his photographs on the gallery building.)

Helms shepherded through Congress legislation that banned NEA patronage of works of art that "promote, disseminate or produce obscene or indecent materials." Targeted by the new law were all "depictions of sadomasochism, homoeroticism, the exploitation of children, or individuals engaged in sex acts; or material which denigrates the objects or beliefs of the adherents of a particular religion or non-religion." To drive home his point, Helms, in the well of the Senate, tore apart photographs by Serrano and Mapplethorpe. Later, prosecutors in Ohio brought criminal "obscenity" charges against the director of the Cincinnati Contemporary Arts Center for exhibiting Mapplethorpe's compositions. Mapplethorpe, who died of AIDS in 1989, was spared seeing the public uproar his photographs elicited. But the shrill calls for censoring artists in what was otherwise a very open society betrayed a turn toward intolerance in the latter part of the decade as well as the opportunism of some politicians who used the culture wars as a "wedge" issue.

The manner in which the Humanities were being taught in the nation's colleges and universities also came under attack during this period. In 1987, Allan Bloom's *The Closing of the American Mind* became an unlikely bestseller after social conservatives welcomed it as a scholarly repudiation of the "multiculturalism" prevalent in American universities. Bloom, a classicist and scholar who taught at Cornell and at the University of Chicago, ridiculed African-American Studies, Women's Studies, Ethnic Studies, and other programs that arose in the 1960s and had become part of the standard curriculum at many universities. Only by returning to the classic texts of Western Civilization could a decaying American university system be saved, Bloom argued. Had Bloom concluded his tract with a simple appeal for resurrecting the Western canon his ideas might not have been so widely discussed. But he also asserted that American college students, even during an era of conservative ascendancy, were being "indoctrinated" and were "unified only in their relativism and in their allegiance to equality." Bloom even compared what was taking place at American colleges to German universities in the 1930s.

Bloom's foreboding about the growing prominence of multiculturalism on college campuses, which he called "an intellectual crisis of the greatest magnitude" and a "crisis of our civilization," turned out to be the perfect elixir to fuel the culture wars. For Bloom, acknowledging the history of minorities or women did not present examples of people contesting unjust power relations or nonviolently working out differences, but rather, was leading to a new form of "tyranny." Bloom, a nominally closeted gay man, believed the liberalism in the universities was spreading a new kind of prejudice. One of the great ironies of Bloom's authoritative indictment of multiculturalism was its timing. He identified the "crisis" not in a period of liberal dominance, but when conservatives for years had been setting the agenda of the nation's political discourse. *The Closing of the American Mind* also affected the debate about the nature of American freedom at a time when millions of people living under real tyranny in Eastern Bloc countries were looking to the openness and pluralism of American society as an inspiration that progressive change might be possible in their own societies.

REVIEW QUESTIONS

1. What were some of the significant developments in consumer electronics technology that took place in the 1980s that changed the way Americans related to television, Hollywood movies, popular music, and the workplace?
2. What was it about the content of rock 'n' roll and pop music lyrics that stirred such controversy in the mid-eighties and sparked the public battle between musicians like Frank Zappa and the Parents Music Resource Council? What role did MTV play in fostering this debate?
3. What new breakthroughs took place in the eighties among popular music genres? What was it about Madonna's music and public persona that generated so much controversy (and publicity) for her work? What did pop music artists discover about their potential power to raise awareness of social causes?
4. What was it about the paintings of the young artist, Jean-Michel Basquiat, that catapulted him to the top of the New York City art world?
5. What were some of the major controversies surrounding publicly funded art? Did these conflicts mirror the debate at the time about popular music lyrics?

mysearchlab CONNECTIONS SOURCES ONLINE

READ AND REVIEW

Review this chapter by using the study aids and these related documents available on MySearchLab.

Study Plan
Chapter Test
Essay Test

Documents
Frank Zappa, Testimony to the U.S. Senate (1985)
Statement by the rock musician on record labeling.

Patricia Morrisroe, "Yuppies—The New Class" (1985)
Morrisroe describes the movement of young urban professionals into New York's Upper West Side neighborhoods.

RESEARCH AND EXPLORE

Use the databases available within MySearchLab to find additional primary and secondary sources the topics within this chapter.

5

Foreign Policy at Mid-Decade

CHAPTER OUTLINE

The Philippines, Haiti, and Libya   Afghanistan
Mikhail Gorbachev   Reykjavik
South Africa

THE PHILIPPINES, HAITI, AND LIBYA

Dating back to the U.S.-Philippine War of 1898 to 1907, the United States had a special relationship with the 7,100-island archipelago as a colonial ward. At the start of World War II, when the Japanese sent General Douglas MacArthur packing (vowing to return), the Philippines had become central to America's ability to project its power in Southeast Asia. In the postwar period, Colonel Edward Landsdale and the CIA had crushed the Hukbalahap rebellion and installed the regime of Ramon Magsaysay. Later, when things were going badly for the United States in Vietnam, American policy in the Philippines was to build up the anti-communist government of Ferdinand Marcos (as well as Suharto in Indonesia) as a bulwark against the rising tide of Asian communism. By the mid-eighties, however, the Philippines was seen as a foreign policy crisis for the Reagan administration as Marcos, like Anastasio Somoza and the shah of Iran before him, fell into disfavor with his own people.

The June 1982 Israeli invasion of Lebanon set the stage for President Reagan to send in 1,600 American Marines to serve as "peacekeepers." The civil war in Lebanon, with regional actors Israel and Syria intervening and the superpowers squaring off behind opposing sides, created the possibility of a wider war. On October 23, 1983, 241 American military personnel were killed when a pair of Shia suicide bombers drove an explosive-laden truck into the U.S. Marine barracks near the Beirut airport. It was the largest loss of American soldiers since the Vietnam War, and the attack compelled Reagan to pull out all U.S. troops by April 1984.

In 1983, Philippine Senator Benigno "Ninoy" Aquino Jr., who was a popular opposition leader, was assassinated, and his widow, Corozon, reluctantly took up the mantle of her fallen husband's leadership. Ms. Aquino always believed Marcos had a hand in killing her revered husband, which was not a far-fetched assumption. Philippine religious organizations had reported that in 1985 alone there had been 602 disappearances, 1,326 cases of torture, and 276 political executions. Human rights groups sometimes compared the Marcos government to the junta in Argentina that "disappeared" 9,000 political dissidents between 1976 and 1982. The Reagan administration's chief concern in the Philippines was protecting the two giant U.S. military bases, Subic Bay Naval Base and Clark Air Base, which were prized military installations in the Pacific and of immense strategic importance to the Pentagon. Complicating the situation was a communist insurgency on some of the islands, the "New People's Army," which had about 18,000 men under arms and had ignited fighting with government forces that caused 1,200 civilian deaths in 1985. The U.S.-trained military at Marcos's disposal had a force of over 200,000 soldiers.

In November 1985, responding to mounting political pressure, Marcos agreed to hold elections the following February. He reasoned that given the lack of coherence among his opponents and his control over the levers of power he would be able to manipulate the results and quell the calls for greater liberalization. The only leader who could have given Marcos a run for his money was Benigno Aquino and when his widow, "Cory," stepped forward it hindered his plans to rig the election. When the Philippine dictator declared himself the winner based on widespread fraud he was surprised to see an unprecedented outpouring of popular anger as Aquino's supporters filled the streets of Manila and other Philippine cities.

At first, Reagan stood by the election results and defended Marcos's actions. Some of his foreign policy advisers urged him to stand by Marcos as a valued friend against Soviet expansionism. In the end, Secretary of State George P. Shultz realized that trying to maintain Marcos's government was not only spreading unrest and anti-American sentiment in the region, but it was also alienating local elites. He feared that if Marcos did not give up power it would be fertile ground for a more radical alternative than the moderate Aquino. The protests reached the point of paralyzing the country and, with U.S. support, the defense minister and his vice chief of staff threw their support behind Aquino. After the defections of the top military brass it took only 78 hours for the regime to crumble. On February 26, 1986, four U.S. Air Force helicopters shuttled Marcos, his wife Imelda, and an entourage of 88 to exile in Hawaii ending 20 years of authoritarian rule. The last time there was a transfer of power in the Philippines was in 1965. "People power" had declared Aquino the winner in massive ongoing protests. For the Philippines' 56 million people it was their first real taste of popular democracy.

Marcos excoriated the United States for what he called a "coup," and he tried to manipulate Philippine politics from his sanctuary in Honolulu, Hawaii. The former Philippine leader had been the poster boy for "crony capitalism" and his friends and allies had mastery over a vast network of state-owned enterprises. He denied looting the Philippine treasury but after he fled a thorough inspection of the Malacanang Palace revealed that a great deal of wealth had gone missing. Philippine authorities of the Aquino government charged Marcos with absconding with 36 suitcases and crates filled with more than $100 million in cash, diamonds, and gold. The U.S. media reported that he and his wife Imelda owned $300 million worth of New York City real estate, and some estimates of the amount of loot Marcos had squirreled away in Swiss bank accounts and other offshore havens were as high as $2 billion. In the end, the Reagan administration pointed to its deft handling of the Philippine crisis to make its case for increasing aid to the Nicaraguan counter-revolutionaries (contras). "We see Nicaragua, much more than the Philippines," explained Shultz, as "a government at odds with its people."

In Haiti, American relations with the governments there, as in the case of the Philippines, had a long history. President Woodrow Wilson's 1915 military intervention of the island set the stage for a succession of regimes hospitable to U.S. strategic and financial interests in the Caribbean. In the 1950s, the United States threw its support behind the anti-communist strongman, Francois "Papa Doc" Duvalier, who in 1957 declared himself "President-for-Life." In 1971, he transferred power to his pudgy 19-year-old son, Jean-Claude, who became known as "Baby Doc." For years, Amnesty International and other human rights organizations had published blistering reports documenting terrible human rights abuses in Haiti under Duvalier, which included torture, arbitrary detentions, rape, enforced disappearances, and extrajudicial executions. The AIDS epidemic had also become a neglected public health emergency on the island that undermined its already strained economy. The Duvaliers' lavish lifestyle (Baby Doc had spent $3 million on his wedding in 1980) stood in stark contrast to the misery of the vast majority of Haiti's 6 million people. Eight out of ten Haitians were illiterate and most of them had a per capita income of $150 a year. Yet like other anti-communist dictatorships in the Western Hemisphere, Baby Doc's relations with the United States improved markedly during the Reagan presidency.

In March 1983, Pope John Paul II visited Haiti where he threw his support behind the impoverished masses; "I am with you," he said. The pope sided with Haiti's downtrodden, which was the same stand taken by many Catholic clerics in El Salvador and Guatemala only to be singled out as "communist sympathizers" by the governments. Following the pope's trip to Haiti, anti-Duvalier protests escalated. Duvalier's response to the unrest was to cling to power by using his notorious Tonton Macoute death squads to terrorize dissidents and guard the interests of the tiny ruling elite. Like Marcos in the Philippines, Duvalier also ran a bogus election where he was reaffirmed as "President-for-Life" in a plebiscite winning 99.98 percent of the vote. By the mid-eighties, the 34-year-old Duvalier's misrule was bringing Haiti to the brink of civil war. In Port-au-Prince, Gonaives, Cap Haitien, and other cities tens of thousands of people demonstrated against the regime, which sometimes escalated into full-scale rioting with looting and the burning of tires and cars on the streets. In early 1986, Duvalier declared a "state of siege" and in a week 26 people were killed. The U.S. State Department advised Americans not to travel to Haiti.

As with Marcos the Reagan administration's first response was to bolster its long-time anti-communist ally. But as the situation inside Haiti deteriorated Secretary Shultz realized that the time was coming when Baby Doc would have to go. In early February 1986, Duvalier was forced into exile at the United States' insistence in the name of maintaining stability. In the dark of night, the Duvalier family was whisked to France via a U.S. Air Force jet. The new government of Haiti consisted of a five-person junta, headed by Lieutenant General Henri Namphy, the commander of the Duvalier armed forces, who promised a new beginning. As was done in the case of Marcos, Swiss authorities froze Baby Doc's bank accounts to honor claims pending from the Haitian government. Duvalier's fortune was estimated at that time to be about $400 million.

The 1980s were also a period of renewed hostility with Libya. Skirmishes between the U.S. and the Mediterranean Muslim country marked the earliest military actions taken by the Reagan administration. In April 1981, egged on by the hawkish Secretary of Sate

Alexander Haig, U.S. warplanes enforced the status of the Gulf of Sidra as "international waters," which Libya claimed as its territorial waters. The U.S. warplanes shot down two Libyan MIG fighter jets that attempted to ward off American forces. Thereafter, the Libyan leader, Colonel Muammar Gaddafi, became one of President Reagan's favorite targets of ridicule. There was a five-year lull in direct confrontations between the United States and Libya until March 1986 when the U.S. Navy sunk three Libyan ships in the Gulf of Sidra in two separate incidents. The U.S. forces also attacked a Soviet-built missile base onshore. A Libyan armed forces official claimed that 56 Libyans had died in the fighting. On April 5, when a bomb tore through the La Belle discotheque in West Berlin frequented by American soldiers killing two American servicemen and wounding 200 others (including 50 U.S. military personnel), the Reagan administration immediately attributed the blast to Libya claiming it was in retaliation for the Gulf of Sidra clashes.

Administration officials cited an intercepted message from Tripoli to the Libyan Embassy in East Berlin as evidence that the Berlin terrorist attack came from Gaddafi. General Bernard Rogers, the Supreme Commander of NATO in Europe, said the U.S. had "indisputable evidence" that a Libyan terrorist network had been behind the La Belle bombing. "We have taken enough punishment and beating," said Secretary Shultz. "We have to act." The information, however, was later found to be less than convincing. According to German Chancellor Helmet Kohl, the U.S. had passed on intelligence summaries to West German authorities that were incomplete and by no means "proved" that Libya had been solely responsible for the attack. It turned out that Tripoli had not been responsible for the Berlin incident (although Gaddafi had been involved in other acts of terrorism).

In the days following the terrorist bombing the drumbeat for war grew louder as the Reagan administration maneuvered the U.S. Navy into positions off the coast of Libya. The chair of the Joint Chiefs of Staff, Admiral William Crowe, wanted time to make sure he had enough firepower at his disposal for a response, and CIA Director Casey needed to get his agents out of Libya. Leaks to the press forced a brief postponement of the operation. But the media coverage leading up to the U.S. air strikes against Libya amounted to nothing short of cheerleading. The administration's assertion that Libya had been behind the Berlin disco bombing was hardly questioned. The U.S.-Libya standoff in the days following the West Berlin attack was among the most tense of any during Reagan's presidency. When asked if Gaddafi might retaliate with terrorist acts inside the United States, Reagan said grimly: "We certainly do not overlook that possibility." During the lead up to the intervention Reagan called Gaddafi the "mad dog of the Middle East" who was "not only a barbarian, but flakey." Government officials in West Germany and elsewhere in Europe expressed their concerns that an American strike might prompt more terrorism that would occur primarily in Europe.

Ten days after the La Belle bombing Reagan ordered "Operation El Dorado Canyon." On April 16, U.S. warplanes bombed sites throughout Libya, including the Bedouin tent compound Gaddafi used as his headquarters. According to disputed accounts from the regime, the U.S. bombing killed 15 people, including Gaddafi's two-year-old adopted daughter. The U.S. sorties against sites in Tripoli and Benghazi marked the first time since World War II that American planes left bases in Britain for a bombing run. Reagan's decisive blow against international terrorism boosted his approval rating. But the U.S. assault also served to shore up Gaddafi's domestic support by burnishing his nationalist credentials. He milked the American aggression for maximum political benefit, and even converted a bombed-out building to a museum as a testimony to his valor in standing up to the Americans. Two years later, agents allegedly working for Gaddafi blew up Pan American Airlines Flight 103 after it departed London Heathrow Airport bound for New York. The plane exploded over

Lockerbie, Scotland, killing 243 passengers and 16 crewmembers, as well as many people on the ground (189 were Americans). There was no U.S. retaliation. In the decades that followed Gaddafi appeared to have changed his ways, ditching his nascent nuclear program and offering generous oil leases to European, Asian, and American oil conglomerates.

MIKHAIL GORBACHEV

On March 11, 1985, following the death of Soviet Premier Konstantin Chernenko, Mikhail Sergeyevich Gorbachev became the U.S.S.R.'s new General Secretary of the Communist Party. Born in 1931, in Stavropol in the Northern Caucasus to a Ukrainian/Russian family, Gorbachev was reared on a farm where he identified with the problems and culture of Russia's often oppressed farm workers. As a child, he had witnessed firsthand his rural community victimized by Josef Stalin's disastrous collectivization schemes. During the 1950s, he came of age as a college student at Moscow State University (the best in the country) at a time when Stalin's crimes were being publicly aired. With his ambition, talent, and expertise in agronomics, Gorbachev swiftly rose through the ranks of the Communist Party, becoming the national party secretary in charge of agriculture in 1978. Two years later he was the youngest voting member of the politburo. The 54-year-old Gorbachev was the first Soviet premier to have been university educated since Vladimir Lenin.

Gorbachev's tactical virtuosity surprised old-guard Kremlin officials as they watched him outmaneuver his rivals. He brought to power with him other reformers, most notably his Georgian foreign minister, Eduard Shevardnadze, and he pushed through a comprehensive policy called *glasnost*, or "openness," which relaxed many of the restrictions on the free movement and expression of Soviet citizens. *Glasnost* included the stunning reversal of 75 years of the official suppression of religious freedom. For decades, the mistreatment of Soviet Jewry and other religious minorities had been an essential concern of American presidents from both political parties. Gorbachev's other major policy of *perestroika*, or "restructuring," prodded the Soviet state's bureaucratic behemoths toward market-oriented reforms and greater accountability, which had implications for Warsaw Pact nations and Russia's foreign policy.

A month after coming to power Gorbachev halted the deployment of new SS-20 missiles aimed at West Europe. In August 1985, he ordered a unilateral moratorium on all Soviet nuclear testing and invited the United States to join in. Two months later, he cut the number of SS-20s. Gorbachev believed Brezhnev's decision to target West Europe with intermediate-range missiles was a mistake. When Reagan began stationing Pershing IIs and nuclear-tipped cruise missiles in West Germany and other NATO countries his worst fears were realized. Although the Reagan administration rebuffed Gorbachev's moratorium on testing (which Gorbachev extended without U.S. compliance through February 1987), the test ban was extremely popular in Europe and in the United States among those who supported a nuclear freeze. By the summer of 1985, West Europe was experiencing an outbreak of what some commentators called "Gorbamania," which was a collective sigh of relief after years of rising East-West tensions and an uncertain transition. But the nature of Gorbachev's relationship with the United States was yet to be seen.

Unlike most analysts and politicians in Europe, including British Prime Minister Margaret Thatcher who admired the new Russian leader, many of Reagan's neoconservative supporters had no interest in succumbing to Gorbachev's charms. The Heritage Foundation concluded that Gorbachev was just another Stalinist who brought "no essential change in the Soviet political scene." *National Review* branded Gorbachev's foreign policy "vintage Stalin," and *Commentary* saw *glasnost* as a trick devised to "harness the power of the West to promote the Soviet Union's own objectives." Ambassador Kirkpatrick left the administration in April 1985 highly critical of any rapprochement with the Soviet Union (she was succeeded by General Vernon Walters). When the first of four pivotal summit meetings between Reagan and Gorbachev was being planned, conservative columnists warned that Reagan was "walking into a trap." Fortunately, Secretary of State Shultz and U.S. Ambassador to the Soviet Union, James Matlock, did not share these biases.

In November 1985, in Geneva, Switzerland, Reagan and Gorbachev met for the first time in a tranquil lakeside setting where Soviet and American arms negotiators had been at loggerheads for many months. Their freewheeling discussions covered the topics of Russia's abysmal human rights record, its occupation of Afghanistan, and the plight of Soviet political dissidents. But the primary sticking point came over Reagan's perseverance in reinterpreting the 1972 Anti-Ballistic Missile (ABM) Treaty to allow Strategic Defense Initiative (SDI) testing outside of laboratory settings. It was a contentious matter that could derail any new treaty restricting the superpowers' dangerously bloated nuclear arsenals. The president's uncompromising stance on SDI mirrored the opinions of hard-liners in his administration who welcomed SDI as a means of torpedoing new arms control agreements. Just as Gorbachev was obligated to lock horns with hard-liners inside the politburo, Reagan too was going to have to brush back hard-liners inside his own government if progress was to be made in nuclear arms control.

Gorbachev was willing to negotiate a comprehensive treaty, but he remained steadfast against any new ABM system. Soviet arms experts understood that "Star Wars" technology was years away from being effectively deployed (if ever), and that the Soviet military could disrupt any new space-based ABM system relatively cheaply with decoys and other counter measures. Therefore, he believed that Reagan's advocacy of SDI was "bizarre" and regarded it as being, if not a bargaining chip, a continuation of the arms race in outer space. At the close of their first meeting, holding Star Wars in abeyance, the two leaders agreed to sign a joint communiqué that confirmed both sides' understanding that a "nuclear war cannot be won and must never be fought." It represented a new direction in U.S.-Soviet relations, which if put into practice undercut the need to stockpile or modernize nuclear weapons. But on the day when Gorbachev's moratorium on nuclear testing was to end, the United States detonated an underground nuclear blast in the Nevada desert. Despite having a new Soviet leader who was clearly prodding his country in a direction the United States had long wanted, in the eyes of many U.S. defense officials, Gorbachev's actions on behalf of a state known for its misinformation and lies seemed simply too good to be true. Yet Gorbachev's olive branch to the West had prompted some members of Reagan's national security establishment to take the first behind-the-scenes steps to sideline the more vociferous neoconservatives among their ranks.

During this volatile period in superpower relations, two disasters occurred that exposed the limits of both U.S. and Soviet technology. On January 28, 1986, the U.S. space shuttle, *Challenger,* burst into a giant fireball 73 seconds after liftoff; and on April 26, 1986, the worst nuclear power plant disaster in history to that time happened at the Chernobyl reactor in the Soviet Ukraine. The space shuttle explosion revealed the malfunctioning that could beset American missile technology, while Chernobyl illustrated the perils of Russian nuclear technology. For two superpowers, both armed to the teeth with intercontinental ballistic missiles (ICBMs) capable of lobbing hydrogen bombs on each other in a matter of minutes, these dual disasters were sobering.

The *Challenger* blast took place over the Atlantic Ocean off the coast of central Florida when the spacecraft fired its thrusters to reach a velocity capable of leaving the Earth's gravity well. All seven crewmembers were killed instantly, including Christa McAuliffe, a science teacher from New Hampshire who had volunteered to become the first teacher in space. Most people growing up in the 1980s can recall where they were when the *Challenger* exploded much like the baby boom generation remembered the assassination of President John F. Kennedy.

Investigators attributed the *Challenger* tragedy to faulty "O-Rings," a type of mechanical gasket inside the rocket booster that could have been replaced at little cost. Reagan postponed his State of the Union Address and chose instead to speak from the Oval Office about the tragedy. "This is truly a national loss," he said. The fact that a science teacher was on board and children across the nation were watching the liftoff as part of their science curriculum, Reagan spoke directly to them: "And I want to say something to the schoolchildren of America who were watching the live coverage of the shuttle's takeoff. I know it is hard to understand, but sometimes-painful things like this happen. It's all part of the process of exploration and discovery. It's all part of taking a chance and expanding man's horizons. The future doesn't belong to the fainthearted; it belongs to the brave. The *Challenger* crew was pulling us into the future, and we'll continue to follow them."

In contrast to the U.S.'s open investigation into the *Challenger* catastrophe, when the Chernobyl nuclear reactor melted down in the Soviet Ukraine releasing large quantities of radioactive gas into the atmosphere, the Soviet government's secretive handling of the accident reminded the world of the totalitarian nature of the regime. Throughout the spring and summer of 1986, the Soviets tried to hide the extent of the damage from what was later proven to be an out-of-control radioactive graphite fire that contaminated an area the size of Switzerland. "The tragedy of Chernobyl," Gorbachev recalled, "was that it was exploited as alleged proof that we had no intention of really 'opening up,' that we remained treacherous and not to be trusted."

In Ukraine and beyond, hundreds of workers and local residents suffered from radiation poisoning, and dozens of people died within the first few weeks. The number of fleeing refugees was on a scale not seen in Europe since World War II. Tens of thousands of people were hastily evacuated and nearly 400,000 people had to be permanently relocated out of areas of high radioactivity, including all 50,000 residents of the town of Pripyat. After burning off 180 tons of nuclear fuel, the 200 tons that remained melted down into the shape of a giant elephant's foot in the center of Reactor Number 4. Nuclear fallout was detected all over Europe—East and West—polluting lakes and rivers and thousands of acres of farmland. Soviet technicians spent months sealing off the reactor with a thick concrete "sarcophagus."

The word "Chernobyl" has since become synonymous with disaster. It drove home the dangers of nuclear energy and renewed the debate about the safety of all nuclear facilities. The dual disasters of the *Challenger* and Chernobyl pointed to the deep-seated flaws within the technological triumphalism that both superpowers had been projecting to the world (and to each other) since the early 1960s. They also showed that governments and corporations never could realistically control every contingency that might arise within the complex technological systems they built and managed, which had frightening implications for each nation's high-tech nuclear arsenals.

SOUTH AFRICA

"Apartheid," which is a word derived from Afrikaans meaning "separateness," codified a system of strict racial segregation in South Africa dating back to 1948. The black majority, about 74 percent of the population (22 million people), lived under a regime with limited civil rights. A white minority (about 5 million people) held power over the key institutions of government and owned 87 percent of the land, including the resource-rich areas with the most developed infrastructure. Inside South Africa, the preeminent black political organization actively opposing apartheid was the African National Congress (ANC). Formed in 1912, the ANC spent decades trying to rally blacks to rise up in opposition to white minority rule.

In March 1960, South African police fired into a crowd of protesters who were demonstrating against a law requiring blacks to carry special passbooks to travel inside their own country. The "Sharpeville Massacre" (as it was called) killed 66 blacks and wounded 200 others, and drove home the point that the nonviolent tactics of the American civil rights movement were futile in the context of South Africa. A number of ANC activists at that time went underground and took up armed resistance. In 1962, the South African government jailed ANC leader Nelson Mandela and he languished as a political prisoner for the next 27 years. "Free Nelson Mandela!" became a rallying cry for antiapartheid activists all over the world.

Throughout the 1960s and 1970s, the wave of independence movements that swept Africa led the South African government to use its economic, political, and military power to stave off changes in its domestic status quo. The white minority saw the black political associations in the former Portuguese colonies of Mozambique and Angola as threats, as well as those in neighboring Namibia, because they worked in solidarity with the ANC. South Africa therefore armed and financed regional paramilitaries and used them as surrogates to harass its neighbors, known as the "Frontline States." In Angola, South Africa (with the CIA) sponsored the National Union for the Total Independence of Angola (UNITA) headed by the flamboyant tribal leader Jonas Savimbi. UNITA exploited ethnic and class divisions and waged a guerrilla war against the newly independent socialist government. Savimbi jockeyed for U.S. support by claiming to lead, like the Nicaraguan contras and the Afghan Mujahideen, a dedicated band of anti-Soviet "freedom fighters." So successful were UNITA's hit-and-run attacks against civilian targets in Angola that the government requested assistance from Cuba, which sent in 30,000 soldiers as a counterbalance. UNITA's "anti-communist" struggle became a cause célèbre for the American Right, earning high praise from President Reagan.

South Africa also kept up a military presence in neighboring Namibia. The Reagan administration defended the occupation with a policy of "linkage," which stipulated that the U.S. would only support a South African withdrawal from Namibia if Cuban troops withdrew from Angola. In November 1985, when the United Nations voted in favor of economic sanctions against South Africa to protest its occupation of Namibia both the United States and Britain vetoed the measure. In a strange twist that brought to light the incongruity of Reagan's Africa policies, the socialist Angolan government dispatched Cuban soldiers to protect oil installations and other facilities owned by American corporations against sabotage attacks from Savimbi's "freedom fighters."

By the early 1980s, South Africa was the final holdout of white settler rule on the continent, and Prime Minister P. W. Botha adopted a "Total Strategy" to reassert economic and political hegemony in the region. The effort was intended to blunt the effects of neighboring states' nationalist movements focusing on the injustices of apartheid inside South Africa. Through its economic leverage, military operations, and support of proxies, South Africa damaged the economies and infrastructure of its neighbors and threw them into turmoil in a classic divide-and-conquer strategy. From 1980 through 1985, South Africa's destabilization policies cost its neighbors an estimated $10 billion. In 1986, Jesse Jackson testified before a subcommittee of the House Banking Committee where he compared the apartheid state to "an octopus with tentacles that have a suffocating stranglehold on the economies of all of the states in Southern Africa." The "Total Strategy" might have succeeded had it not been for the efforts of American blacks and their allies in the United States, who even in a period of conservative ascendancy succeeded in reorienting U.S. Africa policy. They pressed the Reagan administration to distance itself from the apartheid regime and advanced the cause of turning South Africa into an international pariah.

Reagan's policy toward South Africa was called "Constructive Engagement." This framework, as was the case elsewhere in the world, situated the apartheid regime in the context of the East-West power struggle with the Soviet Union. Reagan appreciated the Botha government's ferocious anticommunism and saw it in terms of Jeane Kirkpatrick's "authoritarian" typology. This Cold War orientation meant standing by anti-Soviet friends, such as Jean-Claude Duvalier in Haiti and Ferdinand Marcos in the Philippines, long past the time their regimes were viable. Similarly, official U.S. criticism of South Africa all but ceased as the administration expedited trade between the two countries, welcomed South African military officers to the Pentagon, and pushed for opening a new South African consulate. Early in his first term Reagan had complimented the Botha regime, telling an interviewer that South Africa was "a country that has stood beside us in every war we've ever fought." (The Afrikaner political elite in World War II had openly identified with the Third Reich.) Meanwhile, the South African government's feared security services, the "Bureau of State Security" (BOSS), ruthlessly enforced the apartheid laws with riot control, attack dogs, water canon, mass arrests, and occasionally by shooting into crowds.

In November 1984, Randall Robinson of TransAfrica, Mary Francis Berry of the U.S. Civil Rights Commission, and the District of Columbia's delegate Walter Fauntroy organized a series of sit-ins at the South African Embassy in Washington DC. The daily arrests of nonviolent activists were evocative of the civil rights movement, and the action kindled an upsurge in antiapartheid protests throughout the United States. Apartheid's racial segregation laws resembled the Jim Crow system that had ruled the American South for most of the twentieth century. The "bantustans," where millions of black South Africans languished, with their rural poverty, low quality land, unemployment, and alcoholism, shared stark similarities with Native American Indian reservations in the United States. Jesse Jackson had made South Africa a centerpiece of his foreign policy during the 1984 campaign and his tough stand against apartheid gained the overwhelming support of civil rights organizations.

College students across the United States enjoined their educational institutions to divest any holdings they might have in companies that did business with South Africa. Soon "shanty towns" sprung up on campuses in solidarity with the living conditions of blacks in the bantustans. Thousands of university students across the country confronted their colleges' administrators by squatting in makeshift encampments they often erected right next to administration buildings. In April 1985, students organized a National Anti-Apartheid Day protest, which coordinated pro-divestment rallies on 60 campuses. The antiapartheid activism on the part of America's college students stood in contrast to the reputation for apathy among young people in the 1980s popularized in the mainstream media. By 1989, over 80 percent of colleges and universities were forced to institute some form of divestment from corporations and banks that had holdings in South Africa.

Throughout 1985 and 1986, there was a flurry of activity in both chambers of Congress as lawmakers attempted to put an end to the Reagan administration's soft touch toward South Africa. Representatives Ronald Dellums of California, William Gray of Pennsylvania,

Throughout the 1980s, American college students took part in major demonstrations and civil disobedience to demand that their university administrators divest from corporations that did business with the apartheid government in South Africa. Shown in the photograph is a group of University of California (UC) students protesting a UC Regents meeting in San Francisco in June 1985. Student activism was central in bringing attention to the antiapartheid struggle, and students worked in solidarity with the Congressional Black Caucus and civil rights groups to expose the racist nature of the regime.

and Howard Wolpe of Michigan, along with the Congressional Black Caucus, cosponsored legislation obliging U.S. corporations to comply with economic sanctions against the regime. In the Senate, Edward Kennedy introduced his own similar measure. The administration opposed sanctions arguing that their negative effects would only hurt the black populations of South Africa's neighbors. African-American and human rights groups disagreed, and lobbied for comprehensive sanctions against South Africa, which made the antiapartheid struggle one of the most significant social movements of the 1980s.

In June 1986, the House approved a sanctions bill on a voice vote by an overwhelming majority. Two months later, Kennedy and his cosponsors succeeded in pushing through the Senate a more limited version of the House's bill and sent it to the White House for Reagan's signature. When Reagan vetoed the bill, Congress overrode him. And on October 2, 1986, official U.S. policy toward South Africa for the first time consisted of an array of detailed economic penalties. Amidst the campus activism and the new legislation coming out of Congress, some American corporate giants, including Coca-Cola, General Motors, IBM, and Kodak, pulled out of South Africa or sold off their

South African subsidiaries. Toward the end of the 1980s, apartheid was buckling under the weight of its own anachronistic contradictions. By February 1990, Nelson Mandela was freed from prison, and he would go on to serve as South Africa's first black president from 1994 to 1999. In 1993 he was awarded the Noble Peace Prize.

AFGHANISTAN

In 1893, during the period of the British Raj in India, Sir Mortimer Durand had in mind Great Britain's colonial interests when he drew up a key border of modern Afghanistan. Known as the "Durand Line," it split roughly in half the territory of the Pashtuns, the largest ethnic group in the country. Traditionally, the region had been a vital passageway on the "Silk Road" linking Asia and the Middle East and consists of thousands of scattered villages and decentralized tribal mini-states. The Afghans' ability to bury their tribal, ethnic, and sectarian differences to fight against foreign intruders gave the country the reputation of being the "graveyard of empires." In the nineteenth century, the British fought two inconclusive wars in Afghanistan, and in late 1979, when the Soviets intervened the Red Army became bogged down in a costly guerrilla war.

Adhering to the Kremlin's own version of the "domino theory," Soviet leaders feared that if Afghanistan became an Islamic state modeled on the Shia theocracy in Iran the "contagion" might spread to the Soviet Union's Muslim republics. By controlling the government in Kabul and introducing reforms devised to secularize and modernize Afghan society, KGB Chief Yuri Andropov and other Soviet foreign policy specialists believed they could stem the tide of Islamic fundamentalism. In the late-1970s, the Russians propped up a satellite government, the Democratic Republic of Afghanistan (DRA), and through it a heavy-handed rural development program like the ones going on in the Soviet Islamic states.

The opening shots of the anti-Russian revolt in Afghanistan were fired in the town of Herat in March 1979 when tribal leaders rebelled against Soviet efforts to dictate compulsory education for girls. When militants in Herat murdered a dozen Russian officials and their families, the Soviet-backed Afghan security services violently repressed the uprising. Thereafter, the regime faced considerable armed opposition from a cross-section of Afghans. That summer President Carter signed an intelligence "finding" authorizing the CIA to give assistance to what became known as the "Mujahideen." Throughout the Arab world, thousands of young men regarded the Russians as atheistic "infidels" and longed to prove themselves in "jihad" (holy war) against the occupiers. Money and arms from the United States and Saudi Arabia flowed into Afghanistan while the CIA worked closely with Pakistani President Zia-ul-Haq and his Inter-Services Intelligence (ISI) agency to work out the logistics of what grew into a major U.S. commitment.

During the debates within Carter's National Security Council (NSC), National Security Adviser Zbigniew Brzezinski entertained the idea that arming the Mujahideen might taunt the Soviets to invade. "We didn't push the Russians to intervene," he later explained, "but we knowingly increased the probability that they would." In December 1979, when the Soviet Union poured combat troops over the border into Afghanistan (at the invitation of its client in Kabul), Brzezinski and other foreign policy professionals hoped it would drain resources and preoccupy Moscow. By the time Reagan became president the Soviet occupation had grown to over 100,000 soldiers. Nicaragua and Afghanistan became two fronts in a wider war, and arming anti-communist insurgents engaged in "low-intensity warfare" became known as the "Reagan Doctrine." By the end of 1981, the Mujahideen had received over $100 million in arms and assistance, mostly from the United States and Saudi Arabia and funneled through Pakistan's ISI. Cold War imperatives trumped concerns about the extremist religious ideology of what was a network of stateless Islamic fanatics.

At the beginning of his second term, Reagan signed National Security Decision Directive (NSDD)-166 authorizing the transfer of sniper rifles, explosives, TOW anti-tank missiles, and mortar targeting devices linked to U.S. Navy satellites to the Afghan guerrillas and their Arab counterparts. In 1985, the United States supplied $500 million in economic and military aid to the Mujahideen (more than all the previous years combined). The CIA also began outfitting the insurgents with high-tech "Stinger" anti-aircraft missiles. The shoulder-fired Stingers used automated heat-seeking guidance systems to bring down countless Soviet helicopters and transport aircraft that chipped away at the Russian air advantage. The cost of each missile was about $35,000, and by the end of the war, it was estimated that the CIA had passed on to the insurgents between 2,000 and 2,500 of these weapons. The Democratic Congress, which gave its enthusiastic blessing to the "freedom fighters" in Afghanistan, appropriated $630 million in fiscal year 1987. It was the largest U.S. covert operation of the 1980s, and by the end of the decade, the United States spent over $2 billion on aid and weaponry to the Afghan fighters and Arab volunteers (sometimes called "Afghan Arabs").

Hollywood got into the act too of pumping up the Afghan cause with the movie *Rambo III* (1988). This sequel to the *Rambo* franchise, which at the time was known as the most violent film ever made in terms of body counts and explosions, starred the action hero Sylvester Stallone as "John Rambo," the lead character in earlier *Rambo* pictures who played the avenging angel of the Vietnam War. By 1988, *Rambo* had been enshrined in the popular culture as the personification of a resurgent America after the years of doubts cast by Vietnam and the Iranian hostage crisis. This time around Rambo battles stereotypical Slavic soldiers on Afghan soil while fighting side-by-side with his Afghan and Arab comrades in arms. The celluloid jihadists hold the moral high ground as they battle for human freedom and dignity against the totalitarian inhumanity of the Soviet Empire. The film is dedicated, in the final credits, to "the people of Afghanistan."

In early 1988, when Gorbachev resolved to pull Soviet troops out of Afghanistan, it marked a tectonic shift in the Soviet Union's international posture. In late 1988 and early 1989, there were a number of skirmishes between Red Army units and Mujahideen guerrillas, but Gorbachev stuck to his original promise and the last of the Red Army soldiers departed Afghanistan on February 15, 1989. On the day when television cameras broadcast the scene of the final Soviet commander, Boris Gromov of the 40th Army, leaving Afghanistan, CIA Director William Webster threw a party at CIA headquarters in Langley, Virginia. On the walls were large photographs of Afghan and Arab jihadists brandishing their Stinger missiles and standing proudly over downed Soviet helicopters and burned-out tanks.

The war was over but Afghanistan was in shambles. A generation of young Afghans had come of age knowing nothing but war and hardship. The superpowers had abandoned the country to a configuration of tribes and warlords that violently vied for power. Within a few years the country slid into a vicious multisided civil war. Gone were the days of *Rambo* movies describing American volunteers fighting communism alongside their Afghan and Arab brothers. Left to its own devices, the war-ravaged country fell into the hands of some of the most ruthless practitioners of Sharia law. Despite the popular

The action movie hero, Sylvester Stallone, played the role of "John Rambo" in a string of 1980s films. Rambo not only had become Hollywood's version of an avenging angel against the stinging memories of the U.S. defeat in Vietnam, but by the late-1980s he had also joined forces with the Afghan Mujahideen and their Arab volunteers in their struggle against the Soviet occupation. The photograph shown is a scene from *Rambo III* (1988), which is set in Afghanistan and features Rambo battling the Red Army and working alongside CIA operatives who supply the guerrillas with arms. *Rambo III* and movies like it in the 1980s offer a glimpse into the popular culture's anti-Soviet obsession even at a time when the Cold War was coming to an end.

notion that the Russian defeat in Afghanistan had been a stunning U.S. victory, a prelude of things to come occurred a few years later when American authorities in New York arrested Ramzi Yousef for setting off a car bomb inside the parking structure of the World Trade Center. Yousef, a Kuwaiti, had been a Mujahideen volunteer who trained in a camp on the Afghan-Pakistan border. In 1998, Brzezinski was asked by a French journalist if he had any regrets about arming the rebels. "What is more important in world history?" he replied. "The Taliban or the collapse of the Soviet empire? Some agitated Muslims or the liberation of Central Europe and the end of the Cold War?"

REYKJAVIK

On October 10, 1986, Reagan and Gorbachev met for the second time in Reykjavik, Iceland, which was a very different setting than their previous encounter outside a lake in Switzerland. In an unprecedented maneuver that surprised American negotiators, Gorbachev proposed shrinking by 50 percent the nuclear weapons that spanned each nation's "strategic triad" of ICBMs, submarine-launched ballistic missiles (SLBMs), and strategic bombers. It was the first time that the Soviet Union had ever agreed to such a dramatic cut in its nuclear arsenal. When it appeared that the overture was too sweeping, the Soviets' fallback position was to drop their former stipulation that medium-range missiles (mainly the United States' Pershing IIs in West Europe) be counted as "strategic weapons." This change would free up the possibility of a separate, stand-alone agreement to roll back intermediate-range nuclear forces (INF).

The Russian negotiators then unexpectedly tossed out their prerequisite that the French and British arsenals be tallied in the calculus. They would accept the Americans' "zero option" of dismantling all missiles based in Europe. For the first time since the nuclear arms race began the Soviet Union was prepared to negotiate away an entire category of weapons. But if the United States was not willing to consign Star Wars to the laboratory consistent with the 1972 ABM Treaty, all deals were off. When the U.S. negotiating team at Reykjavik rejected what had been its own "zero option" on intermediate-range missiles, which was extremely popular throughout Western Europe, Gorbachev was puzzled. He concluded that Reagan was simply "reluctant to harm the American arms industry."

The deal breaker was the U.S.'s ironclad insistence that there be no restrictions whatsoever on the testing and development of SDI. Although there were members of the Reagan administration who believed that SDI could be easily postponed if it meant a diminution in Soviet missiles, the commitment to Star Wars, in Gorbachev's words, "proved an insurmountable stumbling block." The summit ended abruptly on a sour note when Reagan, bidding farewell, turned to the Soviet leader and said: "You planned from the start to come here and put me in this situation!" Despite Gorbachev's pleas to the contrary and his entreaties to continue the talks, the meeting came to a close. "I'm really sorry," Reagan said. At Reykjavik, unlike Geneva, the two sides couldn't even sign a joint communiqué when the meeting adjourned.

Reporters hounded the American and Soviet negotiators and called the Reykjavik meeting a "failure" and a "setback" in U.S.-Soviet relations. Gorbachev had little experience in foreign affairs but he instinctively refused to allow journalists to cast Reykjavik in a negative light. At his first post-summit press conference he used the word "breakthrough," saying the meeting empowered both sides to "look over the horizon." His public statements opened up diplomatic breathing room to salvage something positive from the talks. Secretary Shultz, who had initially conceded that the summit had been a waste of time, picked up on Gorbachev's remarks and "readjusted" his public stand. Thereafter, like Gorbachev, he too called it a "breakthrough." Shultz worked with Soviet officials behind the scenes to use Reykjavik as a basis for a new round of talks. The secretary of state's gambit reassured Gorbachev, as he recounted in his memoirs, that despite setbacks and rhetorical flourishes from hard-liners in both countries, there were people on Reagan's team with whom he could "do business."

Throughout 1986 and 1987, Gorbachev had his hands full holding off domestic rivals and institutionalizing the complex reforms of *glasnost* and *perestroika*. His radical changes shook the Soviet state to its foundation and met stiff resistance from elements within the vast Russian bureaucracy. But Reagan too confronted his own domestic crises. The same month as the Reykjavik summit the White House would be battered by the biggest scandal of Reagan's two-term presidency.

REVIEW QUESTIONS

1. What do the transitions in the U.S.-backed leadership in the Philippines and Haiti tell us about the U.S. foreign policy goal of promoting democracy during the final decade of the Cold War? Why did relations between the Reagan administration and Libya deteriorate to the point of military confrontation?

2. What concrete steps did Soviet Premier Mikhail Gorbachev take upon coming to power that were aimed at lessening nuclear tensions between the superpowers? How did the Reagan administration respond to Gorbachev's diplomatic overtures? What lessons about the dangers of the U.S.-Soviet nuclear standoff might be learned from the space shuttle *Challenger* explosion and the Chernobyl nuclear plant meltdown?

3. What was it about the nature of the South African government that sparked such intense opposition in the United States during the eighties including calls for economic sanctions and the largest college student demonstrations of the decade? What was the Reagan administration's policy of "Constructive Engagement?"

4. Compare and contrast the policies of the Carter and Reagan administrations regarding the Soviet Union's control of Afghanistan. What was the CIA's role? Was it a smart long-term policy for the United States to arm and equip a stateless network of Mujahideen "freedom fighters" to oppose the Red Army's occupation of Afghanistan? Why or why not?

5. At the October 1986 Reagan-Gorbachev summit in Reykjavik, Iceland what were the key issues at stake that blocked progress on controlling any aspect of the testing, production, and deployment of nuclear armaments?

---

mysearchlab CONNECTIONS SOURCES ONLINE

READ AND REVIEW

Review this chapter by using the study aids and these related documents available on MySearchLab.

Study Plan
Chapter Test
Essay Test

Documents
A Liberal White Journalist on Apartheid (1970s–1980s)
This excerpt from Woods' autobiography discusses the journalist's experiences working for social equality of blacks in South Africa.

Student Anti-Apartheid Newsletter (1986)
Document outlining protests against South Africa on some college campuses.

Mikhail Gorbachev, Speech to the 27th Congress of the Communist Party of the Soviet Union (1986)
Gorbachev provides an early glimpse into some of the major reform impulses that were to become increasingly visible over the next few years.

Mikhail Gorbachev on the Need for Economic Reform (1987)
Gorbachev lays out some specific steps that the leaders of the USSR's economy must take to revitalize the socialist system.

Ronald Reagan, Speech on the Challenger Disaster (1986)
President Reagan's brief statement to the nation speaking about the space shuttle disaster.

RESEARCH AND EXPLORE

Use the databases available within MySearchLab to find additional primary and secondary sources the topics within this chapter.

6

The Reagan Revolution
in Crisis

Contra = counter-revolutionaries [handwritten]

CHAPTER OUTLINE

Contra Resupply   Iran-Contra Hearings
Arms Sales to Iran   More Scandals

CONTRA RESUPPLY

In 1984, after the press reported the CIA's mining of Nicaragua's harbors (an act of war the agency at first denied), Massachusetts Representative Edward Boland successfully amended a defense bill to cut off U.S. aid to the contras (counter-revolutionaries). It was an attempt to grant Congress greater leverage over what the administration was doing in Nicaragua and to clarify Congress's own shifting position on Central America policy. The amendment was clear: "No funds available to the Central Intelligence Agency, the Department of Defense, or any other agency or entity of the United States involved in intelligence activities" could be used to support "directly or indirectly, military or paramilitary operations in Nicaragua by any nation, group, organization, movement, or individual." In anticipation of the congressional ban, the White House began seeking ways to circumvent the law and keep the contra operation going.

Lt. Col. Oliver North is being sworn in here before his testimony to the joint House-Senate committee investigating the Iran-contra scandal in the summer of 1987. An NSC staffer, North was thrust into the public spotlight after the secret arms-for-hostages deals with the Iranians were exposed. North's testimony (after given immunity) revealed a shadowy network of arms merchants who were profiteering from both the sale of arms to the Khomeini regime and the diversion of some of the money to the Nicaraguan contras at a time when Congress banned such assistance. The Iran-contra episode became the biggest domestic and foreign policy crisis of Reagan's two-term presidency.

[handwritten margin notes: "Samoza dictatorship", "Sandinista", "Contras = paramilitaries comprised of Somoza Nat'l Guard", "freedom fighters", "To sidestep, donations from pro-US gov'ts used as aid to contras"]

Adding to lawmakers' anxiety was a cascade of press reports coming out of Central America, often backed by vivid eyewitness testimony from Catholic Church sources, documenting contra raids on health clinics, schools, peasant cooperatives, and other Sandinista-sponsored public institutions. The majority of contra leaders and rank-in-file soldiers came from Somoza's National Guard, and by 1984, CIA Director Casey had reconstituted them into a paramilitary army numbering about 10,000 men and backed up with millions of dollars in covert assistance. Throughout the early 1980s, evidence was mounting that the contras, who Reagan often called "freedom fighters," were waging a terrorist war against Nicaragua's civilian population. As was the case with the death squads in El Salvador, the administration insisted that any reports of atrocities coming out of Nicaragua were either exaggerated by the Sandinistas for propaganda purposes or were the accidental result of civilians being "caught in the cross fire." The overall effect of the armed onslaught was to propel the Managua government to become more paranoid and repressive.

President Reagan told his national security team he did not want to see the counter-revolutionary effort in Nicaragua abandoned and several top National Security Council (NSC) officials took this sentiment as an informal authorization to seek alternative means to sustain the contras. To sidestep the congressional ban they quietly began soliciting funds from third-party governments. Lieutenant Colonel Oliver North, a senior NSC staffer, secured donations from several pro-American governments, including Israel, South Africa, Saudi Arabia, Brunei, South Korea, and Taiwan. These nations viewed their contributions to the anti-Sandinista cause as a means to win favor with the American administration. It was also implied that U.S. money attached to other projects, such as foreign aid and arms transfers, would compensate them for their support. All of these governments faced their own domestic and foreign policy problems where cooperating with Reagan's pet project in Nicaragua could be a good investment. Saudi Arabia became the single biggest benefactor chipping in a million dollars a month and underwriting an additional $24 million. (One $10 million payment from the sultan of Brunei failed to make it into one of North's bank accounts due to a White House error.)

The fund raising also targeted wealthy Republican donors who gave money to a nonprofit, tax-exempt organization called the "National Endowment for the Preservation of Liberty" (NEPL). Oliver North, along with the NEPL's founder, Carl "Spitz" Channell, who was a Grand Old Party (GOP) operative and direct mail consultant, arranged "photo-ops" for patrons with the president. It was later learned that more than half of the $6.3 million reaped from private sources ended up paying for the overhead costs of Channell's NEPL. (One wealthy patron, William O'Boyle, later testified to Congress that North had shown him two different top-secret plans for a U.S. invasion of Nicaragua.) According to the classified notes of one NSC meeting, Reagan preferred to keep these fund raising activities secret because, he said: "If such a story gets out, we'll be hanging by our thumbs in front of the White House until we found out who did it."

On the operational side, North needed a clandestine means to ship arms and equipment to the contras. To finance the transfers without Congress's knowledge he opened a number of Swiss bank accounts and recruited a team of former military and intelligence officers to manage an interlocking collection of front companies and "cut-outs." CIA Director Casey put North in touch with a retired Air Force major general, Richard V. Secord, who had experience running CIA air supply operations in Laos during the Vietnam War. North enlisted Secord and his business partner, Albert Hakim, an Iranian-born entrepreneur who had been a middleman for U.S. arms sales to the shah, to set up what they called "the Enterprise." Soon the Enterprise had pieced together the logistics of an elaborate contra resupply network, worked with international arms merchants, and hired mercenaries. The Enterprise commissioned or leased dozens of aircraft and boats. This privatized NSC intelligence venture, which used the U.S. airbase in Ilopango, El Salvador, as its headquarters, was hidden from Congress from late 1984 to October 1986.

On October 5, 1986, Sandinista troops shot down a Fairchild C-123K cargo plane that had violated Nicaraguan airspace. They arrested the only survivor of the crash, an American soldier of fortune named Eugene Hasenfus. Hasenfus was a former Marine whose primary job was to "kick" supplies to the contras out of low-flying planes at specific rendezvous points. Four days after the plane was downed, the Nicaraguans held a press conference in *Arranged* Managua where they brought forth Hasenfus. He confessed to being part of a larger project *arms/supply* and said he had already flown ten such missions. He also said his plane had taken off from *Iraqs to* Ilopango airbase and divulged the name of his key CIA contact: Felix Rodriguez. *contras*

Rodriguez was a Cuban-American Bay of Pigs veteran who had played a role in some of the earliest U.S. attempts to overthrow Fidel Castro, and had been part of the CIA unit that killed Che Guevara in Bolivia in 1967. White House logs noted that within hours of hearing the news of Hasenfus's detention, the first administration official to whom Rodriguez made a telephone call was Donald Gregg, Vice President George Bush's national security adviser. Rodriguez had worked with Gregg in Vietnam and had frequently contacted him at the vice president's office. Government records also indicated that on May 1, 1986, Rodriguez met with Bush. Despite a particularly damning memo that had been prepared for the meeting listing "resupply of the contras" as a discussion point, both Gregg and Bush denied having any knowledge of what Rodriguez was doing in El Salvador in behalf of the contras.

Back in Washington, Secretary of State George P. Shultz stood firm that Hasenfus's aircraft had been "hired by private people who had no connection to the U.S. government at all." When reporters caught up with Reagan and asked him if the plane had anything to do with the administration, he responded, "absolutely none," and added: "There is no government connection with that at all. . . . We've been aware that there are private groups and private citizens that have been trying to help the contras . . . but we did not know the exact particulars of what they're doing." Behind the scenes, Lieutenant Colonel North requested the FBI and the U.S. Customs Service hold off any investigations of Hasenfus's aircraft. At that time, North must have thought that the furor would blow over because he continued his secret contra activities as if nothing had changed.

ARMS SALES TO IRAN

Side w/ Sadam to combat Iranian rel.

By the fall of 1986, Iranian-backed Shia militants in Lebanon were holding 6 Americans hostage. The CIA's chief of station in Beirut, William Buckley, had been abducted in March 1984 and Director Casey desperately wanted him freed. The Iran-Iraq war complicated U.S. diplomacy in the Middle East because the United States, along with its major Arab allies, sided with the Sunni Baathist regime in Baghdad. In September 1980, the Iraqi regime had annexed strategic islands in the waters of the Persian Gulf that separated Iran and Iraq, and Saddam Hussein's military aggression ignited what would become a devastating eight-year war in the heart of the Middle East. "Tilting" toward Iraq was seen in foreign policy circles as a "realist" attempt to use Saddam as a counterweight to the power of revolutionary Iran. As the war became more costly to both countries (ultimately costing a million casualties on each side), and with Iran in dire need of armaments and spare parts, Reagan's NSC initiated a secret program to exchange arms for hostages. For a time, this policy meant that the United States was arming both sides of the conflict. If the details of the operation were leaked the administration's cover story was that it was reaching out to Iranian "moderates" and trying to broker a settlement of the war.

The covert arms sales apparently began in August 1985, when Reagan's NSC gave Israel the go-ahead to transfer 92 TOW anti-tank missiles to Iran, with the understanding that the United States would replenish the Israel Defense Forces (IDF). These "tube-launched, optically-tracked, wire-guided" missiles were among the most technologically advanced in the U.S. arsenal at the time. The following month, on September 15, 1985, Israel delivered another 408 TOWs to Iran, and on the same day Shia militants in Lebanon freed the Reverend Benjamin Weir, an American Presbyterian missionary who had been held for over a year. The arms deals seemed to have worked. An entry in Reagan's diary from November 22, 1985, reads: "We have an undercover thing going by way of an Iranian, which could get [the hostages] sprung momentarily."

To strengthen the backchannel the White House had opened with the Iranians, Robert "Bud" McFarlane, who at the time was Reagan's former national security adviser, along with Oliver North, secretly flew to Tehran on May 28, 1986, to make direct contacts with the government. Using fake Irish passports they brought with them to Iran a small load of missile parts, a gift-wrapped brace of .357 magnum pistols, a birthday cake decorated with a brass key in honor of the mother of one of their principal liaisons with the Khomeini regime (the arms merchant Manucher Ghorbanifar), and a Bible with an inscription signed by Reagan. In a twist that sounded like something out of a spy novel, North later claimed they carried cyanide pills in the event they were taken captive. The purpose of the trip was to bypass the Israelis and begin direct arms sales with Tehran so that the profits could be more easily diverted to the contras.

North and McFarlane's trip to Iran lasted only three days and ended inconclusively, but it ultimately proved fatal to the overall mission. Five months later, university students in Tehran were spotted passing out leaflets about the meeting, one of which had a photograph of McFarlane in Iran. The story broke on November 3, 1986, when a weekly magazine in Lebanon, *Al-Shiraa*, published a more detailed account. The Iranian government, including the leader of Iran's parliament, Akbar Hashemi Rafsanjani, confirmed the accuracy of the article and within days the news had swept the international press.

In response to a CIA lawyer's concerns about complying with a 1980 intelligence law, Reagan signed a "finding," dated December 5, 1985, which retroactively authorized the three Israeli arms shipments to Iran. The document, with the summary title: "Hostage Rescue—Middle East," does not mention contacts with Iranian "moderates," but states as its goal to "obtain the release of Americans being held hostage in the Middle East." From the start, Secretary of State Shultz and Defense Secretary Weinberger had opposed the clandestine arms deals. They recognized the explosive diplomatic and military consequences if news of the transactions leaked out. Over a period of about 10 months the United States had sent to Iran, through its Israeli conduit, 500 TOWs and 1,500 HAWK missiles along with several truckloads of spare parts. On November 2, 1986, two days before the midterm elections, David Jacobsen, the hospital director of American University in Beirut, who had been a hostage for over two years, was freed. The Reagan administration had sold Ayatollah Khomeini millions of dollars worth of premium military hardware and won the freedom of two hostages. Jacobsen's release was good news. Unfortunately, by the end of 1986 radical Islamic groups in Lebanon had kidnapped 3 more Americans.

After *Al-Shiraa* reported North and McFarlane's trip to Tehran it caused a mad scramble for cover in the White House along with many false and misleading statements. At first, Reagan officials dismissed the story as having "no foundation." A week later, Reagan confessed on TV to the arms exchanges but asserted their primary purpose was to buttress "moderates." He talked about ending the Iran-Iraq war and stopping terrorism; only at the end of his speech did he mention one of his goals being "the safe return of all hostages." Reagan also downplayed the size of the missile deliveries, saying that the United States had given Iran only "small amounts of defensive weapons," which "taken together, could easily fit into a small cargo plane." On the issue of swapping arms for hostages, Reagan was emphatic: "We did not—repeat, did not—trade weapons or anything else for hostages; nor will we." Two weeks later, when Israel's role was becoming better known, Reagan denied that any third country had been part of the arms sales: "We, as I say, have had nothing to do with other countries or their shipment of arms or doing what they're doing."

Reagan's national security adviser, Admiral John Poindexter, and CIA Director Casey, were hauled before Congress where they gave the House and Senate intelligence committees *Denial of* patently false testimony about the arms deals. Poindexter had already destroyed thousands of *Involvement* incriminating documents, including what he believed to be the only copy of the presidential "finding" of December 1985 that retroactively authorized Israel's arms sales. (Unbeknownst to Poindexter, the CIA possessed its own draft copy that was soon in Congress's hands.) Colonel North later admitted to throwing a "shredding party" where he systematically trashed files relating to the contra resupply effort. In the course of just one weekend, North and his aides shredded over 5,000 documents. Poindexter and North seemed willing to play the "fall guys" in an attempt to give the president "plausible deniability."

Then on November 25, 1986, in what the historian Sean Wilentz calls "the worst performance of his presidency if not his entire career," Reagan informed the press that there had been a "flaw" in the "implementation" of the Iran initiative. Reagan announced that he had fired North and accepted Poindexter's resignation. He also said he was appointing former Texas Senator John Tower to lead an inquiry into the arms transactions for the administration. He then turned over the podium in the White House pressroom to Attorney General Meese. An audible gasp could be heard among reporters when Meese read aloud a written statement indicating that "certain monies" obtained from the secret arms deals with Iran had been "made available" for use by the Nicaraguan contras. On Capitol Hill, lawmakers from both parties were incensed over Poindexter and Casey's false testimonies and guaranteed a thorough congressional investigation.

Not since the Watergate scandal of Richard Nixon's presidency had Washington swirled with such anticipation of the uncovering of official wrongdoing. The number of domestic laws and regulations that had been potentially violated was staggering. Operatives working for the NSC and CIA had failed to remit the funds earned from secret arms sales back to the U.S. Treasury as required by law, and then they transferred millions of dollars worth of supplies to the contras, which the Boland Amendment expressly prohibited. Reagan, who was often called the "Teflon President" because bad news never seemed to "stick" to him, saw his approval rating slump to a new low. He experienced a record-setting 21-percentage point drop. The crisis, known as "the Iran-contra scandal," came midway through Reagan's second term and threatened to turn the popular president into a lame duck. Meese appointed Lawrence Walsh, a moderate Republican judge who had served in Dwight D. Eisenhower's Department of Justice, to be his special prosecutor in the case. Reagan's more ideological defenders immediately began attacking Walsh's inquiry, even smearing him personally, which took the highly esteemed litigator by surprise.

Appointing the Tower Commission was a smart political move. It bought the administration time to prepare for a vigorous defense before Congress. The press was obsessed with the "diversion" of money to the contras, and White House correspondents still had a warm relationship with Reagan letting him change his story multiple times even while documents, news reports, and witness testimony were contradicting him. The pivotal question for most journalists was determining whether or not Reagan had specific knowledge of the all-important "diversion" of funds. But the media's obsession with the question: "What did the president know and when did he know it?" tended to shift the spotlight away from the arms-for-hostages deals as well as the cover-up.

While both the Tower Commission and the special prosecutor began their inquiries, CIA Director Casey suffered a debilitating stroke and in May 1987 died of brain cancer. Casey's abrupt death left the Congress with many unanswered questions. In another strange twist, shortly before he was to appear before the Tower panel, McFarlane tried to kill himself by taking an overdose of Valium. The story of McFarlane's suicide attempt and his recovery in the hospital, along with the expressions of solidarity from his colleagues in the government and military, stirred a great deal of public sympathy for the beleaguered former White House official.

At the end of February 1987, the Tower Commission issued its rather tepid report. As expected, it added to the public's knowledge of the events surrounding the arms transactions and the resupply of the contras, but it stopped short of examining the more damning revelations of profiteering, obstruction of justice, and conspiracies relating to the cover up. Five days after the report was published, Reagan gave a polished prime-time television address where he apologized for not knowing "the facts" in the case. He implied that the Tower Commission's findings were sufficient for the American people to put the episode behind them and move on. The success of the speech, which was widely praised for its candor, was a sign that Reagan was regaining his political footing after the setbacks of the fall and winter.

IRAN-CONTRA HEARINGS

In spring 1987, the nation braced itself for a dramatic summer of congressional hearings. The scandal revived memories of Watergate as a Democratic Congress prepared once again to investigate a Republican president who had won reelection in a landslide. Pacifica radio and a few other stations aired gavel-to-gavel coverage of the Iran-contra proceedings. The hearings raised fundamental questions about presidential war powers and happened to coincide with the bicentennial of the Philadelphia Convention that created the U.S. Constitution. The American people were given a summer-long seminar on the constitutional role of Congress in foreign affairs, as well as the president's obligation to "take care that the Laws are faithfully executed."

Senator Daniel K. Inouye of Hawaii cochaired the Joint House-Senate Iran-contra Committee along with the Indiana Representative Lee Hamilton. They decreed October 1987 as the arbitrary deadline and both cochairs had a deep aversion to partisan clashes that might politicize the inquiry. Inouye and Hamilton treated the Republican minority on the committee with deference and made available to the ranking member, Representative Dick Cheney of Wyoming, ample resources for his own staff and counsels. They also accorded the Republicans great leeway to call their own witnesses and to put together a rigorous defense, which they did. Despite Inouye and Hamilton's stacking the committee with Democratic moderates, congressional Republicans (on and off the committee) disparaged the investigation as a witch hunt by liberals to discredit the president.

Senator Inouye opened the hearings on May 5, 1987, and they quickly turned into political theater. The retired Air Force major general, Richard Secord, who ran the day-to-day functioning of "the Enterprise," was the first witness called to testify. He went through four days of sometimes grueling questioning. As his testimony continued, with the help of the Republicans on the panel, Secord said he had been motivated by nothing more than serving his country and stopping Soviet expansionism in Central America. But he also admitted, under oath, to destroying steno books, telephone logs, and telexes at his office in McLean, Virginia. During one round of questioning, Democratic Senator Paul Sarbanes of Maryland asked him to clarify his testimony that aiding the contras had been his sole objective:

SARBANES: If the purpose of "the Enterprise" was to aid the contras, then why did you charge [contra leader Adolfo] Calero a mark-up that included a profit?

SECORD: We were in business to make a living, Senator, we had to make, we had to make a living, I didn't see anything wrong with it at the time, it was a commercial enterprise.

SARBANES: Oh, I thought the purpose of "the Enterprise" was to aid Calero's cause.

SECORD: Can't I have two purposes? I did.

Source: Testimony of Richard Secord, Senate Hearing (May 8, 1987).

Two purposes
Patriotism &
profit

The point was damning because such opportunism is not normally associated with selfless acts of patriotism. Secord and his Iranian business partner, Albert Hakim, had personally profited from both the U.S. arms sales to Iran and the resupply of the contras. But despite the revelations of crass profiteering, destroying government documents, and lying to Congress, hundreds of letters and telegrams flooded the offices of committee members accusing the Democrats of abusing their power. The committee's two lead attorneys, Arthur Liman and John Nields, were ridiculed as being out-of-touch East Coast liberals seeking to tarnish Reagan. Caught off guard by what appeared to be the public's negative reaction, the Democrats began softballing their questions.

Effects of Red Scare still apparent

The Democrats' hands were also tied by their own contradictory signals they had sent regarding Reagan's Central America policy. In the run up to the 1986-midterm elections, House Democrats passed $100 million in assistance for the contras. "Centrists" in the party had instigated this change while they were up for reelection in conservative districts hoping to avoid being labeled "soft" on communism in Nicaragua. The congressional Democrats' contra aid package smacked of political expediency and effectively nullified the Boland Amendment, which undercut the Iran-contra committee's case against the administration. Still, while the amendment was in effect it had been the law of the land.

On the 24th day of the hearings, Lt. Col. Oliver North entered the Senate Caucus Room wearing his crisp Marine Corps uniform and the visual effect was stunning. Prior to North's testimony his skilled Beltway lawyer, Brendan V. Sullivan, who had coached the witness for weeks in preparation, had secured a grant of immunity from criminal prosecution based on anything that North might say during the hearings. North therefore talked freely about shredding documents and deleting files on the White House's PROF computer system (an early form of e-mail). He confessed to lying to Congress and to the CIA, and to concocting false chronologies for lawmakers with the intent of deceiving them. He even admitted that he had falsified financial records to use Iran-contra money to install an alarm system at his home.

On the second day of North's testimony, when Sullivan placed a large stack of favorable telegrams on the table "proving" his client was a hero in the eyes of most Americans, North played the part of the aggrieved patriot. He cast himself as standing above the opportunistic Washington politicians who preferred grandstanding to fighting the communists. "Lying does not come easy to me," he said. "But we all have to weigh in the balance the difference between lives and lies." North said he had no choice but to lie to Congress to prevent the Soviet Union from learning about the Iran initiative. But when committee counsel John Nields pointed to evidence from North's own memos that the Soviets already knew about the operation, it was clear that many of his lies were intended to keep the project secret, not from the Soviets, but from Congress. This line of questioning yielded an awkward pause in the committee room as North whispered back and forth with Sullivan before sheepishly affirming that Nields was correct.

Subsequent testimony from other witnesses, including a young State Department aide, Robert Owen (who said he had been a "foot-soldier" for North), though less dramatic, filled in the blanks of both the secret arms sales to Iran and the resupply of the contras. The arms transfers had undermined Secretary Shultz's "Operation Staunch," which was a U.S.-directed diplomatic initiative to press other nations to deny the Iranians weapons. (The Department of Justice had even set up a sting operation to try to nab international arms dealers who sold arms to Iran.) Reagan's categorical statements that the United States would never do business with terrorists made the revelations of the arms-for-hostages swaps impossible to square with the administration's stated policy goals in the Middle East.

An estimated 50 million Americans watched some portion of the Iran-contra hearings on television. After 41 days of testimony from dozens of witnesses Senator Inouye read an authoritative final statement before gaveling the proceedings to a close. His expertise on national security affairs had the added gravitas of his own military service in World War II where he lost an arm. Senator Inouye said that a "junta" within the NSC had usurped executive decision-making functions and "privatized" American foreign policy. The president had handed over unprecedented power to a cabal of active and former military and intelligence personnel, he said, while crucial policies defining the parameters of war and peace had been wrapped in a fabric of lies, deception, and misinformation. Coordinating this "secret team" from the White House was a little known Marine lieutenant colonel. Inouye called it "a government within a government" that possessed its own financing mechanism, its own "backchannel" system of worldwide communications, its own army, navy, and air force.

In the final analysis, the Iran-contra operation failed in its most basic goals. The hostage taking in Lebanon continued as those who were set free were replaced with others. The profiteering of "the Enterprise" and the NEPL meant that the contras did not get much in the way of arms and supplies, and no communication channels were opened with authentic Iranian "moderates." (In fact, the Iranian middlemen who North and McFarlane dealt with were agents of the Khomeini regime.) And when the program was uncovered it was a major international embarrassment that raised the level of costs and risks for the United States in Central America and in the Persian Gulf.

Even before the Iran-contra hearings got underway, public opinion polls were not tracking in Reagan's direction. A March 1987 *Newsweek* poll found that 32 percent of Americans believed Reagan should consider resigning before the end of his term. Yet it's a sign of Reagan's resilience that what would become a legendary speech took place at a time when his administration was engulfed in its most serious crisis. Given Reagan's difficulties at home at the time, his speech in West Berlin was largely drowned out by the crisis in Washington. But in subsequent years when parts of it were replayed, particularly after the Berlin Wall came down two-and-a-half years later, it became one of the most lasting images of his presidency.

Beginning in the 1950s, in Communist East Berlin, there had been a surge of people fleeing west in search of political freedom and a chance for a better life. If an East German citizen made it into West Berlin, he or she could apply for asylum, and many of those who defected were highly educated professionals, which caused a "brain drain." By 1961, the crisis became so acute that Soviet Premier Nikita Khrushchev, along with his East German allies, built the Berlin Wall as a means of stemming the tide. In 1962, President John F. Kennedy had delivered one of his most memorable speeches at the city hall in West Berlin to a crowd of several hundred thousand Berliners. Twenty-five years later, when President Reagan spoke in West Berlin, hammering away at the similar themes of freedom and liberty, a generation of people had grown up who had difficulty imagining a world where the Berlin Wall did not exist.

West German Chancellor Helmut Kohl felt he owed Reagan the opportunity to speak in Berlin to atone for the president's disastrous May 1985 trip to Germany when he visited a military cemetery in Bitburg that included the gravesites of soldiers who served in Adolf Hitler's Waffen-SS, the Nazi Party's fighting force. On June 12, 1987, as the Iran-contra committee was grilling his top national security aides at home, Reagan spoke to a gathering of 200,000 at the Brandenburg Gate that divided East and West Berlin: "We welcome change and openness; for we believe that freedom and security go together, that the advance of human liberty can only strengthen the cause of world peace. There is one sign the Soviets can make that would be unmistakable, that would advance dramatically the cause of freedom and peace. Secretary General Gorbachev, if you seek peace—if you seek prosperity for the Soviet Union and Eastern Europe—if you seek liberalization: come here, to this gate. Mr. Gorbachev, open this gate. Mr. Gorbachev, tear down this wall."

In the fall of 1987, the Reagan administration suffered other setbacks in addition to Iran-contra. On October 19, the Dow Jones industrial average lost nearly 23 percent of its value in a matter of hours (508 points). The "Black Monday" stock market crash highlighted the downside of the deregulatory zeal of the administration's early years. Four days after the Wall Street crisis, which was the biggest one-day decline since 1929, the Democratic-controlled Senate rejected Reagan's nominee to the Supreme Court, Robert Bork, to succeed the retiring Justice Lewis Powell. (The Senate's action added the term "to be Borked" to the American political lexicon.) Reagan's choice of Richard Nixon's former Solicitor General to be named to the nation's highest court, like Iran-contra, dredged up unpleasant memories of the Watergate scandal. Bork had played a key role in Nixon's October 1973 purge of the Department of Justice (known in Washington as the "Saturday Night Massacre"), which was an attempt to hinder the investigation into Executive Branch wrongdoing. Bork's past association with Watergate, along with other factors, doomed his Senate confirmation to be a Supreme Court justice.

After the Senate rejected Bork's nomination by a vote of 58 to 42, Reagan nominated Douglas Gingsburg, only to see him take his name out of the running after the public learned that he had smoked marijuana in college. Anthony Kennedy, a law professor from Sacramento, California, was Reagan's third choice and he glided to Senate confirmation with a vote of 97 to 0. (The bruising Senate battle over Bork was a far cry from Reagan's other two appointments: Sandra Day O'Connor, who succeeded Justice Potter Stewart, sailed through the Senate with 91 votes in 1981, and the Senate unanimously confirmed Antonin Scalia in 1986 following Reagan's elevation of William Rehnquist to be chief justice.) Still, the Bork and Ginsburg debacles showed that in Reagan's last 18 months in office, with Democratic majorities in both chambers, he could no longer count on getting his way with Congress.

The Iran-contra scandal precipitated a major shake-up in the administration. In addition to the departure of North, Poindexter, and the death of CIA Director Casey, Casper Weinberger resigned as defense secretary, and Donald Regan was removed as White House chief of staff. Howard Baker, the moderate former Republican senator from

Tennessee stepped in as chief of staff. Frank Carlucci, a veteran Washington defense official who had succeeded Poindexter as national security adviser became the defense secretary, and Reagan named President Carter's former director of the FBI, William Webster, to head the CIA. Weinberger's military aide, Army Lieutenant General Colin Powell, became the national security adviser (the first African American to serve in the post). In his final months in office, Reagan projected a far more conciliatory tone both internationally and with Congress than the swashbuckling actions of his first term.

By March 1988, despite numerous immunity deals, Special Prosecutor Walsh had amassed enough evidence to win a guilty plea from Robert McFarlane on four counts of withholding information from Congress. Walsh also successfully returned indictments against North, Poindexter, Secord, and Hakim on 23 separate counts. Ultimately, 11 people connected to the Iran-contra operation were convicted of a wide range of crimes, including perjury, obstruction of justice, conspiracy, and financial abuses. Reagan publicly stood by his former subordinates and the strategy of circling the wagons apparently worked. By the time his term ended, his approval rating was back to where it was before the public learned about "the Enterprise." Throughout, the administration (with the help of congressional Republicans) was largely successful in shielding Vice President Bush from any Iran-contra fallout. (At the time, he was considered to be the presumptive GOP nominee for president in 1988.) Later, an appeals court overturned both North's and Poindexter's convictions, and when Bush became president he pardoned Weinberger and five others who had been convicted for Iran-contra offenses.

Throughout 1987, in Geneva, Switzerland, U.S. and Soviet negotiators had been working on a draft agreement they called the "zero-zero" (or "double-zero") option scrapping the superpowers' land-based European missiles in two categories: medium and short-range. Medium range missiles were capable of knocking out targets 1,000 to 3,000 miles away, while short-range missiles had a reach of 300 to 1,000 miles. Both Reagan and Gorbachev had political motives for agreeing to an accord: Gorbachev needed a de-escalation of Cold War tensions to further his reforms and mollify hardliners inside his government. For Reagan, a foreign policy win could lift him out of the Iran-contra morass and rebuild the shattered confidence of NATO allies. The Intermediate-Range Nuclear Forces (INF) Treaty not only froze in place the deployment of new intermediate-range missiles, but also for the first time dispensed with an entire category of weapons. "By signing the INF treaty," Gorbachev later wrote, "we had literally removed a pistol held to our head."

In December 1987, Gorbachev came to Washington for his first state visit, which included the signing ceremony of the INF Treaty. He appeared with Reagan at a press conference in the White House where both leaders' ability to charm the international press was on full display. After the political setbacks Reagan had suffered throughout 1986 and 1987—the loss of the Senate, Iran-contra, the stock market crash, and the contentious Bork hearings—his third summit with Gorbachev, this time in the U.S. capital, had been a resounding success. Within three years of being implemented the last of the Soviet SS-20s was dismantled, bringing the total number of missiles purged on both sides to nearly 2,700. In Gorbachev's view, the INF Treaty "represented the first well-prepared step on our way out of the Cold War." Opinion polls in the United States and Europe indicated that any sign that Reagan and Gorbachev could work together to lower the likelihood of a nuclear conflagration was immensely popular. Just after his summit with Gorbachev, Reagan's approval rating topped 60 percent for the first time since the disclosure of Iran-contra.

After the U.S. Senate ratified the treaty, Reagan answered Gorbachev's visit with a trip of his own to Moscow. His arrival on May 29, 1988, marked the first time a U.S. head of state had visited the Soviet Union in 14 years. In his memoirs, Gorbachev recalls one exchange in Moscow that occurred near the *Tsar-Pushka* (The Tsar of Cannons) when a reporter asked Reagan if he still viewed the Soviet Union as an "evil empire"? Without hesitating Reagan answered: "No." The following day another journalist queried Reagan about why he had changed his mind. "Mr. Gorbachev deserves most of the credit as the leader of his country," he said. "And it seems to me that with perestroika things have changed in the Soviet Union. Judging from what I read about perestroika, I could agree with a lot of it."

MORE SCANDALS

In May 1986, the Wall Street financier, Ivan Boesky, famously said at the University of California, Berkeley business school commencement: "I think greed is healthy." Eighteen months later, he was convicted for insider trading, sentenced to three years in prison, and fined $100 million. (Boesky became the template for the lead character, Gordon Gekko, in Oliver Stone's perfectly timed Hollywood film, *Wall Street* (1987) that recounted the dirty tricks that epitomized the "go-go" capitalist ethic of the period.) As part of Boesky's plea deal with federal prosecutors, he gave up Michael Milken as a co-conspirator. Known as the "junk bond king," the business press had fallen over itself praising Milken, calling him "the premier financier of his generation" (*Fortune*); "the chief architect of America's corporate restructuring" (*Forbes*); and "probably the most influential American financier since J.P. Morgan" (*The Economist*). Milken had built his empire out of his Los Angeles arbitrage firm, Drexel Burnham Lambert, and became a major underwriter of exotic securities. He pioneered new methods of financing based on the speculative value of bonds that were technically "junk." Milken's creative accounting in the context of a deregulated Wall Street greased the wheels for corporate raiders to engage in a wave of leveraged buyouts (LBOs) and hostile takeovers that piled up (for a time) unimaginable profits and commissions. LBOs were particularly damaging to the real economy because they entailed buying companies and then selling them off piece by piece. The financiers made out like bandits while the workers lost their jobs and often their pensions when the companies were liquidated.

Federal authorities dusted off the old RICO statute (the Racketeer Influenced and Corrupt Organizations Act), normally used against mafia titans, to prosecute Milken. He pleaded guilty to six felonies of conspiracy and a host of tax and mail frauds and was sentenced to 10 years of imprisonment. (He served less than two years in prison.) Milken also paid what was then the biggest single fine in American history: $900 million. In 1989, Drexel shelled out $650 million in penalties before going bankrupt a year later. Boesky and Milken became the poster boys for the shady deals and widespread "control frauds" that were taking place on Wall Street throughout the 1980s. Their criminal convictions marked an end to an era of fast money and high-stakes gambling that had put the "real" economy at risk and were a factor in the October 19, 1987 stock market crash.

When two prominent Christian evangelicals, the Reverends Jim Bakker and Jimmy Swaggart, became embroiled in their own public humiliations it added to the growing sense that no sector of American society was immune to disgrace. Reverend Bakker, along with his wife, Tammy Faye Bakker, controlled a media empire that included the "Praise the Lord" (PTL) television and radio network, as well as a Christian-themed amusement park in Fort Mill, South Carolina, called "Heritage USA." Reverend Swaggart owned a television network and dozens of charitable organizations with headquarters all over the world. The Bakkers and Swaggart, along with the Reverend Jerry Falwell of the Moral Majority (one of the largest political lobbying groups for evangelical Christians),

Pat Robertson of the Christian Broadcasting Network's *The 700 Club,* and Oral Roberts of Oral Roberts University, were all role models for millions of social conservatives.

In early 1987, circumstances compelled Bakker to admit to having a sexual relationship with a young church volunteer named Jessica Hahn. He later confessed to paying Ms. Hahn $265,000 in "hush money" in an attempt to keep the affair hidden. To salvage his ministry, Bakker used his TV show as a platform to inform his flock that he had committed the sin of adultery and that he was relinquishing control of PTL. Tammy Faye, who was known for her heavy makeup, wept by her husband's side, her cheeks streaked black by tears mixed with mascara. Falwell stepped in to manage PTL and mitigate the public crisis.

Notwithstanding his confession of the extramarital affair, Bakker still claimed he was resigning only because his rival, Swaggart, had hatched a "diabolical plot" to purloin PTL and Heritage USA. Ms. Hahn subsequently sold her story to *Playboy* magazine and even posed for a photo spread. According to Hahn, Bakker told her while soliciting sex: "When you help the shepherd, you're helping the sheep." As embarrassing as the sex scandal, it was the Bakkers' financial improprieties that brought them down. For years the couple had been dipping into the collection plate and spending lavishly on luxury trips, fancy cars, and even an air-conditioned house for their family dog. (Bakker later went to prison for fraud.) Swaggart, for his part, denied having any interest in "stealing" PTL, but seemed to relish in condemning Bakker's sex and money scandal, which he called "a cancer that needed to be excised from the body of Christ."

But Swaggart's air of moral superiority soon evaporated when he found himself mired in his own sex scandal after his trysts with a New Orleans prostitute were brought to light. Like Bakker, Swaggart went before his TV congregation in an emotional appeal where he too confessed and begged for salvation. "I have sinned against you, my Lord!" a tear-drenched Swaggart bewailed during a gut-wrenching crying jag where he yelped for God's forgiveness. He (and the Bakkers) became the butt of jokes and ridicule on late-night TV. (The rock musician and PMRC foil, Frank Zappa, wrote a series of songs skewering the fallen reverends, and he performed the satire across America as part of his final tour in 1988.) In government, high finance, and even among highly esteemed religious leaders, the public revelations of wrongdoing and hypocrisy signaled an end of the era of restored faith in America's dominant institutions that had been one of the hallmarks of the Reagan Revolution.

REVIEW QUESTIONS

1. Why did President Reagan and his National Security Council (NSC) believe it was vital to U.S. national security to keep the arms flowing to the Nicaraguan "contras" even during a time when Congress had explicitly banned such military assistance? What were some of the early sources of secret financing for the operation?

2. What were the Reagan administration's goals for opening "backchannel" communications with the Islamic Republic of Iran? What were the U.S. objectives for the transfer of TOW missiles and other armaments to the government of Ayatollah Khomeini? Were these transactions "arms-for-hostages" swaps? Why or why not?

3. What was the purpose of the congressional Iran-contra hearings during the summer of 1987? What were some of the key revelations about the operation the committee uncovered? What was Oliver North's role in the operation? What makes the Iran-contra scandal different from other Washington scandals?

4. How did the Iran-contra scandal affect Reagan's presidency midway through his second term? How did the Reagan administration address the crisis? What Constitutional issues did the Iran-contra revelations raise? How did Reagan regain the trust of NATO allies and the American people following the scandal? Did his warmer relations with Mikhail Gorbachev help Reagan politically? Can Reagan's presidency be viewed in terms of "pre-Iran-contra" and "post-Iran-contra?"

5. What were some of the important scandals involving Wall Street financiers and evangelical preachers in the latter part of the decade? What were the political effects of the public revelations relating to these scandals?

---

mysearchlab CONNECTIONS SOURCES ONLINE

READ AND REVIEW

Review this chapter by using the study aids and these related documents available on MySearchLab.

Study Plan
Chapter Test
Essay Test

Documents
Ronald Reagan, Support for the Contras (1984)
In this speech, Reagan portrays the Marxist Sandinista government of Nicaragua, which had been democratically elected, as "a communist reign of terror."

Senator Daniel Inouye, Closing Statement to the Iran-Contra Select Committee (1987)
Inouye's remarks at the end of the House and Senate Iran-contra committees 12 weeks of public hearings.

The Intermediate Nuclear Forces Treaty (INF Treaty (1987))
Text of the 1987 agreement between the United States and the Soviet Union on nuclear weapons.

RESEARCH AND EXPLORE

Use the databases available within MySearchLab to find additional primary and secondary sources the topics within this chapter.

Map Discovery
Conflict in Central America, 1970–1998

Video
Oliver North Hearing
Evangelical Religion and Politics, Then and Now

7

A Bumpy Ride to a New World Order

CHAPTER OUTLINE

THE SAVINGS AND LOAN DEBACLE

Throughout the 1980s an almost religious faith in "free markets" often hamstrung federal and state regulators, even those in charge of financial institutions. What were looked upon in previous administrations (and Congresses) as the normal oversight functions of the Federal Home Loan Bank Board (FHLBB), which appraised the health of the nation's savings and loans (or "thrifts"), were now judged "wasteful" in a straight cost-benefit analysis. As early as 1982, some bank examiners found that the economic "shock therapy" that Federal Reserve Chair Paul Volcker had prescribed as a means to whip inflation, wreaked havoc in the savings and loan industry. On a market value basis, some projections suggested that the savings and loan sector was insolvent by as much as $150 billion, and the Federal Savings and Loan Insurance Corporation (FSLIC), which guarantees

---

On November 9, 1989, the world's preeminent symbol of police-state repression, the Berlin Wall, came crashing down to the surprise of most international observers, including President George Herbert Walker Bush. Soviet Premier Mikhail Gorbachev's reforms that encouraged greater openness not only inside the Soviet Union, but also in Eastern Bloc countries, and the resistance and activism of the people living under those regimes, had loosened the East German government's totalitarian control. The result was the birth of what President Bush called a "new world order."

depositors, had a reserve of about $6 billion. What followed was a concerted bipartisan effort to hide the scope of the problem mainly because it would entail new estimates of the federal budget deficit at a time when tax cut legislation was pending.

Reagan's first FHLBB head, Richard Pratt, was a dyed-in-the-wool proponent of deregulation and Congress codified this trend in 1982 by passing the Garn-St. Germain Depository Institutions Act. The act remanded key provisions regulating thrifts back to the states and some states took advantage of their new jurisdiction to decree further deregulation. Savings and Loans (S&Ls) in Texas, California, and Arizona, for example, were among the least regulated and were responsible for the most egregious abuses and the biggest losses. The Garn-St. Germain Act also empowered state-chartered S&Ls to convert to federal charters, which licensed some managers to play state and federal regulators against each other.

In the early 1980s, the number of bank examiners and yearly audits dropped precipitously. One of Chairman Pratt's more costly reforms was to hold in abeyance conflict-of-interest rules that had been in place for years that prevented executives from abusing their control of S&Ls for personal gain. Worse still, the Economic Recovery Tax Act of 1981 (ERTA) authorized new tax shelters that incentivized dicey real estate deals for tax (as opposed to market) purposes. These policies subsidized over-building and an unsustainable commercial real estate and housing boom, particularly in the Southwest. S&L executives took advantage of the new rules, gamed the tax code, and pumped up real estate bubbles in regional markets using FSLIC-insured deposits.

In early 1983, Reagan appointed his old friend and former press secretary in Sacramento, Edwin J. Gray, to head the FHLBB. At first, Gray continued the deregulatory trajectory of his predecessor but soon the gravity of the situation began to unnerve him. His faith in the self-correcting mechanisms of markets was profoundly shaken after he realized that private developers and S&L insiders were making personal fortunes by building on essentially worthless real estate and arranging all manner of kickbacks and payouts that were nearly impossible to sort out. Through "goodwill accounting," "mark-to-market" purchases, and other schemes, S&L managers were free to exploit raises, bonuses, and stock options to enrich themselves using federally guaranteed funds.

The culminating event occurred when Gray hired a Texas real estate specialist to help him analyze how bad the S&L mess had gotten. From a small plane the contractor videotaped aerial views of the I-30 corridor that runs through Garland, Texas near Dallas. He documented miles and miles of unfinished housing units, many of them consisting of no more than concrete slabs. When Gray watched the film in March 1984 he told a member of his staff that he wanted to throw up. Gray showed the footage to Representative Fernand St. Germain, the Rhode Island Democrat who chaired the House Banking Committee and coauthored the deregulation bill. St. Germain became more upset with Gray for bringing to light the economic carnage in Texas than he was with the abuses that caused it. According to Gray, politicians in this period were "so ideologically blinded" they "couldn't understand the difference between thrift deregulation and airline deregulation." (The House Ethics Committee later investigated St. Germain for discrepancies in his own financial records, and he lost his House seat in 1988.)

Chairman Gray became an unlikely hero in the S&L saga and did everything he could to contain the damage. He shut down the conveyor belt of new S&L charters, increased capital requirements, and ordered more examinations and greater supervision. Politicians connected to the powerful interests that were benefitting from the real estate bubbles, especially in Texas, California, Arizona, and Florida, were outraged by Gray's actions and orchestrated an effort to unseat him. In a climate of hot housing markets, with CEOs registering extraordinary earnings and investors up and down the food chain making money, Gray's attempt to put the brakes on the good times required a Herculean effort. By the time his term ended in June 1987, it was clear that despite the flak he caught, Gray's moratorium on new charters prevented the crisis from becoming even worse. But given that the potential losses to the S&L sector exceeded the FSLIC funds by a factor of 20 or more, the cost to taxpayers of a potential bailout shot skyward.

Charles Keating, owner of the California-based Lincoln Savings and Loan, marshaled his allies in the U.S. Senate to undermine Gray's work. Keating was a well-known campaign contributor with a reputation for buying political influence. (He once told a business associate that securing a California S&L charter was like having "a license to steal.") Michael Milken, the junk bond guru, cobbled together the financing for Keating to purchase Lincoln Savings, securing a credit line of $125 million. In his correspondence with his Senate allies, Keating called Gray a "mad dog" and persuaded a bipartisan cadre of senators to help Lincoln Savings fend off regulatory action, which the press dubbed the "Keating Five." Among them were the Republican senator from Arizona, John McCain, and the Democrats Dennis DeConcini (also of Arizona), John Glenn of Ohio, Alan Cranston of California, and Donald Riegle of Michigan.

When Lincoln Savings subsequently went belly up, costing taxpayers over $3 billion as well as the life savings of 23,000 bondholders and small investors, the public learned of the "Keating Five's" role in protecting their friend even while he was defrauding depositors. The Senate Ethics Committee decided that Cranston, DeConcini, and Riegle had crossed the line in trying to block the FHLBB on behalf of Keating, and although Cranston was the only one to receive a formal reprimand, the committee criticized all five of them for exercising "poor judgment." In the end, Keating was slapped with multiple criminal convictions in federal and state courts for fraud, racketeering, and conspiracy, and served four-and-a-half years in prison.

After the catastrophic wave of S&L bankruptcies in the late-eighties, the U.S. government had no choice but to try to recoup the losses that thrift executives had dumped on taxpayers. At the end of Reagan's second term, the White House's own economic team conceded that a significant share of the blame for the S&L debacle was the direct result of overly aggressive deregulation. It wasn't until Reagan left office when the full cost of the taxpayer bailout became known. Estimates vary, but the General Accounting Office (GAO) calculated that the total outlay of the S&L crisis, including interest, cost American taxpayers $341 billion.

ELECTION 1988

Running for public office for the first time in the Republican primaries was the Reverend Pat Robertson who had a large following among the core "values" voters of the GOP. He was a founding father of the "Christian Coalition," a political action committee that was the brainchild of the young Republican operative Ralph Reed. Robertson's campaign was a sign of the dissatisfaction among religious conservatives who felt there had been a lack of progress on social issues. The Republicans, who were swept into office in 1980 with the help of Christian voters, authored a total of 21 school prayer bills and 31 bills limiting abortion rights in the House of Representatives. But they remained bottled up in

Congress. After eight years of a Republican administration that got most of what it wanted on taxes and defense social conservatives had little to show for their efforts.

In the 1980 and 1984 elections, Christian conservatives had been practically king-makers inside the GOP. But by 1988 rifts had developed between prominent segments of the evangelical movement. Robertson appealed to "Charismatic" Christian evangelicals, but he had trouble lining up members of the mainline Protestant sects behind his candidacy. The Bakker-Swaggart sex scandals didn't help the religious Right's cohesion. A further splintering resulted with the rise of the National Christian Action Coalition and the Religious Roundtable. Despite its divisions, the movement remained formidable, especially in the South and Midwest and Robertson's candidacy institutionalized the Christian Right as a grassroots political force. It began playing an active role in the Republican primaries similar to that of labor unions in the Democratic primaries. In addition, there was a resurgence of Randall Terry's militant antiabortion movement, "Operation Rescue," which mobilized thousands of people disillusioned with the failure to whittle away at *Roe v. Wade*, the landmark 1973 Supreme Court ruling that constitutionally protected women's reproductive rights. Between May 1988 and August 1990, Operation Rescue staged 683 "blockades" of women's health clinics with a total of 41,000 arrests. Some commentators compared the scale of the "pro-life" mobilization, as well as its nonviolent tactics, to the civil rights movement of the 1960s.

The former Senate majority leader, Robert Dole of Kansas, who was popular among Republican base voters, also threw his hat into the ring in 1988. Dole had been on the Republican ticket with Gerald Ford in 1976 and political analysts saw him as Vice President Bush's only realistic rival (or possible running mate). In the Iowa caucuses of February 1988 Vice President Bush finished third behind both Dole and Reverend Robertson. But after a few missteps, such as calling the World Wars "Democrat wars," and braving unfair and often mendacious attacks from the Bush campaign, Dole withdrew from the race after a poor showing in the remaining primaries.

Vice President Bush, who was the presumed Republican nominee, had avoided the taint of Iran-contra, but he had the dilemma of never being totally accepted by movement conservatives. Bush had the solid support of the business community, especially those interests tied to financial services, defense, and oil, and he had political followings in Texas, where he won his first elective office as a representative in 1964, and Connecticut, where his father, Prescott Bush, had served as U.S. senator. However, many Republicans perceived him as representing the moderate Rockefeller wing of the party. His long resume, which included stints as ambassador to the United Nations, chair of the Republican National Committee, envoy to China, and CIA director, for him accomplished little in winning support among voters who were suspicious of Washington insiders. He had the added burden of serving eight years under the shadow of a charismatic president beloved by Republicans.

In a column published at the end of Reagan's second term the liberal *New York Times* editorialist, Anthony Lewis, pointed to "the intangible costs of the Reagan years," which included "hostility to the role of government," an "indulgence toward private greed," and an "insensitivity to the needs of the weak in our society." After two terms of Reagan's brand of cheery optimism fused with a kind of benign neglect of the underprivileged, his vice president was compelled to run on a platform that promised a "kinder, gentler America." (When Nancy Reagan first heard Bush speak about a "kinder, gentler nation" she reportedly asked a friend: "kinder and gentler compared to what?") In 1988, yarns about "welfare queens" or recasting "ketchup as a vegetable" no longer had resonance

After winning the 1988 election, President Bush appointed Lee Atwater, who managed his campaign, to be the chairman of the Republican National Committee (RNC). Atwater (seen in the photograph with the president) pioneered new techniques in negative campaigning and was a master at driving opposing candidates' "negatives" upward through personal attacks and character assassination. Atwater died of a rare brain cancer at the age of 40 while serving as RNC chair but his scorched-earth political tactics have, in subsequent years, become mainstays of American presidential campaigns.

after years where the poor in American society had clearly lost ground. A more compassionate message from the Republican presidential candidate reflected the public mood.

Bush's campaign themes might have accentuated a newfound compassion, but there would be nothing "kind" or "gentle" about the political operation his campaign manager, Lee Atwater, was going to run. Atwater was an ambitious South Carolina Republican operative who specialized in "opposition research" and had worked for North Carolina Senator Jesse Helms. In 1980, in the South Carolina primary, Atwater helped Reagan defeat Bush by successfully tarring Bush as a northeastern liberal who would take people's guns away. Now, working for the vice president, he set out not so much to sell Bush's image, but to take the bark off any rival, Republican or Democrat, who stood in his way. "Republicans in the South could not win elections by talking about issues," Atwater explained. "You have to make the case that the other guy, the other candidate, is a bad guy," he said. Atwater had his work cut out for him; not since Martin Van Buren, 152 years earlier, had a sitting vice president won the White House through direct election.

There were many factors responsible for the callousness of the 1988 presidential campaign: Bush's lukewarm popularity among primary voters, the shadow that Reagan cast over all GOP contenders, and the simple fact that a Republican administration had been in power for eight years. But there was also an awareness that the period of ebullience that distinguished the Reagan years was coming to an end. Since Bush could do little to elevate his own popularity other than wrapping himself in Reagan's legacy, his campaign strategists calculated that his best chances for winning was to drive up the "negatives" of his opponents. After the televangelist, Pat Robertson, beat Bush in the Iowa caucuses with an outpouring of Christian conservatives, Atwater knew he would have to be even more aggressive. He would have the opportunity to apply his scorched-earth techniques that worked so well in the South to a national campaign. "Let me tell you about my negative theory," Atwater clarified to reporters. "When a candidate reaches a negative factor of 35 percent in the polls, and his positive rating is within five points of that—he's terminal."

On the Democratic side, the party establishment that four years earlier had nominated Walter Mondale coalesced around the candidacy of Massachusetts Governor

Michael Dukakis. Dukakis was a pragmatic politician who efficiently managed the government of a liberal state. But he could come off as a drab technocrat. "This election is about competence—not ideology," Dukakis declared, polishing his own stereotype. But Lee Atwater would soon teach him that the 1988 presidential race was going to be about competence *and* ideology.

Dukakis chose the senior senator from Texas, Lloyd Bentsen, to be his running mate giving the ticket regional and ideological balance. With a Massachusetts liberal and a moderate Texan as the nominees, some Democrats believed they had a winning team reminiscent of the triumphant 1960 race where Massachusetts Senator John F. Kennedy and Texas Senator Lyndon B. Johnson narrowly defeated the sitting Republican vice president, Richard Nixon. Throughout the summer most opinion polls showed Bush neck and neck with Dukakis. These poll numbers only led Atwater to redouble his efforts.

GEORGE H. W. BUSH AND DAN QUAYLE

Bush never enjoyed the kind of cordiality from the press that Reagan received. Typifying this trend was the Washington media's conjuring out of thin air a phenomenon questioning Bush's "strength" that became known as the "wimp" factor. (*Newsweek* even ran a cover story about it.) It was an unfair portrayal of a World War II veteran who had served as the youngest U.S. Navy aviator flying 58 combat missions. But the "wimp" trope affected Bush's decision to choose a vice presidential running mate who would not overshadow him. He bypassed more experienced figures who were better known and with more gravitas in favor of the 41-year-old junior senator from Indiana, Dan Quayle. Quayle was an heir to the Pulliam publishing empire and his scant legislative record and negligible political clout made him a curious choice. So paltry was Quayle's resume that the creator of the syndicated comic strip *Doonesbury*, Garry Trudeau, characterized him as a feather floating in midair (and Bush as a disembodied voice). However, Quayle was popular among social conservatives and, unlike other potential running mates, had no chance of eclipsing Bush who was struggling to get out from under Reagan's shadow and construct his own identity in the eyes of voters.

When the vice presidential candidates, Senators Lloyd Bentsen and Dan Quayle, squared off in their sole debate in Omaha, Nebraska, it afforded one of the more memorable moments of the campaign. Quayle's age and inexperience had been a topic of discussion and he dispelled this criticism by pointing out that John F. Kennedy was about his age when he ran for president. Bentsen, who was a veteran Washington politician who rose through the ranks in the Senate to become chair of the powerful Finance Committee, turned to the candidate and said: "I knew Jack Kennedy, I worked with Jack Kennedy, and you, Senator, are no Jack Kennedy." Bentsen's rebuke drew a noisy reaction from the audience and a stern admonishment from Quayle. Afterwards the exchange came to define the debate when the cable news shows ceaselessly ran the clip. Bentsen was widely seen as the "winner" of the contest.

Another standout of the 1988 campaign came in the form of a series of commercials attacking Dukakis's record on crime. During the Democratic primaries, questions were raised about an obscure Massachusetts prison furlough program. The issue piqued Atwater's curiosity and he searched for a recidivism case in Massachusetts he could use to paint Dukakis as being "soft" on crime. He soon discovered the case of William Horton who was a South Carolina native convicted for the 1974 murder of a gas station attendant in Lawrence, Massachusetts, and sentenced to life imprisonment. In 1986, Horton had qualified for a weekend furlough but never reported back to prison. He was later arrested in Maryland after raping a woman and beating her fiancé. The weekend pass system had been in place before Dukakis's governorship but he generally supported its rehabilitative goals. Allies of the Bush campaign produced a series of anti-Dukakis television and radio commercials that spotlighted the Horton case. The advertisements (ads) were as controversial as they were effective and rank among the most notorious ever run in a modern American presidential campaign.

One ad, shot in ominous black and white, features scores of hardened criminals in dingy shirts and blue jeans traipsing in and out of jail through a revolving door. The most menacing among them, an African American, is the only one who glances upward into the camera and peers directly into the eyes of the viewer. Another commercial with a scary mug shot of a disheveled "Willie" Horton glowering at his captors, was clearly crafted to play on deep-seated racial stereotypes. The Willie Horton spots were evidence of Atwater's "Southern Strategy" of past Republican campaigns. Jesse Jackson, as well as the leaders of the nation's major civil rights organizations, deplored the overall visual effect of the Willie Horton ads as "racist." Since they were the fruit of "independent expenditures" from an organ not directly linked to the Bush campaign, Atwater pretended he had nothing to do with them while defending the "free speech" rights of those responsible. Privately, Atwater said he was going to "make Willie Horton Dukakis's running mate." In the context of the late-1980s, with Alabama and South Carolina still flying the Confederate flag over public buildings, and Arizona, Idaho, Montana, New Hampshire, South Dakota, and Wyoming refusing to honor Martin Luther King Jr.'s birthday, the racial component of a black rapist in a campaign commercial was clear.

Amidst the relentless attacks, Dukakis tried to remain above the fray and his half-hearted attempts to counter Atwater's take-no-prisoners offensive only reinforced the narrative that he lacked conviction. This perception was further fortified during Dukakis's second and final debate with Bush in Los Angeles when the CNN correspondent and moderator, Bernard Shaw, opened the debate by asking him a hypothetical question about whether or not he would choose the death penalty for a criminal who had raped and murdered his wife Kitty. The Democratic candidate's response was a disquisition on the ineffectiveness of capital punishment filled with deadening statistics. The exchange left the impression that Dukakis was incapable of showing passion even when the situation warranted it.

Adding insult to injury, Dukakis campaign advisers, in an attempt to bolster their candidate's persona as a potential commander-in-chief, scheduled a tour at a General Dynamics production facility in Sterling Heights, Michigan. Dukakis accepted what he thought at the time would be a light-hearted invitation to take a short ride in an M1 Abrams tank. The spectacle of the diminutive Dukakis poking his head and shoulders out of a giant armored vehicle, wearing an ill-fitting helmet, smiling and waving to the cameras, became an indelible visual of the 1988 campaign. The Bush team seized upon the unflattering photo-op (Atwater told the press Dukakis looked like "Rocky the Flying Squirrel") and ran the videotape with a voice-over narration savaging Dukakis's "weakness" on national defense. Dukakis, who had served in the U.S. Army, was a critic of Reagan's Star Wars and other parts of the defense buildup. The "Dukakis-in-a-tank" motif has since entered the American political lexicon as a shorthand term denoting any embarrassing photo-op or public appearance that takes place in the heat of a campaign.

In the end, the Bush-Quayle team won 53.4 percent of the popular vote to Dukakis and Bentsen's 45.6 percent, and beat the Democratic ticket in the Electoral College by 426 to 111. Nearly all incumbents were reelected in the House of Representatives with the Democrats picking up two net seats (giving them a 260 to 175 majority). In the Senate, the numbers held with the Democrats increasing their majority by a single seat, 55 to 45. Bush had no coattails. Reagan succeeded in passing the torch to his chosen successor but the status quo of divided government continued.

The acrimony of the 1988 campaign seemed light-years away from the more upbeat tone four years earlier. It expounded the efficacy of the dark arts of negative campaigning that tend to drive down voter turnout and undermine civil discourse. (Voter turnout was 50.1 percent, low even by American standards.) Pleased with his success, President Bush elevated Atwater to chair the Republican National Committee. Atwater, after contracting a pernicious form of brain cancer that would take his life at the age of 40, admitted that he had behaved unethically and apologized to Dukakis and other politicians he had slimed during his career. Perhaps more than any single individual in recent history Lee Atwater was responsible for institutionalizing jaundiced tactics as normative in modern presidential races. Atwater's deathbed confession aside, there was little hope that the political techniques he perfected would recede from American politics any time soon for the simple fact that they can be decisive in winning elections.

THE BERLIN WALL

The seeds of the monumental events of November 1989 that brought down the Berlin Wall were planted back in August 1975 when 35 nations, including the United States, unanimously approved the Helsinki Accords. The multilateral agreement contained many parts that were seen at the time to be purely symbolic in nature, such as guarantees for the "equal rights and self-determination of peoples." But Helsinki's "Final Act" recognized the sovereignty of East Germany and other Soviet satellites and forbid "armed intervention or threat of such intervention against another participating State." In effect, the Helsinki Accords were an ironclad assurance that neither NATO nor the United States would take military action against the Warsaw Pact. They solidified the status quo of a divided Germany and put to rest the idea that someday there might be an attempt to reunify the country by force of arms. An international organization sprung up, "Helsinki Watch," with the express purpose of monitoring and publicizing human rights abuses in signatory states. In the late-1970s, grassroots clubs and community groups proliferated in Eastern Bloc countries that petitioned their governments to honor the pledges laid out in Helsinki.

Even with Mikhail Gorbachev's reform agenda and the popular struggles going on in Eastern Europe (such as *Solidarity* in Poland) in 1987 and 1988, East Berlin did not appear to be a city on the brink of a revolution. The pro-Soviet German Democratic Republic (GDR) routinely dispersed nonviolent protestors, as it did in January 1988, when the Stasi security services arrested over a hundred people who were commemorating the 1919 murder of the revolutionaries Rosa Luxemberg and Karl Liebknecht. Erich Honecker, the 77-year-old GDR premier who had been in power for eighteen years, renounced Gorbachev's *perestroika* and *glasnost*. In the spring of 1989, his regime held municipal elections where government candidates won 98.9 percent of the vote.

But events began moving quickly in May 1989 after the Soviet-sponsored government in Hungary decided, as part of its own Gorbachev-style restructuring, to turn off the electrified fence that sealed the country's western border. Officially, the Hungarian frontier with Germany remained "closed," but when news of the relaxed border control spread to East Germany people began flooding across it. In a matter of weeks, there were over 25,000 GDR citizens "on holiday" in Hungary and by September the number had swelled to 60,000. Hundreds of people sought refuge inside the West German Embassy in Budapest, and when the Hungarian government acknowledged it would take no action against GDR nationals going to Austria, another 22,000 people dashed across the border. Following these momentous events even a crusty authoritarian like Honecker had to realize he had a major public-relations disaster on his hands.

That October, Gorbachev visited East Germany to attend an event celebrating the 40th anniversary of its founding and he took the opportunity to spur Honecker toward greater liberalization. But the GDR leader made it clear he had no interest in following Gorbachev's reformist path. Within weeks spirited demonstrations broke out in Leipzig and other East German cities, and some GDR officials close to Honecker believed that he might be contemplating a "Tiananmen Square"-style solution to the unrest. Four months earlier, in June 1989, the Chinese communist government cracked down on pro-democracy protesters in Beijing killing scores of people and jailing thousands. Believing that Honecker might follow China's lead, GDR authorities, coordinated by Egon Krenze, staged a coup d'etat against the septuagenarian and removed him from office. Krenze flew to Moscow to confer with Gorbachev and upon his return gave assurances to carry out an East German version of *perestroika.*

Despite the promises of greater openness from the socialist regime the protests in Leipzig grew past 300,000 people, and in early November, tens of thousands of East Germans were participating in daily rallies on the streets of Berlin. Czechoslovakia (today split into the Czech Republic and Slovakia), like Hungary, loosened its border enforcement and another 30,000 GDR citizens emigrated. Then, on November 9, 1989, the Krenze government, trying to stabilize the situation, agreed to permit East Germans to visit West Germany. The change in policy, divulged almost inadvertently at a press conference by the foreign minister, had the effect of rendering the Berlin Wall obsolete. People came from all over Europe to help Berliners tear down what had become since its construction in 1961 the world's most famous symbol of police-state oppression. They converged on the wall with picks and sledgehammers and battered down its ugly concrete edifice as Stasi guards stood by watching.

The spectacle of thousands of joyous people demolishing the Berlin Wall came to symbolize the power of ordinary people, even under a "totalitarian" state, to win their newfound freedom. It was a poignant sign that in the final months of the decade the world was entering a new era. By Christmas 1989, one in six East Germans, about 2.4 million people, had crossed into West Berlin to sojourn with friends and relatives or just to look around. There was a colossal shopping spree as GDR citizens voraciously snapped up consumer goods that had been denied them under the communist economy. President Bush remained cautiously optimistic about events in Berlin: "I'm very pleased," he told reporters, "but I can't say that I foresaw this development at this stage." A week after the earth-shaking events in Berlin, *USA Today* published an opinion poll showing that 43 percent of Americans attributed the change to Gorbachev. According to the same poll only 14 percent gave Reagan the credit. In Germany, the polls were even more skewed: 70 percent of the people believed Gorbachev had brought about the new German reality, while only 2 percent hailed the former U.S. president. The path had been cleared for reunifying

Germany, which had been split in two since the end of the Second World War, and on October 3, 1990, less than a year after the fall of the Berlin Wall, Germany was reunified.

CHANGE COMES TO THE SOVIET BLOC

By the end of the decade roughly a quarter of Soviet citizens were 30 years old or younger, and the values and beliefs these young people held had drifted far away from those of the older generation who ran most of the state bureaucracies. Gorbachev became their leader and his *glasnost* reforms granted them unprecedented contact with the consumer culture of the capitalist West. Throughout the Communist world there was a fascination with American and European commercial products, which were of great interest due to their relative scarcity. The Croatian journalist, Slavenka Drakulic, in *How We Survived Communism and Even Laughed* (1993), details the sense of awe many people living in the Eastern Bloc felt toward the free exchange of ideas and goods represented in Western popular culture. As a professional woman whose writings were routinely censored, she recounts the significance of having even limited access to American media:

> Fed up with advertising, a Western woman only browses through such magazines superficially, even with boredom. She has seen so much of it, has been bombarded by ads every single day of her life, on TV, in magazines, on huge billboards, at the movies. For us, the pictures in a magazine like *Vogue* were much more important: we studied their every detail with the interest of those who had no other source of information about the outside world. . . . Here, the images make you hate the reality you live in, because not only can you not buy any of the things pictured (even if you had the money, which you don't), but the paper itself, the quality of print, is unreachable. The images that cross the borders in magazines, movies, or videos are therefore more dangerous than any secret weapon, because they make one desire that "other-ness" badly enough to risk one's life by trying to escape. Many did.

> *Source:* Slavenka Drakulic, *How We Survived Communism and Even Laughed* (New York: HarperPerennial, 1993), 28–29.

People living in Eastern Bloc countries might have enjoyed a superior standard of living compared to previous generations, but most citizens did not look to their own history as the measure, but to the West and its cornucopia of consumer choices. To move in the direction of capitalist societies, as more of their people wished to do, communist leaders had little choice but to accommodate freer markets and private ownership, which undermined Soviet-style socialism at its core. Some reformers believed they could reinvigorate the socialist project with greater openness. But millions of people living under those stultifying regimes had little interest in "reforming" a system they saw as anachronistic and corrupt. By 1989, as events in East Germany showed, most people in these societies were ready to abandon postwar notions of socialism altogether.

The costs of the Afghan occupation only added to the economic hardships the Soviet Union was experiencing. The whole endeavor had become a testimony to the failures and vanity of the communist leadership. The war, along with the plummeting revenues from global oil sales, hit ordinary Russians hard and strained the Kremlin's ability to bankroll its clients from Poland to Cuba. The Soviet Union depended on oil exports for more than half of its yearly foreign exchange revenues. Economists figured that each time the world price of oil dropped by $1 per barrel it equaled a loss of about $500 million annually in hard currency going to Moscow. In 1986, when world oil prices fell precipitously it denied the Soviet Union badly needed funds and pushed it toward becoming what one American Russian specialist called an "economic halfway house."

Fewer than one in ten people in the Soviet Union had access to a private telephone, and the government strictly controlled typewriters and photocopiers because of their potential to distribute "subversive" materials. Yet by the mid-eighties, about a third of the population had access to audiocassette recorders as well as the means to press LP record albums. In the field of computer technology the Soviet government tried to play catch up by using KGB front companies to purchase computers on the world market. But these efforts were futile in keeping pace with the computer revolution in the United States and West Europe. By the middle of the decade, there were over 25 million microprocessors in the United States alone (and that number was about to soar), while in the Soviet Union there were less than 200,000.

Under Gorbachev, the state-run media system tolerated Western-style exposés to be printed in *Pravda*, the major daily newspaper, and even to be aired on state TV. Russian muckrakers eagerly tackled topics such as poverty, alcoholism, drug addiction, the rising number of abortions, and the war in Afghanistan. Gorbachev's reforms also relaxed restrictions on movies, books, and other literature that had been previously forbidden. By 1989, there were 90 million television sets in the Soviet Union and the authorities abided Russian-language translations of family TV shows from Britain and France. As VCRs and cassette players became ubiquitous in the West they made their way into Eastern Bloc countries where the pirating and black-market distribution of American movies and music became a cottage industry. Young Russian urbanites built their own counterculture and rock 'n' roll scenes. Ironically, it was the sons and daughters of Soviet apparatchiks who had the greatest access to the West and played an essential role in disseminating its influences. Their parents' invaluable technical work led to a higher level of tolerance toward the Western-leaning predilections of their children.

In the 18 months following the reunification of Germany the Soviet Union went through convulsive changes, including a failed coup attempt against Gorbachev, and the ultimate dissolution of the country into 15 independent republics. The senior American diplomat, George Kennan, who had been the architect of U.S. "containment" policy, shared his astonishment at the sea changes he had witnessed: "Reviewing the history of international relations in the modern era," he wrote in 1995, "I find it hard to think of any event more strange and startling—and at first glance more inexplicable—than the sudden and total disintegration and disappearance from the international scene . . . of the great power known successively as the Russian Empire and then the Soviet Union."

Gorbachev's moratorium on nuclear testing, along with his scaling down of military aid to Soviet satellites and ending the Afghan War, oriented the U.S.S.R. away from direct military competition with the United States that had characterized previous decades. Reagan's defense buildup, including the Strategic Defense Initiative (SDI), put added pressures on the Soviet Union's capacity to maintain the status quo in the superpower rivalry. The first Polish pope gave Catholics under Soviet rule fortitude in standing up to the regimes. And Deng Xiaoping's market reforms in China showed that a communist state could adjust to changing global realities. There was no single "cause" for the collapse of Soviet communism in the late-1980s and early-1990s (especially those emanating *outside* of the Soviet Union and the Eastern Bloc). But the attractive power of Western technology and consumer culture; the falling price of oil; Gorbachev's restructuring; the social movements in Warsaw Pact countries; and the general lack of belief in state socialism among the people living under those regimes, all played their roles in pulling down the "iron curtain" that separated East and West, which British Prime Minister Winston Churchill had identified back in 1946.

THE WAR ON DRUGS

In the United States, as Cold War tensions ebbed and the nation breathed a collective sigh of relief after 40 years of "containing" international communism, a new "threat" to U.S. "national security" arose, this time in the form of the sale and use of illicit drugs. The "drug war" became boilerplate for Democratic and Republican politicians as they tried to outdo each other in passing stricter anti-drug laws such as mandatory sentencing guidelines that tied the hands of judges and granted greater power to prosecutors.

Despite the increasingly alarmist rhetoric attached to drug use, throughout the eighties there had been a kind of glamour associated with certain drugs. Powder cocaine, for example, largely because of its expense and cache among affluent young people, became the status drug of the decade, as rock stars, actors, and comedians were known to use it. The Hollywood movie *Scarface* (1983), directed by Brian De Palma with a screenplay by Oliver Stone, portrayed Miami, Florida as the nation's epicenter for cocaine-based gangsterism and sketched out the political economy of the drug world. Television mirrored this glorified drug imagery with NBC's popular cop show, *Miami Vice* (1984–89), which also chronicled the flashy underbelly of the cocaine world along with its ties to Latin America.

By the summer of 1986, news accounts were flooding the airwaves and print media about a new drug called crack cocaine. In June 1986, *Newsweek* proclaimed the crack "epidemic" to be the biggest story since Watergate, and two months later *Time* called crack "the issue of the year." Television news shows broadcast numerous segments about drugs, the majority of them following the twists and turns of the crack saga. Over the course of a year, *The Washington Post* ran 1,565 stories covering various aspects of the drug problem, leading the paper's ombudsmen later to concede that the paper had lost "a proper sense of perspective." When two promising young athletes—Len Bias and Don Rogers—died of cocaine abuse, countless news commentators joined politicians in the outcry for "tougher" drug laws.

In this context of lurid media descriptions about the damaging societal effects of drug use the Congress passed the Anti-Drug Abuse Act of 1986. It freed up the U.S. military to pursue narcotics control operations, enacted capital punishment for some drug-related crimes, loosened the evidentiary requirements in drug trials, and imposed mandatory minimum sentences for the distribution of cocaine. Federal prison sentences for first-time drug offenders shot up to five-to-ten years and there were more severe penalties for selling crack cocaine than powder. Since it was more likely that blacks would be convicted for possessing crack than whites, it set in motion sentencing guidelines that were demonstrably discriminatory. Leaders of the Congressional Black Caucus (CBC) and civil rights organizations were torn between those who believed the penalties were necessary to protect vulnerable black communities, and those who felt the law disproportionately victimized African Americans. In the end, only six members of the CBC voted against the legislation, which passed in the House by a vote of 341 to 11, a testament to the bipartisan consensus on drug policy.

As the election year 1988 unfolded, politicians in Washington pumped up the volume on the drug problem and passed a spate of amendments to federal drug laws that defined new penalties. Public housing officials tied to the Housing and Urban Development department (HUD) and other federal agencies were mandated to evict any tenant remotely connected to a drug crime. The new federal codes also barred people who were convicted of a drug felony from ever qualifying for a student loan; called for wider use of the death penalty in drug cases; and set a five-year minimum prison sentence for possessing cocaine base (with or without the intent to sell). Law enforcement authorities now had the power to seize the property of small-time dealers through "forfeiture" provisions without having to go to court. In addition, the revised drug bill inaugurated a cabinet-level director of the Office of National Drug Control Policy, (which the press dubbed the "Drug Czar"), charged with coordinating federal law enforcement efforts with the Department of Defense and intelligence agencies. President George H.W. Bush, who called drug use "the most pressing problem facing the nation," appointed William Bennett (Reagan's former Education Secretary) to the post. When a 17-year-old high school student was arrested for selling crack in Lafayette Park across from the White House, the case became fodder for political campaigns.

States and municipalities followed the federal government's lead and enacted their own minimum sentencing laws and ordinances for drug crimes. In New York City, for example, narcotics convictions shot up from 7,201 in 1980 to 34,366 in 1988. In California there was an average of 300 new prisoners locked up each week as the total inmate population jumped from 22,000 in 1980 to 97,309 in 1990. After spending $3.3 billion on a prison-construction boom, California still closed the decade with its correctional system stuffed to 180 percent of its capacity. Nationally, between 1985 and 1990, the number of people incarcerated doubled from approximately 500,000 to over a million, and in 1990 the prisons in every state in the Union (save Kansas) were filled above capacity or at court-ordered maximums. Longer prison sentences for crack abusers affected African Americans disproportionately while white middle-class users of powder cocaine received lighter sentences even when caught with the same amount of the narcotic.

Midway into President Bush's term the Sentencing Project, a Washington, DC-based organization that advocates non-punitive drug policies, reported that the number of people behind bars in the United States for drug offenses was unprecedented, and that an astounding one-fourth of young black men were under some form of control of the criminal justice system. Yet despite the incarceration rate and the new federal, state, and municipal laws and ordinances drug use in America continued to rise. One unfortunate by-product of the 1988 election's obsession with the Willie Horton recidivism case was that it opened up to ridicule government-run rehabilitation programs. Rehabilitation efforts were now widely seen as tantamount to coddling criminals (even though they are generally less costly to taxpayers), and politicians did not dare open themselves up to the charge of being "soft" on crime.

In December 1988, a subcommittee of the U.S. Senate Foreign Relations Committee, (the Subcommittee on Terrorism, Narcotics and International Operations), published a report titled "Drugs, Law Enforcement and Foreign Policy." The committee's lengthy document, largely ignored by the press, examined some of the more complicated aspects of the international drug trade and the flow of drugs into the United States. It also cites Lt. Colonel Oliver North's own heavily redacted notebook entries that allude to his suspicions that people connected to the Nicaraguan contras were engaged in drug trafficking. An appendix to the report, "Narcotics and the North Notebooks," points to evidence that some planes used to re-supply the contras (which were cleared from going through normal U.S. Customs) also carried cocaine, and that drug money might have been funneled back into the operation. North's notebooks also show that on September 22, 1986 he met in a London hotel with the Panamanian dictator, General Manuel Antonio Noriega, to co-ordinate their activities in arming the contras. North shared his idea with National Security Adviser John Poindexter of using "Project Democracy" funds, raised from the secret U.S. arms sales to Iran, to pay Noriega for his services.

THE U.S. INVASION OF PANAMA

A week after jubilant crowds had torn down the Berlin Wall, in El Salvador there was a massacre that reminded the world that Eastern Bloc nations did not have a monopoly on egregious human rights abuses. In the United States, people active in the movement to end American aid to the Salvadoran government, most notably the Committee in Solidarity with the People of El Salvador (CISPES) and their allies among Catholic organizations, were jolted by the murders of six prominent Jesuit priests at the University of Central America in San Salvador. Included among them was Father Ignacio Ellacuría, the Spanish-born rector of the university, their housekeeper, Elba Ramos, and her 16-year-old daughter. Each victim was marched into a back garden, ordered to lie face down, and shot in the back of the head. Father Ellacuría was a theologian and intellectual the Far Right in El Salvador despised for trying to broker a peace settlement between the government and the Faribundo Marti National Liberation Front (FMLN). Members of a Salvadoran Army unit, including an officer who later became El Salvador's defense minister, covered up the military's role. They had targeted the educators because of their criticism of the security services. Some of the soldiers had attended the U.S. Army School of the Americas (SOA) at Fort Benning, Georgia (now renamed the "Western Hemisphere Institute for Security Cooperation"). The atrocity touched off a long-standing, largely Catholic protest movement, "SOA Watch," which organized annual vigils and demonstrations at Fort Benning each November commemorating the 1989 killings.

In Panama, General Manuel Antonio Noriega's ties to the United States dated back to the mid-1960s when as a young officer he received training in military intelligence at the SOA. Over the years Noriega had become a valued U.S. "asset" who helped secure the Canal Zone from the subversion spreading throughout Central America. In 1969, after then Captain Noriega affirmed his loyalty to General Omar Torrijos by thwarting a coup attempt, Torrijos appointed him head of the country's "G-2" intelligence service. From that powerful post Noriega built up the Guardia Nacional into a ruthless internal security service. Noriega loathed the Sandinistas and his willingness to do anything to destroy the rising power of leftist guerrillas in Central America made him a useful backer of the contras. The CIA had paid him at least $365,000 for his assistance, and some reports put the amount as high as $200,000 a year.

In 1981, when General Torrijos, with whom President Carter had negotiated the Panama Canal Treaty, was killed in a plane crash it paved the way for Noriega to consolidate power. (The treaty with Torrijos stipulated that the canal would be transferred to Panamanian sovereignty at the close of 1999.) Noriega's ties to CIA Director William Casey strengthened his political position inside Panama as a favored U.S. ally in the war against the Sandinistas. Between 1981 and 1986, Noriega's government served as a conduit for U.S. money and arms going to the contras and also yielded airfields and logistical support.

However, by the time George H. W. Bush was sworn in as president Noriega had already become an embarrassment, especially after a federal court in Florida indicted him for drug trafficking and money laundering. The February 1988 indictment linked Noriega to the infamous Medellín drug cartel of Columbia. (A widely-circulated 1976 photo of the then Colonel Noriega meeting with George H. W. Bush when he was CIA Director added to the president's chagrin.) Noriega had been well-trained in the techniques of surveillance and intelligence and he used these skills to counter internal machinations against him. He was also good at rigging elections. Reagan and Bush, both critics of the Panama Canal Treaty, approved intelligence operations to oust Noriega, which included an October 1989 coup attempt that Noriega foiled. Democrats and Republicans alike pressed the Bush administration to be more aggressive in overthrowing the Panamanian strongman. Congress voted for economic sanctions against the regime, which appeared to be going down the same path as Jean-Claude "Baby Doc" Duvalier in Haiti and Ferdinand Marcos in the Philippines, where formerly trusted anti-communist allies were ousted from power after they had become liabilities.

On December 20, 1989, President Bush ordered into Panama 27,500 American troops, along with 300 aircraft (including advanced fighter jets). The stated goals of "Operation Just Cause" were to protect the Canal Zone and Americans living in Panama, stop the drug traffic flowing through the isthmus, and arrest General Noriega. The superior American forces quickly overwhelmed the segment of the Panamanian Defense Forces (PDF) that remained loyal to Noriega. In Panama City and in Colon, U.S. troops blasted away at targets that served Noriega's command and communications structure. When U.S. Marines attacked the Commandancia (Noriega's headquarters), the fighting spilled over into the neighborhoods of El Chorrillo where the United States unloaded with "smart bombs" and other explosives. The battles destroyed some apartment buildings and El Chorrillo was where most of the civilian casualties occurred. Within a week of the start of the invasion, Physicians for Human Rights estimated that 300 civilians had been killed and another 15,000 were made homeless. Looting broke out in parts of Panama City enjoining the Americans to divert resources to securing the capital.

The Pentagon skillfully managed the news media for "Operation Just Cause" as it had done with great success during the October 1983 invasion of Grenada. Access to the combat zones was strictly limited as journalists were again amassed in "pools" highly dependent upon Department of Defense briefings. American authorities disseminated a barrage of damaging information about Noriega's "fascination with witchcraft" and "black magic," as well as his sexual proclivities with his mistress. The colorful descriptions of Noriega's private life, which one anonymous U.S. official called "kinky," added to the stories about his brutal treatment of rivals and his links to the Columbian drug cartels. This elaborate and titillating narrative took the limelight away from Noriega's earlier training in U.S. military schools and his former ties to the CIA that had enabled his rise to power in the first place.

From the early morning hours of December 20, when the invasion began, until Christmas Eve, Noriega had eluded his would-be captors among the American Special Forces. They conducted over forty operations across Panama, many of them simultaneously, with the goal of apprehending Noriega, but each time they came up empty. Finally, early Christmas morning, Noriega arranged for asylum in the Vatican Embassy at Punta Paitilla in Panama City. The papal nuncio, Monsignor Jose Sebastian Laboa (Pope John Paul II's emissary in Panama), found himself in the unenviable position of harboring a wanted felon with a $1 million bounty on his head as U.S. military forces surrounded the embassy. Secretary of Defense Dick Cheney, who arrived in Panama to spend Christmas with the American soldiers, told reporters that he was "delighted that General Noriega has finally been run to ground. I think it's clear at this point," he said, "that the Panamanian people have no use for him, that he had to take sanctuary in a foreign embassy."

What followed was a series of negotiations between U.S. officials and the papal nuncio to persuade church officials to hand over Noriega. The Bush administration wanted

Noriega extradited to Florida to stand trial. Secretary of State James Baker III wrote a letter to the Vatican arguing that Noriega's alleged involvement in drug dealing and murder meant that he didn't meet the Roman Catholic Church's moral standards for asylum. To push the process along American military officers tried out some new psychological warfare or "psy-war" techniques, which involved setting up in front of the embassy a sound system capable of filling an arena and blaring ear-splitting rock 'n' roll and tape-loops of annoying noises to try to flush Noriega out. Klieg lights glared at the facade of the building at night while the loudspeakers crushed the nunciature with sound. Among the songs played were "No Place to Hide," "Voodoo Chile," and "You're No Good." A crowd of Panamanians gathered outside each day to chant their ridicule of Noriega. American soldiers also shot out a garden light at the compound and harassed Monsignor Laboa every time he came and went. The Vatican officials who lived and worked in the embassy pleaded with the United States to cease the racket so that they could get some sleep (they claimed the noise was having little effect on Noriega). Pope John Paul II expressed his strong disapproval of the U.S. military's heavy-handed "psy-war" tactics outside his embassy and after about a week the audio assault ceased.

Monsignor Laboa meanwhile tried to reason with Noriega telling him that he could not escape the Americans by remaining locked up indefinitely inside the nunciature. Noriega realized that if he tried to flee his life would be in danger, and surrendering to the Americans started to look like a more desirable option. He tried to retain a semblance of dignity by demanding that he wear his PDF uniform as a condition for turning himself in to U.S. authorities. After an 11-day standoff, on January 3, 1990, a shackled and defeated Noriega submissively boarded an American military plane that took off for Homestead Air Force Base outside of Miami. He would stand trial in the United States. At the time of his arrest it was reported that Noriega had stashed away inside a filing cabinet at his home $5.8 million in denominations of 10s, 20s, 50s, and 100s; U.S. officials confiscated the cash during the invasion.

After being tried and convicted of drug smuggling, as part of a twelve-count racketeering indictment, Noriega was sentenced to forty-years in prison. The lengthy prison term was important for the Bush administration. The loss of 23 American lives, with 300 wounded, along with 600 Panamanians killed and $2 billion in economic damage would have been hard to justify had Noriega won asylum in a third country. Like the Grenada invasion six years earlier, the American people rallied around the president. Lee Atwater, the chair of the Republican National Committee, called the successful outcome of the invasion a "political jackpot" for Bush.

American and international diplomats oversaw elections in Panama that brought to power a civilian government headed by President Guillermo Endara. A significant amount of the U.S. aid President Bush had promised the new Panamanian government failed to materialize after the appropriations request became bogged down in Congress. In November 1990, a few weeks before the first anniversary of the invasion, the Endara government still had such a tenuous grasp on power that it had to call in the U.S. military to help put down a rebellion by police officers who were protesting their working conditions and low pay. The television footage of American soldiers pointing their rifles at Panamanian police as they lay on the ground with their hands behind their heads were evocative of scenes from the intervention a year earlier.

Throughout the 1980s, the Reagan administration and its allies in Congress had argued that the contra war in Nicaragua, the U.S. military aid to El Salvador and Honduras, and the invasion of Grenada, were all vital steps in countering Soviet power in the region. President Reagan had painted a dire picture of the threat: "Using Nicaragua as a base, the Soviets and Cubans, can become the dominant power in the crucial corridor between North and South America. Established there, they will be in a position to threaten the Panama Canal, interdict our vital Caribbean Sea lanes, and, ultimately, move against Mexico." In one of his State of the Union addresses, Reagan called Nicaragua a "Soviet ally on the American mainland" and asked: "Could there be any greater tragedy than for us to sit back and permit this cancer to spread?" Senator Jesse Helms, who chaired the Foreign Relations Committee until January 1987, expressed his fears about a possible Russian take over of Mexico where millions of "foot people" would flood across the border.

Going back to the nineteenth century, Central America and the Caribbean had been seen as the United States' "backyard." In the 1850s, the American freebooter, William Walker, "the grey-eyed man of destiny," had inserted himself briefly as the dictator of Nicaragua. The Spanish-American War of 1898 secured U.S. dominance of Cuba and Puerto Rico, and in 1903, Panama became a de facto U.S. protectorate after President Theodore Roosevelt seized the country "and let Congress debate." The "Roosevelt Corollary" to the Monroe Doctrine institutionalized U.S. military power in the region; and President William Taft's "Dollar Diplomacy" sealed its finances in the hands of U.S. investors. President Woodrow Wilson's 1915 invasion of Haiti set the stage for a string of pro-U.S. governments there. Major General Smedley Butler described his role in this aggressive U.S. policy in his famous essay *War Is a Racket* (1935). Historians have noted dozens of U.S. military interventions in Central America and the Caribbean long before the Russian Revolution of 1917. But in the years following the Cuban uprising that swept Fidel Castro into power in January 1959 the stated purpose of U.S. policy—from the Bay of Pigs and the 1965 invasion of the Dominican Republic to the contra war and the intervention in Grenada—had been justified to "contain" or "roll back" Soviet influence.

But President Bush's December 1989 invasion of Panama, like during the nineteenth and early twentieth centuries, demonstrated that the United States would not hesitate to protect its interests in its "backyard" with or without the justification of fighting international communism. The drug war accommodated a new rationale well-suited for the post–Cold War environment. The Panama invasion, as part of this emphasis on combating drugs, occurred at a time when U.S. policymakers were searching for a post–Cold War paradigm for applying the tenets of American global power. The "New World Order" of 1989 to 1990, at least in Central America, looked a lot like the older world order where U.S. military imperatives would be decisive with or without a Soviet menace in the hemisphere.

REVIEW QUESTIONS

1. What lessons can be learned from the Savings and Loan scandal of the late-1980s? What role did deregulation play in fomenting the crisis? Why were American taxpayers saddled with paying for the bailout of the S&L industry? Could the debacle have been avoided? Why or why not?
2. What important political innovations took place during the 1988 presidential campaign that have influenced the way subsequent elections have been run? Why did Vice President George Herbert Walker Bush feel it necessary to make the call for a "kinder" and "gentler" America a central theme of his campaign?

3. What was the chain of events in the late-1980s that led to the destabilization of the totalitarian regimes of East Europe? What was the role of "people power" in beginning the process of dismantling East German Communism? Why did the Berlin Wall come down in November 1989? Did the events in East Europe catch the administration of George H.W. Bush by surprise?

4. What were some of the sociological, technological, cultural, and economic forces at work that contributed to the sweeping changes inside the Soviet Union and its satellites in the late-1980s? What role did Mikhail Gorbachev and his reforms of *perestroika* and *glasnost* play? What are some of the myths often associated with the end of the Cold War?

5. What does the U.S. invasion of Panama in December 1989 tell us about the "new world order" that was developing as the Cold War was receding? What does "Operation Just Cause" have in common with U.S. military interventions in Central America that took place earlier in the 20th century? What was the justification for overthrowing a government that had been a staunch U.S. ally in the fight against the spread of Soviet Communism in Central America?

---

mysearchlab CONNECTIONS SOURCES ONLINE

READ AND REVIEW

Review this chapter by using the study aids and these related documents available on MySearchLab.

Study Plan
Chapter Test
Essay Test

Documents
Ronald Reagan, Speech at the Brandenburg Gate (1987)
Reagan summarizes his administration's policies on nuclear weapons in Europe and on the changes that were slowly emerging in the Soviet Union.

Vice President George Herbert Walker Bush, Acceptance Speech (1988)
Bush's acceptance speech at the Republican National Convention in New Orleans.

RESEARCH AND EXPLORE

Use the databases available within MySearchLab to find additional primary and secondary sources the topics within this chapter.

Map Discovery
Events in Eastern Europe, 1989–1990

Video
Ronald Reagan at the Berlin Wall
The Collapse of the Communist Bloc
George Bush Presidential Campaign Ad: The Revolving Door

Legacies of the Eighties

In 1982, when the Equal Rights Amendment (ERA) failed to win enough states for ratification it telegraphed a shift in the national discourse away from the priorities of the women's movement of the previous decade. The antiabortion activism targeting women's health clinics that began in earnest with Operation Rescue, and worked in concert with other "pro-life" groups, also pulled the debate on reproductive choice away from the tenuous consensus of *Roe v. Wade*. Women's organizations responded by utilizing Political Action Committees (PACs), direct mail operations, and mobilizing large demonstrations in support of reproductive rights. The National Organization for Women, the National Abortion Rights Action League (NARAL), the National Women's Political Caucus, and Emily's List (established in 1985), all became adept at lobbying for women's interests in Washington and in the states. By the early 1990s, women in the House of Representatives more than doubled, going from 21 to 48; and the number of female state legislators increased from 800 to 1,270.

President Reagan appointed the first woman to the Supreme Court, Sandra Day O'Connor, and Representative Geraldine Ferraro became the first woman to be nominated on the presidential ticket of a major American political party. After 1984, however, neither party would nominate a woman over the next five presidential elections. In later decades, there was the first woman secretary of state, Madeleine Albright, and the first woman speaker of the House, Nancy Pelosi (Democrat of California). The Supreme Court's 2009 ruling that struck down a sex discrimination case against Goodyear Corporation illustrated that the fight for pay equity has continued since the 1980s. The Court's decision prompted Congress to pass, and President Barack Obama to sign into law, the Lilly Ledbetter Fair Pay Act, which removed the statute of limitations on sex discrimination lawsuits. In 2011, when the House voted to zero-out the budget for Planned Parenthood it signaled that women's reproductive rights remain, as they were in the 1980s, contested territory.

The mobilization of the lesbian, gay, bisexual, and transgendered (LGBT) community to combat the spread of HIV/AIDS in the 1980s went a long way toward changing the tenor of the public's perception of gay rights. Gay activists succeeded in countering the antigay bigotry that had overshadowed much of the mainstream discussion of AIDS and the pressure on pharmaceutical companies and research institutes to find a cure bore fruit (even spinning off a number of antiviral drugs that have applications beyond HIV). Over the next 20 years, AIDS was no longer a death sentence but could be managed through drug therapy. The recurring instances of violence against gay people, exemplified by the 1998 killing of Matthew Shepard outside Laramie, Wyoming, tragically confirmed that the gay rights movement still had a long way to go. After Shepard's murder, advocates of gay rights tapped the organizational infrastructure that arose during the height of the AIDS epidemic to lobby for hate crime legislation. In recent years, new battles over marriage equality and legal safeguards against discrimination in the workplace have taken center stage where AIDS activism once stood.

The early 1980s saw an unraveling of the consensus on protecting the environment of the Nixon, Ford, and Carter years. Federal agencies charged with regulating corporate polluters, most notably the Environmental Protection Agency (EPA), which business grudgingly accepted but the public believed was vital to the nation's health, came under systematic political and budgetary assault. Early in Reagan's presidency, the misdeeds of some of his industry-friendly appointees at the EPA provoked Congress to step in. Had Reagan simply sustained the status quo on the environment (even half-heartedly) he could have avoided what became the biggest domestic scandal of his first term. After years of drift and deferring to Congress leadership on environmental issues, the March 1989 Exxon Valdez oil spill awakened the nation once again to the importance of enforcing strict environmental protocols.

In 1982, Secretary of the Interior James G. Watt established the Mineral Management Service (MMS) by secretarial order. Over the years the MMS, which was in charge of collecting royalties from oil and mining companies as well as enforcing regulations, routinely used wording and policy guidelines drawn up by the American Petroleum Institute, the oil industry trade group, for its own rules governing oil and gas extraction. On Earth Day 2010, when British Petroleum's Macondo oil well blew out in the Gulf of Mexico causing the biggest oil spill in U.S. history the legacy of the 1980s loomed large. Congressional investigators and the Department of Interior found that lax regulation on the part of MMS had been largely responsible for the oil spill. Since the 1980s, environmentalists have fought to protect old-growth forests, demanded safeguards for endangered species in "free trade" agreements, and lobbied for higher fuel efficiency standards for cars and trucks, as well as have been in the forefront in pressing for policies to address the problem of global climate change.

President Reagan's decision to match the Soviet Union's SS-20 medium-range nuclear missiles that targeted NATO countries with the U.S.'s own Pershing IIs put Europe on a hair trigger. The heightened nuclear tensions spurred protests on both sides of the Atlantic. In June 1982, one of the largest demonstrations in American history took place in New York City's Central Park calling for a freeze on the testing, production, and deployment of nuclear weapons. Later, when India, Pakistan, Israel, and North Korea joined the nuclear club every president since Reagan has claimed nuclear nonproliferation as a top U.S. priority. The 1986 Chernobyl reactor meltdown called into question the safety of nuclear power, and in the years since, despite constant industry pressure, there have been few new nuclear power plants built in the United States. The 2011 tsunami-induced nuclear disaster at Japan's Fukushima Daiichi reactor was widely compared to Chernobyl and reopened the debate on whether nuclear power's benefits outweigh its potentially devastating environmental costs.

Reagan's brand of conservatism fused an ebullient celebration of free markets and conspicuous consumption with a social agenda that (on the surface at least) appeared to further the goals of social conservatives. Sometimes the *laissez-faire* proclivities of his administration contradicted the Religious Right's desire for a return to more whole-some "family values." Nowhere did this tension play out more fully than in the arena of popular culture. While Washington politicians exulted in free enterprise, there was also an effort to control the content of the entertainment industry (including music lyrics, pornography, movies, and the arts). The mass marketing of VCRs and cable television (especially MTV) exploded at a time when the inconclusive "culture wars" were being fully enjoined. The "culture wars" have become a recurring phenomenon in American politics, especially during election cycles and in the partisan hothouse of Washington. In the 1990s, President Bill Clinton was often maligned for participating as a college student in anti-Vietnam War protests and his political opponents tried to yoke him to the more polarizing countercultural "excesses" of the 1960s. Jesse Jackson's two presidential campaigns in 1984 and 1988, along with the "Rainbow Coalition" and his community organizing in the city of Chicago, opened the door for future black candidates. Yet in 2008, the election of the first African-American president unleashed a flood of attacks painting him as being somehow culturally "foreign" if not "un-American." The nation's first black president was subjected to barbs and criticism similar to those leveled at "multicultural-ism" 30 years earlier.

From the time of the assassination attempt in March 1981 Reagan enjoyed a largely compliant press. The Washington press corps seemed content to cast him as the "Teflon president," while Beltway journalists played catch up to the White House's communications machine. At the dawn of the 24-hour news cycle, Reagan's public relations specialists brought the "bully pulpit" into the modern media age. They looked after the tiniest details of the president's public appearances with a keen eye not only to an event's stated purpose, but also to its optics and atmospherics. Through stage-managed events they could construct politically advantageous narratives that went beyond the rhetoric. Presidents since then have used similar media management techniques, but often with less satisfactory results.

The Democratic Party establishment in Washington DC of the 1980s had cultivated ties to many of the same corporate special interests that also financed the Grand Old Party (GOP). Democratic strategists believed that by lurching rightward they could stay on the good side of Reagan's personal popularity (and his nationwide constituency). This stance is understandable given the historic shellacking the Democrats took in the 1984 election. Even when congressional Democrats seemed to have the upper hand, such as during the Iran-contra scandal, they rarely pressed their advantage. This dynamic between America's two dominant political parties has had a long life.

Both Presidents Reagan and Bush could count on a significant number of congressional Democrats to cross party lines and vote for key elements of their agendas. The tax cuts for high earners and corporations, deregulation, the military build up, aid to the Nicaraguan contras and the Afghan Mujahideen, the invasions of Grenada and Panama, drug policy, and even the "culture wars," all had substantial Democratic support. Forty-eight House Democrats voted for Reagan's sweeping Economic Recovery Tax Act (ERTA) of 1981; a Democratic Representative coauthored the bill that deregulated the Savings and Loan (S&L) industry (with catastrophic results); and a Democrat was a driving personality in Congress behind arming the Mujahideen in Afghanistan. Of the five senators who were part of the S&L influence-peddling scheme known as the "Keating Five," four were Democrats. Ironically, at the moment a sizeable *bloc* of Democratic legislators in

Washington were accommodating the prerogatives of the Republican administrations, GOP strategists were doing everything in their power to portray them as radical left-wingers outside the American mainstream. This political dynamic has also played out in the decades since.

Reagan had spent nearly his entire public career alerting Americans to the dangers of Soviet communism, and he was successful at using the Cold War to gain the upper hand against his political opponents. He insisted that the military buildup and the arming of the Nicaraguan contras and Afghan Mujahideen were necessary steps in rolling back Soviet influence. In early 1985, after Mikhail Gorbachev came to power in the Soviet Union there was an opportunity for a new beginning in U.S.-Soviet relations. When Gorbachev announced a unilateral moratorium on nuclear testing and asked the United States to join in, it impeded efforts to stoke the Cold War. Even when the U.S. and U.S.S.R. were still at loggerheads over key components of the nuclear arms race, marked by the deadlocked summit at Reykjavik, Gorbachev's persistence in resetting relations with the United States, and the popular backing he earned from people living in NATO countries, made it more difficult for Reagan to keep up the level of anti-Soviet rhetoric of his first term. In West Europe, the popularity of Gorbachev's reformist path gave impetus to a thaw in East-West relations. With regard to foreign policy, Reagan's presidency, therefore, can be evaluated in terms of "pre-Gorbachev" and "post-Gorbachev."

The Iran-contra revelations of November 1986 shattered the administration's credibility, and Reagan's approval rating plummeted a full 21 percentage points. The arms sales to Iran not only wounded the president domestically and obligated him to spend political capital managing the crisis, but they also undermined U.S. efforts to isolate Iran through banning international weapons sales to the Khomeini regime. The revelation of the secret Iranian arms transactions, which had all the hallmarks of an arms-for-hostages swap, caused rifts between the U.S. and NATO leaders whose nationals were also being held hostage in Lebanon. American foreign policy entered a protracted period of crisis, which meant that softening the attitude toward Gorbachev's overtures was a wise political move both at home and abroad. Reagan's presidency, therefore, might also be thought of in terms of "pre-Iran-contra" and "post-Iran-contra."

The successful negotiation of the Intermediate-Range Nuclear Force Treaty (INF Treaty) in December 1987, which for the first time eliminated a category of nuclear weapons, won overwhelming approval from the populations of the United States and Europe. The INF Treaty went a long way in helping Reagan mend fences with America's NATO allies and to regain his political bearings at home. During his final year in office Reagan's popularity shot back up not because he stubbornly adhered to right-wing ideology, but because he was far more conciliatory on both the domestic and diplomatic fronts.

With the fall of the Eastern Bloc and the U.S.S.R. in the early 1990s, there was a period of drift in U.S. foreign policy. Many theorists seized upon the end of the Cold War to declare it an unmitigated triumph for Western capitalist democracy. There was talk of "the end of history" and a "new American century" with the United States bestriding a "unipolar" world. But the U.S. global military posture to counter Soviet power was replaced with a messier multipolar era of "globalization." During the presidency of George Herbert Walker Bush, the idea of a "peace dividend" surfaced where the United States might be able to divert tax dollars previously earmarked for defense to neglected domestic needs, such as health care, education, and infrastructure. The December 1989 invasion of Panama, where the United States ousted a former anti-Soviet ally, marked a significant departure from earlier justifications for the use of American military power. Later, when international terrorism replaced the U.S.S.R. as the major threat to U.S. national security, politicians from both parties no longer talked about "peace dividends" and Pentagon spending was maintained at Cold War levels.

In the 1990s, President Bill Clinton adopted many of the public policies associated with the Reagan era, such as welfare "reform," deregulation, "free trade" agreements, and a near total lack of interest in enforcing antitrust laws (even in telecommunications, pharmaceuticals, and energy). The PAC system of financing campaigns metastasized in subsequent decades to the point where it would embarrass most 1980s politicians, and Congress and the courts have derailed attempts at strengthening campaign finance laws.

The insider trading scandals that sent some of the most celebrated personalities on Wall Street to prison, the stock market crash of October 1987, and the collapse of the S&L industry, all pointed to the downside of the freewheeling capitalist ethos of the 1980s. However, the S&L crisis, even with its $300 billion taxpayer bailout, did not dissuade politicians in later years from pushing through even more far-reaching legislation deregulating the financial sector. When a Democratic president and a Republican Congress passed the Financial Services Modernization Act of 1999 and the Commodity Futures Modernization Act of 2000, Washington politicians seemed to be taking a trip "back to the future." Reagan's chair of the Federal Reserve, Alan Greenspan, who served until 2006, assured Congress that these new deregulation laws were necessary to free big banks from the antiquated rules left over from the 1930s.

Like the Garn-St. Germain Act of 1982 that deregulated the S&Ls, these laws laid the groundwork for a speculative housing bubble and a massive taxpayer bailout after the bubble burst. The second time around, however, at stake was not only the solvency of 1,000 S&Ls and a few regional real estate markets, but also the overall health of the U.S. economy. After the mortgage meltdown of 2008, the United States endured high unemployment, a moribund construction sector, constricted consumer demand, and huge budget deficits at the federal, state, and local levels. The austerity budgets and wholesale denuding of the public sector in the wake of the crisis promise to have unpredictable effects on civil society in the United States well into the twenty-first century.

If opinion polls can be trusted most Americans today are just as cynical about the role of government in society (if not more so) as they were in the 1980s. Tax cuts for the wealthy and corporations, "free trade" agreements that have resulted in a net loss of American jobs, corporate and financial deregulation, cuts in social programs, the lack of enforcement of antitrust laws, expansive military expenditures, and so on, have continued from the Reagan-Bush years to the present. Wages have remained stagnant for most workers and the gap between the rich and the average American worker has grown to levels not seen since the Gilded Age of the 1890s. In the 30 years from 1980 to 2010, working people in the United States have become less secure economically, and this greater insecurity has affected their attitudes toward politics and government. This condition was not the product of uncontrollable market forces, but was the result of conscious policy choices that continue to flourish despite their often-demonstrable failures. In that sense, the legacy of the 1980s in America lives on.

mysearchlab CONNECTIONS SOURCES ONLINE

READ AND REVIEW

Review this chapter by using the study aids and these related documents available on MySearchLab.

Study Plan

Chapter Test

Essay Test

Documents

George H. W. Bush, Inaugural Address (1989)
Bush speaks about the goals of his presidency.

RESEARCH AND EXPLORE

Use the databases available within MySearchLab to find additional primary and secondary sources the topics within this chapter.

Video
President Bush on the Gulf War
Modernity's Pollution Problems

BIBLIOGRAPHY

Michelle Alexander, *The New Jim Crow: Mass Incarceration in the Age of Colorblindness* (New York: The New Press, 2010).

Martin Anderson and Annelise Anderson, *Reagan's Secret War: The Untold Story of His Fight to Save the World from Nuclear Disaster* (New York: Crown Publishers, 2009).

Carrie N. Baker, *The Women's Movement Against Sexual Harassment* (New York: Cambridge University Press, 2008).

Dean Baker, *The United States Since 1980* (New York: Cambridge University Press, 2007).

Letitia Baldrige, *Letitia Baldrige's Complete Guide to Executive Manners* (New York: Simon & Schuster, 1985).

Lucius Barker and Ronald Waters, eds., *Jesse Jackson's 1984 Presidential Campaign: Challenges and Change in American Politics* (Urbana, IL: University of Illinois Press, 1989).

Bob Batchelor and Scott Stoddart, *The 1980s, American Popular Culture through History* (Westport, CT: Greenwood Press, 2007).

Coral Bell, *The Reagan Paradox: U.S. Foreign Policy in the 1980s* (New Brunswick, NJ: Rutgers University Press, 1989).

Paul Berman, ed., *Debating P.C.: The Controversy over Political Correctness on College Campuses* (New York: Dell Publishing, 1992).

William K. Black, *The Best Way to Rob a Bank Is to Own One: How Corporate Executives and Politicians Looted the S&L Industry* (Austin: University of Texas Press, 2005).

Allan Bloom, *The Closing of the American Mind: How Higher Education Has Failed Democracy and Impoverished the Souls of Today's Students* (New York: Simon & Schuster, 1987).

Sidney Blumenthal, *Our Long National Daydream: A Political Pageant of the Reagan Era* (New York: Harpers & Row, 1988).

Richard Bolton, ed., *Culture Wars: Documents from the Recent Controversies in the Arts* (New York: The New Press, 1992).

Douglas Brinkley, ed., *The Reagan Diaries* (New York: Harper Perennial, 2007).

Cynthia Brown, ed., *With Friends Like These: The Americas Watch Report on Human Rights & U.S. Policy in Latin America* (New York: Pantheon, 1985).

Will Bunch, *Tear Down This Myth: How the Reagan Legacy Distorted Our Politics and Haunts Our Future* (New York: Free Press, 2009).

Martha Burt, *Over the Edge: The Growth of Homelessness in the 1980s* (New York: Russell Sage Foundation, 1992).

Lou Canon, *President Reagan: The Role of a Lifetime* (New York: Simon & Schuster, 1991).

David Colburn and Jeffrey Adler, eds., *African-American Mayors: Race, Politics, and the American City* (Urbana, IL: University of Illinois Press, 2001).

Steve Coll, *Ghost Wars: The Secret History of the CIA, Afghanistan, and Bin Laden, from the Soviet Invasion to September 10, 2001* (New York: Penguin, 2004).

Robert M. Collins, *Transforming America: Politics and Culture During the Reagan Years* (New York: Columbia University Press, 2007).

David Cortright, *Peace Works: The Citizens' Role in Ending the Cold War* (Boulder, CO: Westview Press, 1993).

Kevin Courrier, *Dangerous Kitchen: The Subversive World of Frank Zappa* (Toronto: ECW Press, 2002).

George Crile, *Charlie Wilson's War* (New York: Grove Press, 2003).

Donald T. Critchlow and Nancy MacLean, *Debating the American Conservative Movement: 1945 to the Present* (Lanham, Maryland: Rowman and Littlefield, 2009).

Mary Cross, *Madonna: A Biography* (Westport, CT: Greenwood Press, 2007).

Matthew Dallek, *The Right Moment: Ronald Reagan's First Victory and the Decisive Turning Point in American Politics* (New York: Free Press, 2000).

Mike Davis, *Reshaping the U.S. Left: Popular Struggles in the 1980s* (New York: Verso, 1988).

_____, *Buda's Wagon: A Brief History of the Car Bomb* (New York: Verso, 2007).

Thomas Donnelly et al., *Operation Just Cause: The Storming of Panama* (New York: Lexington Books, 1991).

Susan J. Douglas, "Letting the Boys Be Boys: Male Hysteria, and Political Discourse in the 1980s," in *Radio Reader: Essays in the Cultural History of Radio*, ed. Michele Hilmes et al. (New York: Routledge, 2002).

Marlene Dixon, ed., *On Trial: Reagan's War Against Nicaragua* (San Francisco: Synthesis Publications, 1985).

Douglas F. Dowd, *The Broken Promises of America* (Monroe, Maine: Common Courage Press, 2005).

Katherine Dudley, *The End of the Line: Lost Jobs, New Lives in Post-Industrial America* (Chicago: University of Chicago Press, 1994).

Peter Duignan and Alvin Rabushka, eds., *The United States in the 1980s* (Palo Alto, CA: Hoover Institution Publication, 1980).

Slavenka Drakulic, *How We Survived Communism and Even Laughed* (New York: HarperPerennial, 1993).

Barbara Ehrenreich, *The Worst Years of Our Lives: Irreverent Notes from a Decade of Greed* (New York: Pantheon, 1991).

John Ehrman, *The Eighties: America in the Age of Reagan* (New Haven: Yale University Press, 2005).

John Ehrman and Michael W. Flamm, *Debating the Reagan Presidency* (New York: Roman and Littlefield, 2009).

Bret Easton Ellis, *American Psycho* (New York: Vintage Books, 1991).

Barbara Epstein, *Political Protest and Cultural Revolution: Nonviolent Direct Actions in the 1970s and 1980s* (Berkeley, California: University of California Press, 1991).

Sara Evans, *Tidal Wave: How Women Changed America at Century's End* (New York: Free Press, 2003).

Susan Faludi, *Backlash: The Undeclared War Against American Women* (New York: Crown, 1991).

Geraldine Ferraro, *Ferraro: My Story* (New York: Bantam Books, 1985).

Robert Fisk, *Pity the Nation: The Abduction of Lebanon* (New York: Nation Books, 2002).

Frances Fitzgerald, *Way Out There in the Blue: Reagan, Star Wars, and the End of the Cold War* (New York: Simon & Schuster, 2000).

Steve Fraser and Gary Gerstle, *Ruling America: A History of Wealth and Power in a Democracy* (Cambridge, MA: Harvard University Press, 2005).

Jo Freeman and Victoria Johnson, eds., *Waves of Protest: Social Movements Since the Sixties* (Lanham, MD: Rowman and Littlefield, 1999).

Betty Friedan, *The Second Stage* (New York: Summit Books, 1981).

Francis Fukuyama, *The End of History and the Last Man* (New York: Avon Books, 1992).

John Lewis Gaddis, *The Cold War* (New York: Penguin, 2005).

Reebee Garofalo, *Rockin' Out: Popular Music in the U.S.A.*, 4th ed. (Upper Saddle River, NJ: Pearson Prentice Hall, 2008).

Nelson George, *Post-Soul Nation: The Explosive, Contradictory, Triumphant, and Tragic 1980s as Experienced by African Americans* (New York: Penguin, 2004).

James William Gibson, *Warrior Dreams: Paramilitary Culture in Post-Vietnam America* (New York: Hill and Wang, 1994).

George Gilder, *Wealth and Poverty* (New York: Basic Books, 1981).

Steven Gillon, *The Democrats' Dilemma: Walter F. Mondale and the Liberal Legacy* (New York: Columbia University Press, 1992).

Mikhail Gorbachev, *Memoirs* (New York: Doubleday, 1995).

Greg Grandin, *Empire's Workshop: Latin America, the United States, and the Rise of the New Imperialism* (New York: Henry Holt, 2006).

David Harris, *The Crisis: The President, the Prophet, and the Shah—1979 and the Coming of Militant Islam* (New York: Little, Brown, 2004).

Chris Hedges, *Death of the Liberal Class* (New York: Nation Books, 2010).

Mark Hertsgaard, *On Bended Knee: The Press and the Reagan Presidency* (New York: Schocken Books, 1989).

Phoebe Hoban, *Basquiat* (New York: Penguin, 1998).

Gregory Hodgson, *More Equal Than Others: America from Nixon to the New Century* (Princeton, NJ: Princeton University Press, 2004).

Erik P. Hoffmann, ed., *The Soviet Union in the 1980s* (Montpelier, VT: Capital City Press, 1984).

David E. Hoffman, *The Dead Hand: The Untold Story of the Cold War Arms Race and Its Dangerous Legacy* (New York: Doubleday, 2009).

Robert Hughes, *Culture of Complaint: The Fraying of America* (New York: Oxford University Press, 1993).

James Davison Hunter, *Culture Wars: The Struggle to Define America* (New York: Basic Books, 1991).

Susan Jeffords, *Hard Bodies: Hollywood Masculinity in the Reagan Era* (New Brunswick: Rutgers University Press, 1994).

Chalmers Johnson, *Dismantling the Empire: America's Last Best Hope* (New York: Henry Holt, 2008).

Haynes Johnson, *Sleepwalking through History: America in the Reagan Years* (New York: W. W. Norton, 1991).

Tony Judt, *Reappraisals: Reflections on the Forgotten Twentieth Century* (New York: Penguin Press, 2008).

_____, *Postwar: The History of Europe Since 1945* (New York: Penguin, 2005).

Herman Kahn, *Thinking About the Unthinkable in the 1980s* (New York: Simon & Schuster, 1984).

Robin D. G. Kelley, *Yo' Mama's DisFUNKtional! Fighting the Culture Wars in Urban America* (Boston: Beacon Press, 1997).

Barbara Kingsolver, *Holding the Line: Women in the Great Arizona Mine Strike of 1983* (Ithaca, NY: Cornell University Press, 1989).

William Kleinknecht, *The Man Who Sold the World: Ronald Reagan and the Betrayal of Main Street America* (New York: Perseus Books, 2009).

Stephen Kotkin, *Armageddon Averted: The Soviet Collapse 1970-2000* (New York: Oxford University Press, 2008).

Donald Kuspit, *Art in the 1980s: The New Subjectivism* (New York: Da Capo Press, 1993).

Walter LaFeber, *America, Russia, and the Cold War, 1945-2006*, 10th ed. (New York: McGraw Hill, 2008).

_____, *Inevitable Revolutions: The United States in Central America* (New York: W. W. Norton, 1984).

Saul Landau, *The Dangerous Doctrine: National Security and U.S. Foreign Policy* (Boulder, Colorado: Westview Press, 1988).

Derek Leebaert, *The Fifty-Year Wound: How America's Cold War Victory Shapes Our World* (New York: Little, Brown and Company, 2002).

William E. Leuchtenburg, *In the Shadow of FDR: From Harry Truman to George W. Bush* (Ithaca, NY: Cornell University Press, 2001).

Marilyn Loden, *Feminine Leadership: How to Succeed in Business Without Being One of the Boys* (New York: Times Books, 1985).

Dave Marsh, *Glory Days: Bruce Springsteen in the 1980s* (New York: Pantheon, 1987).

Bradford Martin, *The Other Eighties: A Secret History of America in the Age of Reagan* (New York: Hill and Wang, 2011).

Jane Mayer and Doyle McManus, *Landslide: The Unmaking of the President, 1984-1988* (Boston: Houghton Mifflin, 1988).

Douglas Massey and Nancy Denton, *American Apartheid: Segregation and the Making of the Underclass* (Cambridge, MA: Harvard University Press, 1993).

Constantine C. Menges, *Inside the National Security Council: The True Story of the Making and Unmaking of Reagan's Foreign Policy* (New York: Simon & Schuster, 1988).

Barry Miles, *Zappa: A Biography* (New York: Grove Press, 2004).

Bill Milkowski, *Jaco: The Extraordinary and Tragic Life of Jaco Pastorius* (San Francisco: Backbeat Books, 2005).

Nicolaus Mills, ed., *Culture in an Age of Money: The Legacy of the 1980s in America* (Chicago: Ivan R. Dee, 1990).

Charlene Mitchell and Thomas Burdick, *The Right Moves: Succeeding in a Man's World Without a Harvard MBA* (New York: Macmillan, 1985).

Lorenzo Morris, ed., *The Social and Political Implications of the 1984 Jesse Jackson Presidential Campaign* (New York: Praeger, 1990).

Jack Nelson-Pallmeyer, *School of Assassins* (New York: Orbis Books, 1997).

Sharon Erickson Nepstad, *Convictions of the Soul: Religion, Culture, and Agency in the Central America Solidarity Movement* (New York: Oxford University Press, 2004).

Riki Ott, *Not One Drop: Betrayal and Courage in the Wake of the Exxon Valdez Oil Spill* (White River Junction, VT: Chelsea Green Publishing, 2008).

William Pfaff, *The Irony of Manifest Destiny: The Tragedy of America's Foreign Policy* (New York: Walker & Company, 2010).

Christian Parenti, *Lockdown America: Police and Prisons in the Age of Crisis* (New York: Verso, 1999).

Michael Parenti, *Inventing Reality: The Politics of the Mass Media* (New York: St. Martin's Press, 1986).

—————, *The Sword and the Dollar: Imperialism, Revolution, and the Arms Race* (New York: St. Martin's Press, 1989).

James Patterson, *Restless Giant: The United States from Watergate to Bush v. Gore* (New York: Oxford University Press, 2005).

Rick Perlstein, *Nixonland: The Rise of a President and the Fracturing of America* (New York: Scribner, 2008).

Kevin Phillips, *Wealth and Democracy: A Political History of the American Rich* (New York: Broadway Books, 2002).

William R. Polk, *Violent Politics: A History of Insurgency, Terrorism and Guerrilla War, from the American Revolution to Iraq* (New York: HarperCollins, 2007).

Stephen Prince, ed., *America Cinema of the 1980s: Themes and Variations* (New Brunswick: Rutgers University Press, 2007).

—————, ed., *A New Pot of Gold: Hollywood Under the Electronic Rainbow, 1980-1989* (Berkeley, California: University of California Press, 2000).

Adolph L. Reed Jr., *The Jesse Jackson Phenomenon* (New Haven: Yale University Press, 1986).

—————, *Stirrings in the Jug: Black Politics in the Post-Segregation Era* (Minneapolis: University of Minnesota Press, 1999).

Mark Reid, ed., *Spike Lee's Do the Right Thing* (New York: Cambridge University Press, 1997).

Michael Rogin, *Ronald Reagan: The Movie* (Berkeley, California: University of California Press, 1987).

Tricia Rose, *Black Noise: Rap Music and Black Culture in Contemporary America* (Middletown, CT: Wesleyan University Press, 1994).

Richard E. Rubenstein, *Reasons to Kill: Why Americans Choose War* (New York: Bloomsbury Press, 2010).

Jerry Sanders, *Peddlers of Crisis: The Committee on the Present Danger* (Boston: South End Press, 1983).

Michael Schaller, *Reckoning with Reagan: America and Its President in the 1980s* (New York: Oxford University Press, 1992).

Bruce Schulman, *The Seventies: The Great Shift in American Culture, Society, and Politics* (New York: The Free Press 2001).

Sarah Schulman, *My American History: Lesbian and Gay Life During the Reagan/Bush Years* (New York: Routledge, 1994).

Larry M. Schwab, *The Illusion of a Conservative Reagan Revolution* (New Brunswick: Transaction Publishers, 1991).

Ellen Schrecker, ed., *Cold War Triumphalism: The Misuse of History After the Fall of Communism* (New York: The New Press, 2004).

Harriet Sigerman, ed., *The Columbia Documentary History of American Women Since 1941* (New York: Columbia University Press, 2003).

David Sirota, *Back to Our Future: How the 1980s Explain the World We Live in Now—Our Politics, Our Everything* (New York: Ballantine Books, 2011).

Kiron Skinner et al., *Reagan: In His Own Hand: The Writings of Ronald Reagan That Reveal His Revolutionary Vision for America* (New York: Simon & Schuster, 2001).

Stephen Small, *Racialized Barriers: The Black Experience in the United States and England in the 1980s* (New York: Routledge, 1994).

Christian Smith, *Resisting Reagan: The U.S. Central America Peace Movement* (Chicago: University of Chicago Press, 1996).

Rickie Solinger, ed., *Abortion Wars: A Half Century of Struggle, 1950-2000* (Berkeley: University of California Press, 2003).

Laura Stein, ed., *Sexual Harassment in America: A Documentary History* (Westport, CT: Greenwood Press, 1999).

Thomas Sugrue, *The Origins of the Urban Crisis: Race and Inequality in Postwar Detroit* (Princeton, NJ: Princeton University Press, 1996).

Graham Thompson, *American Culture in the 1980s* (Edinburgh, U.K.: Edinburgh University Press, 2007).

Hunter S. Thompson, *Generation of Swine: Tales of Shame and Degradation in the '80s* (New York: Simon & Schuster, 1988).

Gil Troy, *Morning in America: How Ronald Reagan Invented the 1980s* (Princeton, New Jersey: Princeton University Press, 2005).

Gil Troy and Vincent Cannato, eds., *Living in the Eighties* (New York: Oxford University Press, 2009).

Gore Vidal, *Armageddon? Essays 1983-1987* (London: Andre Deutsch, 1987).

_____, *Perpetual War for Perpetual Peace: How We Got To Be So Hated* (New York: Nation Books, 2002).

S. Craig Watkins, *Representing: Hip-Hop Culture and the Production of Black Cinema* (Chicago: University of Chicago Press, 1998).

Gary Webb, *Dark Alliance: The CIA, The Contras, and the Crack Cocaine Explosion* (New York: Seven Stories Press, 1998).

Tim Weiner, *Legacy of Ashes: The History of the CIA* (New York: Anchor Books, 2007).

Odd Arne Westad, *The Global Cold War* (New York: Cambridge University Press, 2007).

Leslie Aldridge Westoff, *Corporate Romance: How to Avoid It, Live through It, Or Make It Work for You* (New York: Times Books, 1985).

David Wildman and Phyllis Bennis, *Ending the U.S. War in Afghanistan: A Primer* (Northampton, MA: Olive Branch Press, 2010).

Sean Wilentz, *The Age of Reagan: A History 1974-2008* (New York: Harper Collins, 2008).

Garry Wills, *Reagan's America: Innocents At Home* (Garden City, New York: Doubleday, 1987).

William Julius Wilson, *The Truly Disadvantaged: The Inner City, the Underclass, and Public Policy* (Chicago: University of Chicago Press, 1987).

Lawrence Wittner, *Toward Nuclear Abolition: A History of the World Disarmament Movement, 1971-Present* (Stanford, CA: Stanford University Press, 2003).

Tom Wolfe, *The Bonfire of the Vanities* (New York: Bantam Books, 1987).

Frank Zappa, *The Real Frank Zappa Book* (New York: Poseidon Press, 1989).

Howard Zinn, *A People's History of the United States, 1492-Present* (New York: Harper Collins, 2001).

INDEX